Strictly Bruce

STORIES OF MY LIFE

transworldbooks.co.uk

Strictly Bruce

BRUCE FORSYTH

STORIES OF MY LIFE

BANTAM PRESS

LONDON · TORONTO · SYDNEY · AUCKLAND · JOHANNESBURG

61–63 Uxbridge Road, London W5 5SA
www.transworldbooks.co.uk

Transworld is part of the Penguin Random House group of companies
whose addresses can be found at global.penguinrandomhouse.com

First published in Great Britain in 2015 by Bantam Press
an imprint of Transworld Publishers

A CIP catalogue record for this book
is available from the British Library.

ISBN 9780593075982

Designed and typeset in 11/15pt Minion Pro by Julia Lloyd
Printed in Germany by Mohn Media

Penguin Random House is committed to a sustainable
future for our business, our readers and our planet. This book
is made from Forest Stewardship Council® certified paper.

1 3 5 7 9 10 8 6 4 2

CONTENTS

To my darling wife Wilnelia,
whose creativity was the inspiration for this book.

My wonderful children, Debbie, Julie, Laura, Charlotte, Louise and JJ.

And also my loving parents, my sister Maisie and my brother John.
Writing this book has brought back very happy memories of you all.

INTRODUCTION

For my eightieth birthday my darling wife, Wilnelia, presented me with the most beautiful hardback book of photographs, which told the story of my life. Starting with the old black-and-white shots from my childhood – me in my sister Maisie's arms, me on the beach at Newquay enjoying a family holiday, my dad at work in his garage, and so on – the photos progressed chronologically through my early days in cabaret and variety, the fantastic times I had at the Palladium, and beyond to the hit TV shows of the seventies, eighties and nineties, such as *The Generation Game* and *Play Your Cards Right*. And let's not forget the fantastic years I enjoyed presenting *Strictly Come Dancing*.

Alongside my professional life, there were wonderful shots of my family life, too. All my lovely children, in-laws and grandchildren smiled out at me from the pages. It was a gorgeous gift and I was deeply moved.

Then someone suggested that I should turn Wilnelia's concept into a published book. I was surprised at the suggestion, but at the same time thrilled at the idea. I knew I would love working on such a project. So that is what you have here – a collection of photographs, many from my own personal archive, that help to tell the story of my life. It's eight decades' worth of some of my favourite memories. And I've got a lot of memories! There are stories of friends and family, colleagues and contestants, and perhaps the odd villain, too. It hasn't all been plain sailing but it has been a dream come true.

I have loved every moment of putting this book together – what a wonderful trip down Memory Lane – and I very much hope that you enjoy reading it, too.

Chapter One

ABOUT A BOY

T his is the first ever photograph taken of me, as far as I know. I can't be certain, I don't remember much from back then. It's 1928 in Edmonton, north London. Judging from the size of little Bruce Joseph Forsyth-Johnson, it must be March or April as I was born on 22 February. By the way, just so it's clear right from the beginning, Forsyth-Johnson *is* my name – it was just a bit of a mouthful for a career in show-business, so for professional purposes I shortened it.

The girl holding me is my sister Maisie. She must be ten or eleven years old. She was a darling, lovely person, very much like my mother, with a wonderful sense of humour. Everyone loved her. Many years later, when I was performing in Summer Season and then on television, Maisie used to organize bus trips for groups of her friends to come and watch her brother perform. She was so supportive.

Don't I look adorable? I think so and I'm sure my sister would have agreed. I wonder what she would have said if asked the same question a few years later, after chasing me along our street for the umpteenth time following another Brucie tantrum. I remember making my family laugh a lot at home, but I could also be a horrible child. I know it's hard to believe, but it's true.

You see, from the age of eight or nine I used to love going to the local picture house, especially if a Fred Astaire movie was playing. My parents, Florence and John, would often take me, but occasionally they preferred to go alone. Don't ask me why. When they did, there was hell to pay. My mother had to hide her hat and coat in my father's car before setting off, because if I saw her preparing to leave I would go crazy. And Lord help them (and Maisie) if I spotted the car leaving without me. That would send me into a mad rush, tearing out of the house after them, yelling at the top of my voice, as if there was a fire, with my sister soon in hot pursuit.

Maisie would eventually catch up with me and haul me back home, kicking and screaming. In my world, not being allowed to go to the movies was the *end* of the world. Quite simply, my parents were being disloyal. And if they had decided to take my brother, John, and I caught a glimpse of his head popping up in the back window of the car, well, that just added to my fury.

On those occasions poor Maisie then faced an evening trying to pacify me, which she often did by reading stories out loud. I loved *Aesop's Fables*, but even with those wonderful tales being brought to life, it would still take an age for me to emerge from my bad mood. She had the patience of a saint, my darling sister.

FOR MANY, MANY YEARS, most of my life in fact, I wondered why I had never seen a photograph of my mother holding me as a baby. I always suspected it was because I was such a little horror and drove her mad, even then. While researching this book, however, I found this treasure tucked away in an old envelope at the bottom of a dusty box. As you can imagine, I was thrilled. Perhaps I was an angelic infant after all. I hope so.

IT'S HARD TO IMAGINE I was ever a terror when, as you can see opposite, I look so innocent in that most fetching bathing cap! I'm sure the photo was taken in Newquay, where we almost always went for our summer holiday. 'Golden days' is how I would describe our Newquay holidays. There were always new rock pools filled with tiny fish to explore, little coves to discover and new friends to be made. As kids we had so much freedom. Of course, our parents kept a watchful eye on us, but from a distance.

My parents paid for these two-week vacations through a holiday club, depositing small amounts every week into the fund. And, boy, was it worth it. Newquay was beautiful and unspoiled in those days, a stunning seaside resort, simple, with gorgeous bays when the tide came in and huge expanses of beautiful sandy beaches when it receded. The whole family loved it there.

We always stayed in the same boarding-house, with me sharing a room with John, who was five years older. The place was run by a woman who, I swear, would have won *Masterchef* hands down purely on the strength of her roast potatoes. The amazing aroma drifting out of that kitchen, oh, my word, and the taste . . . I am struggling to think of anything since that has made my mouth water in the same way. Absolutely delicious. Perhaps I'm looking back on those Cornish holidays through a misty lens, but I don't think so.

I NOTICE IN A lot of these early photos that I'm sticking my chest out, as I'm doing here. I think I was so conscious of my physique, my skinniness, that I was determined to make myself look bigger. I wanted to look like a man, just like my brother John. You can see his broad shoulders in this photo. He took after Mum; I was more like my father, very slim.

This is Newquay again. Before we set out on our holidays my father could often be found tinkering away in the garage he owned, making sure the car was ready for the trip. Dad was a skilled mechanic and he ran the garage, which was situated right next to the house in which I grew up, as a business, with petrol pumps and a repair shop.

My mother would have us all dressed and ready to go first thing in the morning, but by late afternoon he would still be at it. As the evening drew in, she would pack us off to bed, fully clothed, until Dad was ready to go. It might be ten or even eleven at night before we finally set off from our small terraced house.

Every year we would stop on Bodmin Moor for a break. My father would unpack his little Primus stove on which Mum cooked eggs and bacon, often in the early hours of the morning. There has never been a better-tasting breakfast anywhere in the world! Something about sitting there with my family, the open landscape stretching as far as the eye could see, breathing in clean fresh air, made it so special.

Dad owned an Armstrong-Siddeley car for a couple of years and on one of the journeys to Cornwall we suffered a flat tyre in the middle of nowhere. With no spare, what could we do? We stuffed the tyre full of grass and carried on, stopping off every now and again beside a convenient field to top up the bits that had fallen out.

For once this is not a Newquay holiday, instead we are at Southend-on-Sea – or, as we used to call it, Southend-on-Mud. We thought that was very funny. It didn't have the beaches of Newquay – Southend's were pebbly, as you can see – but it was still a super place for a day trip or weekend away.

One of the great pleasures of our trips to Southend was a visit to the Kursaal, which was a funfair with the largest (in my mind) big dipper and roller-coaster in the world. Fear, excitement and joy wrapped up in a three-minute ride. Exhilarating.

When the time came to head home, us kids would be miserable, but not for long. Before we left for Edmonton, Dad would take us to one of the seaside stalls along the front, where he would buy saveloys and

pease pudding for our supper. The smell as we ate it in the back of the car . . . another special childhood memory.

That's my mother in the middle, with my sister on the right and a cousin on the left. What I like about this photograph is that I have obviously been in yet another bad mood. I have a distinct memory of acting like an absolute horror one day in Southend. Everyone is clearly ignoring me and I look as if I've been crying. One of my nicknames at home was 'Boo-Boo'. I wonder why?

Anyway, I seem to be cheering up a little. It's hard to make out but there is a coin in my hand, probably given to me by my mother to go and buy my favourite treat – a penny bar of Cadbury's chocolate. I'm sure she hoped it would calm me down. And get rid of me for a bit. Can't say I blame her. My bad behaviour in those days obviously wasn't *my* fault. How could it have been? No, I was merely a victim of circumstance, having been born the youngest of three and desperate for attention . . . or perhaps I was just a right little monster. One of those options sounds more plausible than the other.

I guess I am about five years old here, which would make this 1933. That's important because it's before I took up dancing. Once I started, almost immediately I had something in my life I could latch on to. I adored dancing, I just loved it. From then on I was good as gold. Well, that's how I remember it.

HERE I AM AT Brettenham Road Elementary School, just around the corner from our house. Can you spot little Brucie? No? I'm the handsome devil on the far left of the back row, with the big smile. Now that tells me something. This photo certainly wasn't taken on my first day. I would not

be sporting such a happy grin if it had been. In fact, I wouldn't be there at all as I ran home before lessons had even begun, risking life and limb dodging buses and cars to cross a busy main road. I just didn't want to be separated from my mother. In time I got over that, helped by the fact that we received a free bottle of milk every morning, and I ended up enjoying primary school.

OH DEAR. I KNOW exactly what's happening here. My poor mother used to go through hell when we were on the beach because I was the most embarrassing kid when it came to changing into my trunks or bathing suit. I was so shy I would never risk the humiliation of exposing myself. I couldn't bear the thought of anyone seeing my skinny body. It was almost a complex with me. I would insist on getting changed beneath a towel.

Unfortunately for my dear mother, this modesty-saving routine was not confined to our trips to the beach. At the age of about nine, I started to attend dance lessons at Tilly Vernon's school in Tottenham, a bus ride from our house. By then it had become clear to my parents how much I loved to dance – I hero-worshipped Fred Astaire, and my impromptu 'tap' routines on the linoleum at home were a big giveaway. Being as supportive as they were, they offered me the chance to turn that passion into something more than a hobby. The cost of the lessons was a stretch for Mum and Dad, but they knew how much it meant to me and they managed. That's how lucky I was to have the parents I did – they made everything possible for me.

I took to dance quickly and was soon ready for competitions. This is where the towel comes back in. There were never *any* other boys entering the competitions, which meant I had to change into my homemade outfits (it took my mother hours to sew on all the shiny sequins!) in the girls' changing rooms. Mum would let me know when the girls were all out, then usher me into a corner and hold up her coat to shield me as I undressed. This was not a speedy process. I required constant reassurance that I was not being spied on. 'Now, put your trousers on, Bruce, there's a good boy. No, no, I've checked. No one's here. Yes, of course I'll look again . . . All clear, I promise.' Goodness knows what the judges thought, having to wait for this rake of a boy to make his grand appearance.

At twelve, I decided that Tilly had taught me all she could. In fact I had started to give dance lessons of my own in my father's No. 5 garage. A shilling a lesson and the local girls – with a handful of boys – had the privilege of sharing my years of experience. Lucky them. From Tilly I moved on to a teacher that my mother had heard about, Douggie Ascot, whose daughter, Hazel, had appeared as a child tap-dancer in a couple of films in the late thirties. To me, attending Douggie Ascot's classes seemed like a big step forward in terms of what I was going to learn, with a hint of 'celebrity' thrown into the mix for good measure. I might meet Hazel, for goodness' sake, Britain's answer to Shirley Temple, so they said.

There were two problems, however. Douggie was an excellent teacher, no question, but his studio was in Brixton, a long way from Edmonton. Door-to-door, it took about two hours to get there, requiring a trolleybus ride, a long tube journey and a steep walk at the end. My mother used to come with me and never once complained about how long it took us. She wanted the best for me.

The second problem, and this is the main reason I didn't spend as long with Douggie as I had imagined I would, was that he taught English tap. Thanks to Mr Astaire and the US stars, I had fallen in love with the American version. The difference was significant. In English tap you are very much 'on your toes' whereas across the Atlantic there was a more relaxed, natural style, with bent knees and your weight more on your heels. That's what I wanted to master. And I soon heard of a place where I could make it happen.

Buddy Bradley was an American teacher who taught dance just like I'd seen in the movies. His studio was in Denman Street, just off Piccadilly, which was far more convenient for Mum and me than Brixton. The downside was that we had to cope with some rather unwelcome interruptions from time to time.

This would have been around 1940–41, when air-raid sirens were an all too regular addition to the city's soundscape. Buddy's classes took place on the top floor of the building, so when the warning sounded we had to rush down to the basement for shelter. The moment we heard the all-clear, we would charge back up the numerous flights of stairs to continue our lesson. The Germans were not going to frighten us off.

I loved those classes, learned so much and, as an added bonus, I also met one of my dearest friends there, John Shackell, with whom many years later I would perform professionally. I owe Buddy a very big thank-you for that introduction.

I ADORED PLAYING ON my Lilo. In Newquay Dad would take me around the corner to Fistral Bay where there were big waves. People still surf and hold competitions there, but to my mind being on a Lilo was more exciting. I would be riding the top of the wave rather than inside it. To me it was almost like flying, and absolutely thrilling for a young lad.

MY FATHER'S GARAGE, ALTHOUGH it didn't always look like you see it below. I remember, long before this photograph was taken, there being only one petrol pump, which you operated by hand.

When he was younger, my father worked for the Ford Motor Co., repairing the three-wheeler bicycles that were used for deliveries, bread and suchlike. As a qualified and skilled mechanic he rose to the level of foreman before leaving and opening his own garage.

Talking of the Ford Motor Co., the first car I ever drove was a Model T – I was about fourteen. We were on our way home and had just turned into our street when my father suddenly said, ''Bout time you learned to drive, son.' With that he stopped the car, stepped out, came round to the passenger side and indicated for me to slide behind the wheel. It was a

stretch but I could just reach the pedals. I felt very grown-up indeed.

Three years later, in 1945, I obtained a provisional licence and when the war ended the authorities announced that they were converting all provisionals to full licences. Which means I have never to this day passed a driving test! Maybe I shouldn't have said that.

In truth, having the garage so near to home was a bit of a problem – mainly because my father was always at the beck and call of customers.

We'd often be having supper when a knock at the door announced that someone had run out of petrol. Dad would leave the table, go down to the garage, open up and pump petrol into a can for the stranded traveller. Or it might be a motorist whose car had broken down, resulting in my father driving out to tow it back for repairs. There was no escape for him, yet he still never made any real money from the business. Enough to keep the family going, yes – we didn't have to worry about food or clothes – but that was it.

My FATHER WAS A hard-working man, who loved his job and loved cars. As you can see here, he was meticulous, taking great pride in his work.

In the repair shed he had an acetylene torch, which was primarily used for welding, but for my father it had a secondary function. The long flame proved ideal for lighting his cigarette, which was sometimes just a small dog-end. How he never set fire to his moustache I'll never know.

Having learned to drive, my only real role in the garage was to move the cars around. Other than that, I never became much involved in Dad's work. That was his choice, and a wise one. On one occasion I wandered in to ask if I could help and tripped over a jack that was supporting a car. Thank goodness Dad wasn't underneath as the car crashed to the floor. As for me, I didn't escape entirely unscathed. As I stumbled, the jack flew up and smacked me in the face, nearly knocking my teeth out.

'Get out of here, son,' my father said, once I'd recovered. He then held up his hands, ingrained with oil and grime. 'One day you're going to be on the stage so I don't want you finishing up with hands like these.' My father respected my ambitions and was determined to ensure I had every chance of realizing them. Clean hands were part of that. Or perhaps he was merely interested in self-preservation.

Funnily enough, I remember this being taken. My parents wanted a photograph of me in my Life Boy uniform. I was indoors when they called me out to the back garden, and was in such a rush that I didn't have time to find my whole outfit. Still, I am clearly as proud as can be, standing here with my cap on, sticking my chest out. Of course.

I enjoyed the Life Boys, which was the junior section of the Boys' Brigade. I can still do a reef knot. It's handy when I have to tie two pieces of string together. Which, come to think of it, isn't very often. I remained in the Life Boys for a few years, working my way up the ranks, eventually earning a pink lanyard, which was the ranking system they used. I think it was the equivalent of a sergeant, or maybe a corporal . . . At that stage in my life I entertained thoughts of a life in the navy or air force, until dance began to dominate my world. Soon after I began lessons, I realized dancing wasn't a game to me and a career onstage beckoned. All other notions went out of the window.

I love this photograph, even though I don't know where we are or why we're dressed up. It *was* a long time ago.

My mother is holding some flowers. That brings to mind her garden, her pride and joy. It wasn't large by any means, just normal for a small terraced house, but she made it so lovely. It was her space, just like the garage was my father's. When I was older I used to drive her crazy by practising my golf swing on our little patch of lawn. And, of course, I always replaced my divots. Mother might have been watching!

The way my mother treated me was amazing. She knew I was interested in show-business and she supported me in every way she could. I can honestly say she had more ambition for me than I had for myself, but she never pushed. She didn't have to.

For once I'm striking a pose here, rather than sticking

out that little chest of mine. I think that's because I'm wearing a jacket, which made me feel very mature. As a result I am more relaxed in this photograph. Next to me is John. It makes me smile, looking at him – he'd obviously outgrown his jacket some time ago. Look at the sleeves and the tight fit across his chest. It wouldn't have been long before that suit was mine. Hand-me-downs were very much part of our family life.

I THINK OF THIS as my Billy Elliot photograph – just like in the film, I am the ordinary boy who took dancing lessons.

It must have been taken in the autumn of 1939, not long after war was declared. I'm eleven years old and a new boy at secondary school, wearing what looks like my Higher Latymer School blazer . . . and slippers, naturally. I would dance in anything! By then I'd been going to Tilly Vernon for a couple of years, and I may even have been dancing with joy here, having recently made my first ever television appearance. Yes, at eleven years old I performed a song-and-dance routine on a morning TV programme called *Come and Be Televised* live from Radiolympia. Soon after my debut, BBC Television came off the air for six long years. I don't think the two events were linked.

My mother arranged for me to be on the show. Jasmine Bligh, the presenter, conducted short interviews with people who wanted to perform and then invited them to show the viewers what they could do. Unfortunately there is no recording, but I remember my reply when asked about my ambitions: 'I want to dance like Fred Astaire, be a star and buy my mum a fur overcoat.'

I wonder how many entertainers performing today can say they appeared on the BBC *before* the war? Not many, I bet. But looking at this photograph now, I suspect I could easily have pocketed a few bob even earlier than I actually did – I would have walked away with first prize in any knobbly-knees competition!

My parents were very musical people. In their courting days they had both been members of the Salvation Army. My father played cornet and euphonium and ran the children's drum and fife band, while my mother possessed a beautiful voice. On Sundays when she sang with the Salvation Army band on Edmonton Green passers-by would stop just to listen to her.

MY PARENTS WERE
VERY MUSICAL PEOPLE.

At home my sister was a great collector of records – 78s – and every Sunday morning she would pull out our wind-up gramophone and play a selection. I loved listening to those tunes with Maisie. My favourite was a truly awful song called 'Me And Jane In A Plane', with simple, silly rhyming words about young love. I can only assume that, when I was a little boy, it was the glamour of the subject matter that appealed, rather than the quality of the lyrics. I hope so.

We all loved music. My brother was a very good pianist and his interest lay more on the classical side. My father took up the piano in his sixties, bless his heart. What Dad loved more than anything, though, was a brass band. If the Black Dyke Mills Band was playing on the radio he would never miss them.

Having said all that, sing-songs around the piano were rarely part of life at home, except at Christmas when the extended family would meet up for a party in the evening. Lots of my aunties would do a turn, although rarely my mother. I think she preferred to let the others have a go, even though she undoubtedly had the best voice.

One of the highlights of our Christmas 'variety show' was Uncle Eddie, who was an excellent – wait for it – whistler. Nobody seems to do that any more. Uncle Eddie would stand in the corner and entertain us with a whole range of numbers while someone accompanied him on the piano. An absolute delight, it really was.

Needless to say, I got involved. You've heard of a song-and-dance man? Well, I was the song-and-dance boy at those parties. Then, when I was a little older, my friend Jimmy Perry (no, not the fantastic sitcom writer) and I would perform little comedy routines from shows we had seen, things like Sid Field's famous golfing sketch. At the end of the evening, once everyone who wanted to had done a turn, we would all link arms and enthusiastically kick our legs to a rousing rendition of 'Knees Up Mother Brown'. I'll tell you what, I wish I had the same energy now!

My father didn't really take an active part in any of this – he was quieter than the rest of the family and tended to hide his emotions. This was apparent even when we went to the theatre. My parents used to take me to two shows every week – whatever was playing at the Wood Green Empire, part of Sir Oswald Stoll's variety-theatre circuit, and the Finsbury Park Empire, a slightly better theatre, on the rival circuit run by Sir Edward Moss. Throughout all those raucous, funny shows, I never heard my father laugh out loud.

Now don't get me wrong, that doesn't mean he was having a rotten time of it. As the audience around him screamed with laughter, Dad would sit there calmly with a mile-wide dazzling smile lighting up his face. He enjoyed every moment of those shows. Dad was a wonderful man, the best father imaginable, but if I had faced audiences full of people like him in the early days, I would never have got anywhere!

Dad may not have been demonstrative in that sense, but he had no trouble embarrassing me at the shows. After the curtain fell and we were getting out of our seats, if there had been a male tap dancer in the cast he would say, in a deliberately loud voice, 'Boy, you could knock spots off that dancer we've just seen. You are marvellous compared to him.' I was so embarrassed when people turned around to look at me. Deep down, though, I agreed with him.

FAST FORWARD A COUPLE of years from 'Billy Elliot'. It is now 1941 and I am in the same school uniform, now with a gas mask tucked under my arm (you were told repeatedly that the mask was part of your person and you were never to leave it behind), and what may well be a mouth-organ in my top pocket. However, my education had not been the continuous thread these two photographs might suggest.

When I first attended Latymer School in November 1939, the Blitz was under way, and there were understandable fears that us kids could be caught up in the raids. The decision was taken to evacuate and my schoolmates and I were sent to Clacton-on-Sea. Normally they tried to billet children in twos or threes but for some reason I was placed on my own with a dear old lady. I found the experience very hard indeed, suddenly plucked from home, at eleven years old, and deposited in a strange house. I couldn't stop crying.

My parents came to visit on the first Sunday after my arrival. I was so unhappy that when they drew up in the car I ran out, jumped on to the back seat and refused to get out.

My father didn't know what to do with me, so he went round to my new headmaster's house for a chat, where he was told in no uncertain terms that it would be much safer for me to stay where I was (I don't think the headmaster meant the back seat of the car, specifically). Dad tried to explain this to me, but I was having none of it. I kept pleading and pleading to go home, until eventually my mother suggested that we find a café for a cup of tea so we could talk it over. As we drove into the high street, Clacton Pier was visible at the other end of the road . . . and right next to it was the biggest warship imaginable. Huge. My father took one look at this monster and said, 'Blimey! He's nearer the bloody war than we are! He's coming home with us.' And that was what I did.

Back in Edmonton, with Latymer closed, I attended a school in Enfield, two afternoons a week. That was the extent of my schooling for a couple of years, until the evacuees returned and Latymer reopened. The photograph with my gas mask must have been taken soon after that.

I KEPT PLEADING AND PLEADING TO GO HOME

DURING THE WAR YEARS my mother became secretary of an amateur variety show, made up of friends and neighbours, which put on charity performances to raise money to support various causes, such as the Spitfire Fund, or Aid to China and Russia. My father also helped out, rigging up spare car headlamps as spotlights powered by 12v batteries, and even making me a tap mat on our living-room table so that I had something to lay on the uneven floors of the factories and halls in which we performed.

In the photo opposite I am posing alongside a couple of drum majorettes in a uniform my mother made for me. This is the costume I wore for our big show-stopping patriotic finale, in which half a dozen other dancers and I would leap on to some drums and perform a wild routine in fervent support of our boys at the front. The Nazis never stood a chance.

For a lad barely in his teens, dreaming of a life in entertainment, with his name blazing in lights, this was great fun and a fantastic experience. The horror of war seemed remote as we travelled around and I performed my various routines, including a popular solo number entitled 'Franklin D. Roosevelt Jones' in recognition of the major contribution the US forces were now making.

Back in Edmonton the devastating impact of the fighting was never far away, but it really only came home to me when a land-mine parachuted from a German plane landed a couple of hundred yards from our house. The Home Guard spotted it, initially thought a person was hiding under the parachute and jabbed at it with their bayonets. Eventually they realized what it was and quickly sent for the naval bomb-disposal unit. During all this I was hiding behind a wall nearby, fascinated by the goings-on. It wasn't until I saw the naval personnel retreat to a safe distance, leaving one officer to remove the mine's detonator, that I grasped the real life-and-death danger of war. I was terrified and transfixed in equal measure as that incredibly brave young man crept forward to unscrew an outer panel and defuse the bomb. I still think of that event now, and wonder what became of a genuine hero.

At fourteen years old I left Latymer School to run off and join the circus . . . sorry, to start my professional career. Just before I walked out of the school gates for the last time I was summoned to the headmaster's office. From behind his desk he sized me up.

'I am afraid, Forsyth-Johnson, that there is no way I can possibly give you a good report. The truth is, I don't know enough about you. You have hardly been with us.'

'Don't worry about that, Headmaster. I'm going into a business that judges what you *can do*, not what you *have done*.'

'Indeed? And what business might that be?'

These three photographs are publicity stills I had taken to send out to agents and theatres looking for bookings.

'Show-business, sir.'

He looked at me in disbelief, then said, 'Well, good luck then.' He was not impressed.

These three photographs are publicity stills I had taken to send out to agents and theatres looking for bookings. Right from the start I wanted to make it clear I was an all-round entertainer, not just a dancer. That wasn't enough for me, or my ambitions.

In the second, I am playing the piano accordion, an instrument I learned in order to extend my repertoire but eventually grew to dislike after I took up the piano. It's a similar story with the ukulele banjo I'm strumming in the third shot. I really should have been playing the Hawaiian guitar, the first instrument I learned to play and which I much preferred. Perhaps I thought there wasn't much call for tropical music during the war – with the popularity of George Formby, the ukulele was probably a safer choice if I wanted to find work.

I learned the Hawaiian guitar courtesy of a door-to-door sales pitch. The bandleader Felix Mendelssohn (and His Hawaiian Serenaders) had organized a group of salesmen to go around the houses, with a guitar and an instruction book, offering you the chance to have your own instrument on hire purchase. The deal also entailed weekly lessons. It was a clever idea and I immediately signed up when they came knocking on our door. From there, mastering the better-known ukulele was an easy step.

THE THEATRE ROYAL, BILSTON, in the Midlands, scene of my first ever professional engagement in 1942. What an incredible thrill for a fourteen-year-old boy with grown-up ambitions. At last I was taking my first real steps towards fulfilling my dreams of stardom.

'Theatre Royal' sounds fancy, doesn't it? It wasn't. In fact, it was a hellhole, which was not uncommon after the war broke out. A lot of theatres that should have been condemned remained open because variety shows were one of the very few forms of entertainment on offer to lift the country's spirits. The lack of materials available for on-going maintenance did not improve the situation.

I was offered the booking through a frankly useless theatrical agent from Tottenham. Until the show went out on the road I worked in his office, as a gofer, answering the phone when it rang (rarely), and more regularly picking up milk for his 'egg and milk' breakfast. 'It soothes my ulcer, boy,' he explained.

The show was so awful, I think it may have brought on another.

The Great Marzo topped the bill. How to describe him? I know: 'a hopeless magician'. That's what I thought, at least. Then there was me, way down the list, propping up the other acts with my one and only appearance as 'Boy Bruce, the Mighty Atom'.

Now, my idea for the act wasn't bad at all – a page-boy carrying luggage from the railway station to the hotel, who stops off to see what's inside and proceeds to pull out a variety of instruments and a tap mat, all of which spark off a series of song-and-dance numbers. It was just the execution that left a lot to be desired.

Takings were so poor that at the end of the week there was not enough to pay anyone their agreed fee, so the decision was taken to split what little box-office money there was between the acts according to each performer's billing. As bottom of the heap I received thirteen shillings and fourpence, which was a lot less than a pound. It wasn't even enough to pay for my digs, let alone the train fare home. I had to phone my parents and ask them to rescue me. That was bad enough, but to make matters worse, the dreadful show's dreadful producer had already persuaded Mum and Dad to contribute twenty-five pounds for expenses to save us from cancellation before we had even opened. That was a lot of money in those days, money my parents struggled to afford.

Did any of this make me question my chosen career? Not for a second. I was sorry that my parents had lost money, of course I was, and I wished the show had been better. But, deep down, I was thrilled. At last I was in show-business.

THINKING BACK ON THESE childhood memories, one aspect stands out above all others: the encouragement and support I received from my parents.

They truly were amazing. Finding money they really didn't have to pay for dance lessons; my mother stoking my ambitions, sitting late into many nights making my costumes – satin suits and blouses – endlessly pricking her fingers as she sewed on the sequins, and her sacrifice of two hours each way, accompanying me to dance lessons; my father, with his quiet understanding that his youngest child saw a different path for himself and doing all he could to set me on that route – the tap mat, the spotlights and, most importantly, working to build my confidence. Neither of them lived long enough to see what all their hard work eventually led to. I so wish they had.

I STILL SOMETIMES SHUT MY EYES AND IMAGINE HIS FACE, HIS SMILE

At least my father saw me compère *Sunday Night at the London Palladium*. Unfortunately he died in December 1961, before I had the chance to fulfil one of my most cherished wishes. With his love of cars, I wanted to buy him a Rolls-Royce but I couldn't afford to do so before he was gone. I regret that deeply. I still sometimes shut my eyes and imagine his face, his smile, as I hand him the keys. 'Dad, here is your Rolls-Royce. Why don't you lift up the bonnet, see if anything needs fixing?' He would have adored that, and I would have loved to watch him.

My mother didn't live long enough to see me at the Palladium. She died in 1957, a year before my big break came along. We used to watch the show on television when Tommy Trinder was the compère. She would sit there enjoying every minute of it, then turn to me and say, 'I'd love to see you up there, boy. I'd really love that.'

I do believe she had a hand in making that wish of hers come true. She had done so much for me while she was alive, and yet I'm convinced she felt she still had one more thing to do. When she arrived in Heaven I have no doubt she sought out a very good agent to book me into the Palladium.

John's weary expression suggests I've been up to no good all day.

Chapter Two

MY BROTHER JOHN

We are back to that 1933 trip to Southend with this photograph. It's the summer before my first term at Brettenham Road Elementary School. My sister Maisie is in the middle, with one of her friends, and my brother John is on the right. As you can see, I'm pulling a daft face or maybe on the brink of yet another tantrum. It's hard to tell, but John's weary expression suggests I've been up to no good all day. It's lovely to see my mother clutching another bunch of flowers. I bet my father picked them for her. She looks so happy.

You can just about make out a beach ball at my father's feet. We'll have enjoyed a lot of fun with that as a family. The five-year age gap between my brother and myself meant that we didn't play together much at home. Football, occasionally, but that was about all. And my father was always working so hard in his garage that he didn't really have time either. Holidays were the exception.

My brother was a fairly serious young man. He loved engineering and was terribly interested in the mechanical side of the motor industry. When my father first introduced John to the world of cars, understanding how the engines worked came easily to my brother. He was fascinated by all that, quite the opposite of myself. That didn't worry Dad: he was happy to embrace the difference between his two sons.

WHEN WAR BROKE OUT my brother was determined to become a pilot. In early 1941, as soon as he turned eighteen, John volunteered for the RAF and was immediately stationed in Torquay for basic training. Judging by the wintry look in the photo overleaf, it must have been taken within days of his arrival on the south coast. That's John, top right.

My parents were very proud of my brother and also happy for him, despite the obvious danger. They knew he was realizing an ambition. The RAF offered John an opportunity that would otherwise have been beyond him. How could he have learned to fly while living with us in Edmonton and working in the garage? Lessons would have cost far too much. Without the air force, flying would have remained an impossible dream. I have no doubt that, come the end of the war, John would not have returned to working in the garage but would instead have pursued a career as a pilot, perhaps with a civil airline.

From Torquay, John went to Pensacola, Florida, for flight training. He must have sent home this portrait from there – Tooley-Myron was an American chain of photographic studios. The white flash on his cap indicates that he was a trainee pilot when this was taken.

Seeing my brother's handwriting here generates powerful emotions. Just to know with certainty that there had been a day, more than seventy years ago, thousands of miles away, when John sat down, thought of me and wrote out my name – that's very precious. It's also interesting that he chose 'Brucie'. There's a strong sense of intimacy in his use of that name. Normally it was Bruce or Bru or, yes, Boo-Boo, but 'Brucie' was more affectionate.

Impossible for John to know,

of course, but many years later 'Brucie' became the show-business me, as opposed to the everyday Bruce. Brucie would have driven me, and everyone around him, mad, if he'd existed all the time. When I'm waiting to walk onstage I'm Bruce, thinking about what I'm about to do, in my own bubble. I'm quite serious. I don't want to talk to anyone. Then, when the music starts up and I walk out, this other person, Brucie, turns up and takes over. He's a different character altogether. And thank God he does turn up because without him I'd be lost, I really would.

John was presented with his wings when he was still in the US, which meant my parents never had the opportunity to see him pass out. He was incredibly proud of those wings. Having completed his training, he flew a Catalina flying boat over to England. This was a vital undertaking that many newly qualified pilots who had been based in America undertook, transporting aircraft back home that were essential to the war effort. John would have been nineteen. That's an incredible thing for him to have done. Only a few months previously he had been a kid, learning as much as he could about aircraft, before being taken halfway across the world to learn to fly in little biplanes. Then, in a heartbeat, he found himself piloting that big machine all the way across the Atlantic. A bewildering thought.

This is John in his flying suit, with its fleece-lined boots, gloves and collar. When I look at this I realize just how cold and uncomfortable it must have been up in those military planes.

This is clearly a studio shot, taken somewhere John was stationed. He must have mailed it home, to show us how proud he was of what he was achieving. After he arrived back from Florida, John was sent up to Turnberry, on the west coast of Scotland, to the School of Aerial Gunnery and Fighting. The photograph may have come from there, although I can't say for sure. What is almost certain, however, is that this is the flying suit John would have been wearing when the awful tragedy struck. I will never forget that day.

Friday, 21 May 1943, St Neots near Bedford. I am fifteen years old, having recently joined up with an accomplished accordionist and drummer called Peter Crawford. We've managed to land a handful of cabaret bookings and have recently been taken on by the American Red Cross in a touring party performing at US military bases throughout England. It's been a fantastic experience so far, very professional. They've even supplied us with hand-tailored uniforms and forage caps sporting the US Red Cross badge. I play the accordion, accompanying Peter's drumming, then finish our set with a big tap number. We've even played in front of Hollywood royalty – Clark Gable came to see one of the shows, although unfortunately I didn't get to meet him.

It's been incredibly exciting, but I'm happy now to have a break for a couple of days. It's the start of a free weekend and the cast of the show have decided to enjoy the early-summer weather. We've found a field by a brook, where we can swim and play games. Someone suggests rounders. Great. We all join in. I'm enjoying myself until, running to catch the ball, I trip on the uneven ground and fall heavily on my hand, jamming my finger back at an unnatural angle. It hurts like hell and immediately I feel sick.

My friends gather around me. 'Bruce, are you all right? You look terrible. You'd better go back to the bus for a lie-down.'

The Americans have converted Green Line coaches into 'club-mobiles' for all their shows, with bunks in the back, space up front for our instruments and a small piano strapped to the side. I'm lying down, not feeling at all well, dizzy, nauseous, disoriented . . .

Suddenly I'm in a plane, flying over the sea. No, not flying. I'm plummeting downwards, out of control, at an acute angle. There's nothing I can do. I stagger towards the open door of the aircraft as the dark water rushes towards me. I jump . . .

. . . and I'm falling, out of my bunk and on to the floor of the bus. The jolt wakes me from my troubled sleep. A strange, unpleasant dream, obviously. What makes it particularly disturbing, however, is that I've never been in an aeroplane.

I gave no further thought to that horrible vision until I returned home the following day to visit my parents. Normally my mother would call out cheerfully the moment I walked through the front door. Not this time. I found her sitting in her chair, gazing into space.

'What's up, Mum?' That was when she told me that John had been posted as missing.

It wasn't until many, many years later, after my parents had passed away, that I received a letter and documentation from a Mrs Margaret Morrell, explaining what had actually happened to John that night. She had been undertaking research into accidents that occurred in the Turnberry area during the war, and quite correctly thought I would want to know what she had unearthed.

The sea that night had been unusually calm, which made the low-level exercise that John and his fellow airmen were undertaking all the more dangerous. They were practising laying sea mines, hazardous enough at the best of times, but with no waves to produce whitecaps, flying at virtually zero altitude became treacherous. In the pitch black it must have been incredibly difficult to ascertain the distance between your aircraft and the water.

One of the Wellingtons ditched 'in the drink', as the report stated, and John's plane, plus another, went back to help in the search and rescue. With their lights on, flying just above the water in an attempt to spot survivors, these two Wellingtons collided. Of the eighteen men from the three aircraft that crashed, only seven were picked up. John was not one of them.

In many ways I'm pleased my parents never knew the details of John's accident. I think they would have found it even harder to cope with, had they learned that their son died in a collision between two planes searching for survivors rather than in the course of an active and dangerous exercise.

As it was, when we lost my brother we took it hard and personally. Of course we did. This was *our* tragedy. It was only some time afterwards that we began to understand just how many other families were facing up to exactly the same thing, that shocking grief and despair. The magnitude of what was happening across the globe came home to us. Similar telegrams to the one my parents received were being delivered all over the country – in fact, all over the world. Somehow that realization made us feel less alone. We were sharing our loss with so many millions of others.

John's body was never recovered and this lack of closure, as people say nowadays, was very hard for my mother in particular. For such a long time she clung to the hope that John could have been picked up by a tramp steamer bound for South America and, suffering

WE WERE SHARING OUR LOSS WITH SO MANY MILLIONS OF OTHERS.

from amnesia, ended up on the other side of the world, unaware of who he was. It was agony for her. It would have been far better if my parents had received a telegram confirming John's death.

We went on to enjoy happy times as a family in the years that followed, but never for a moment forgot about John. I think about him often to this day.

JOHN'S LIFE AND DEATH are officially commemorated in two locations. One is at the Runnymede Air Forces Memorial, pictured below, near to my home in Wentworth. His name is there on a panel headed '1943, Royal Air Force, Flight Sergeant'. It's a comfort to have him so close.

The second is on Turnberry golf course. One weekend while I was in the RAF I joined my mother and father at Turnberry. They wanted to be near to where their elder son was lost. We stood on the beach and looked out at the sea. I have been there many times since to play golf, and I always make sure to spend a minute or two by the memorial the people of Kirkoswald parish erected in 1923. It is a large, impressive Celtic cross, situated on a hill overlooking the twelfth green of the Ailsa course. You can see it from some distance away. Originally the memorial was built to commemorate those stationed at Turnberry airfield who died in the First World War. In 1990, sections were added to the base to include the dead from the Second World War.

My big brother is listed there. Alongside his RAF comrades, John's life is honoured.

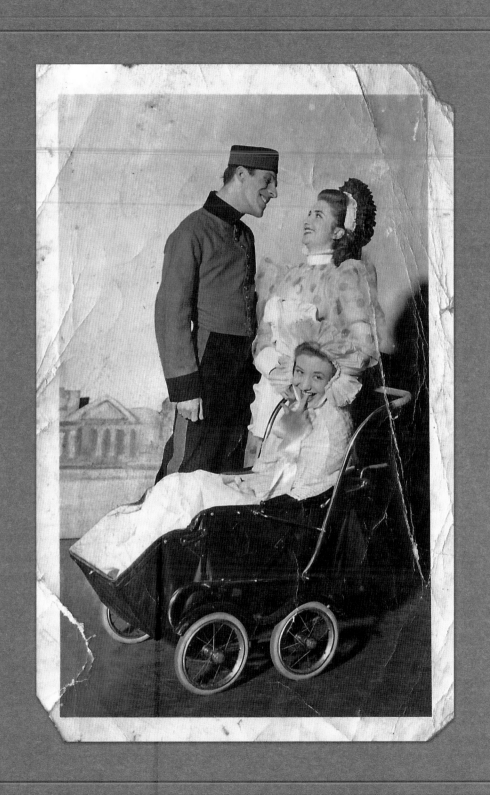

Chapter Three

TAKING TO THE STAGE

know exactly what number I'm performing here at the famous Windmill Theatre in London. It's the very catchy 'When A Soldier Bumps Into A Nursemaid'. The 'nursemaid' I'm serenading is Penny Calvert, a wonderful singer and dancer who, a few years after this was taken, would agree to marry me. The year of the photograph is 1947. How *do* I remember? Well, our literal interpretation of the song is certainly a giveaway, but there is also an inscription on the back, in Penny's handwriting. It gives the song title and year, then 'our first number together'.

This was in the era of national service, and although by 1947 I should already have been called up, my papers had been deferred by a year to allow me to fulfil a series of show-business contracts. Peter Crawford and I had stayed together for a couple of years, the partnership only breaking up when Peter himself was called up in 1945. Directly after that I teamed up with a guy called Les Roy just as the war was coming to an end and together we toured variety theatres (many of them best described as 'grotty') up and down the country.

On 8 May 1945, the day victory in Europe was formally declared, Les and I were performing at the Whitehall Theatre, in Phyllis Dixie's 'Peek-a-Boo' show. Phyllis was often billed as 'England's Popular Pin-Up Girl', but a better description would have been Britain's answer to the American striptease artist Gypsy Rose Lee. This particular show also featured a number of gorgeous dancing girls, who wore very little indeed.

I wonder what it was that attracted Les and me to that particular booking.

Anyway, Les and I and most of the cast watched the VE Day celebrations from the theatre's rooftop. Below us, thousands and thousands of men and women, young and old, were milling around, hugging, kissing and laughing as they waited for Churchill to make his announcement at 3 p.m. The sense of pure happiness that emanated from all those people – I had never experienced anything like it. I don't think anyone ever will again. It was extraordinary.

It was a sunny day, as I recall, and a number of the beautiful showgirls were sunbathing on the roof. Topless. Well, they had to: strap marks were very much frowned upon onstage. To save themselves from painful sunburn, they placed half-crowns on their nipples. From time to time I would pop up to the roof, to ask if anyone had any change.

No one obliged.

Later in the evening Les and I joined the incredible scenes in Trafalgar Square. The thing that stays with me most from that night is the absolute joy that was so clear on everyone's faces, especially the women's. They knew that, at long last, their men were coming home. Music was everywhere, complete strangers hugged and kissed each other, drinks were shared and flags were waved. It was chaos, lovely chaos.

LES AND I CONTINUED touring as a double act for some time, moving up the ranks until we succeeded in making it into the better venues, known as the number-one theatres, before joining the very popular Jack Jackson and His Band in a major revue called *Mayfair Merry-Go-Round*. Les played the drums, very well, while I was on piano, not as good as I would have liked, and it was these professional engagements, still in the top bracket of theatres, which delayed my national service.

When the revue ended, the band was set to embark on a new tour of the number-two theatres. Les chose to stick with them, but I decided the time was right to go it alone. I wanted more than to be merely a member of a band, and in early 1947 I applied for an audition at the Windmill.

I WANTED MORE
THAN TO BE MERELY A
MEMBER OF A BAND

I arrived there at 9 a.m. to find dozens and dozens of other hopefuls waiting alongside me. The morning rehearsals took place on the stage, but it was a slow, slow process and by eleven thirty, with half an hour to go before the theatre opened to the public, I don't think they had managed to see even half the people there. We were told to move upstairs, to the big rehearsal room, where the auditions would continue. That was disappointing. The atmosphere there was nothing like the actual theatre.

Time dragged on and on, until eventually, at round 4 p.m., my turn came. My audience was the theatre's owner, Vivian Van Damm, his casting director Anne Mitelle, plus the remaining performers who were still hanging around.

I start with a song. Halfway through Mr Van Damm interrupts: 'Do you do anything else?'

'Yes, I play the piano.'

After only sixteen bars he interrupts again: 'Do you do anything else?'

'Yes, impersonations.'

I manage a couple before I am halted once again. 'That's all right, old boy. I've seen enough.'

'But you haven't seen my winging yet.' This is the big finish I've been building up to, a routine where I fling my legs out from side to side, very fast. It's my special step. I turn to Molly, the pianist, who has been playing throughout all the auditions. 'Play my last section, please.'

She shakes her head and closes the lid of her piano. 'Mr Van Damm has seen enough.'

I'm furious. I stomp to the middle of the floor. 'If you don't mind, Mr Van Damm, I'm going to finish my routine.' With no accompaniment I burst into my winging finish. It is greeted with absolute silence, but I carry on. When I am finished I grab my music and shoes and storm off in a foul temper. So much for the Windmill. On the way home I begin to think, What do I do now?

'IF YOU DON'T MIND, MR VAN DAMM, I'M GOING TO FINISH MY ROUTINE.'

The following morning my mother wakes me. 'There's someone from the Windmill on the phone for you, Bruce.'

I assume I left something behind. 'Thanks, Mum. I'll be there in a moment.' Downstairs I find to my astonishment that it is Anne Mitelle on the phone.

'I'd like you to come along to the theatre as soon as you can,' she says to me. 'Mr Van Damm was very taken with you yesterday. He would like you to become a juvenile singer and dancer in one of our resident companies.'

To say I'm thrilled . . .

A few weeks later, yes, you've got it, the RAF come calling and I have to swap all those beautiful Windmill showgirls for life on an all-male military base.

Just imagine how I felt!

RAF PADGATE, NEAR WARRINGTON in Cheshire, was where many new conscripts were sent for basic training. Now here is something I bet only a handful of those who passed through the gates would have said: 'I absolutely loved the square bashing at Padgate!' That's what the drilling was called, because you bashed around the parade square in heavy boots.

Not everyone's idea of fun, but to me at times it seemed like a tap dance routine. The timing was critical – start, turn, stop on a certain beat, start again – which is probably why I was so good at it. I guess I had natural rhythm and as a result the flight sergeant appointed me No. 1 Marker. That was terribly important, I can tell you. I would be situated on the far right-hand side of the line and the rest of the squad had to take their mark and set their pace from me. You may have seen troops when they lift up their arms to measure how far apart they are – well, I was the one they all took their measure from. If there was ever a mistake it couldn't be my fault, obviously. Clearly whoever had messed things up hadn't been paying enough attention to yours truly.

It wasn't quite how I had imagined my first starring role!

TIME PASSED VERY SLOWLY in the air force, even though I enjoyed the camaraderie. As you can see here, we had a lot of laughs, and I was fortunate to have been called up with a good bunch of guys. I can guarantee that when this second photograph was taken, I would have bet my week's wages (not that that was saying much) that this was as near to a troupe of Tiller Girls as I would ever manage. Little did I know . . .

After basic training, you had to submit a trade you would like to follow for the rest of your time in the service and, depending on what you chose, you then received your posting. One of my dearest friends, Alan Poore, who was there at the same time as me, put down the same request as I did: 'teleprinter operator'. My reasons were clear: I thought it would help

We had a lot of laughs!

my piano playing. Having listed our trade, we eagerly awaited our posting. Alan was destined for Singapore, lucky devil. Me? Carlisle, 14 Maintenance Unit, three hundred miles from London. Don't laugh.

Carlisle proved to be much more enjoyable than I anticipated. By that stage in my military 'career', I had become a voluntary musician, denoted by a gold harp badge on my sleeve, which allowed me time away from other duties to play at RAF dances. In Carlisle I took full advantage, playing the dance music but also forming a little jazz band. I was determined to keep the performing side of my life as active as possible. I would also sit for hours practising on the small piano in the NAAFI. If anyone wanted a request, I charged a doughnut.

My posting to Carlisle offered an unexpected bonus. Petrol. I owned a little Austin car – registration EMX 906 – that I drove up to Carlisle from Edmonton. That is a long, long way and used up a lot of petrol coupons. Driving home on leave to see my parents would be next to impossible.

Salvation arrived in the shape of my flight sergeant. 'I see you have a car, Forsyth-Johnson.'

'Yes, Flight. But going anywhere is difficult with the petrol shortage.'

'Have you seen all those parked lorries near the main entrance, Forsyth-Johnson?'

I had no idea where this was going. I nodded.

'There must be a lot of petrol in those tanks.'

'Yes, there must be, Flight.'

'All you need is a length of rubber tubing and a couple of cans, which I can provide for you. Then you would have a tankful of petrol all the time, wouldn't you?'

'Yes, Flight.' What's the catch? I wondered.

It turned out that all I had to do was drive him to his girlfriend's house in Carlisle a couple of times a week, and pick him up the following morning before parade. A pretty good deal, I thought, even when I discovered that there were Military Police guards with Alsatian dogs patrolling the compound. It didn't take me long to work out their routine, however, and for the eighteen months or so that I was there, our arrangement worked very well indeed. Well done, Flight.

IF ANYONE WANTED A REQUEST, I CHARGED A DOUGHNUT.

Even so, I was desperate to return to London, to be nearer the world of show-business. Every month I sent in a transfer request but they were all ignored until eventually I received a posting down to Bush House in London, at the top of which was an RAF teleprinter station. I couldn't believe it. Bush House! A stone's throw from the West End. By then I had passed what was known as a 'trade test' with flying colours: my 104 words per minute had earned me the grade of LAC 'Leading Aircraftman'. I was clearly going places although, as it turned out, not where I wanted to go.

For a very happy three weeks I lived at home on my 'living-out allowance', which gave me the freedom to go to all the theatres again. Perfect, until Fate intervened in the shape of a message that arrived while I was on duty. 'Post immediately LAC Forsyth-Johnson to RAF Andover, headquarters Maintenance Unit. Reason for posting – pianist required for pantomime.'

Immediately I went to see my CO. 'Sir, for years I've been trying to get this posting and at last I'm here. It's ideal. I can reacquaint myself with friends and contacts, take up dancing lessons again, and make positive moves for my future career. Now out of the blue I'm being posted away. Can anything be done?'

'I'm afraid not, Forsyth-Johnson. They have a ranking officer at Andover and he has demanded your transfer. You are a voluntary musician and because of that they want you. You have got to go.'

I cursed that harp on my sleeve, but I had no choice.

I KNOW THIS IS a tiny photo but I had to include it. You see, if you squint really hard you can just about make out the two stripes on my arm. Yes, while at Andover I was promoted to the dizzy heights of Acting Corporal, IC! This meant I could be placed 'in charge' (the first time I ever got to say that) of the Signals Unit, responsible for the watch, either during the day or through the night. Surprisingly, I rather enjoyed the shift work this entailed, especially when I took my turn at the night watch and had lower-ranked aircraftmen to make me tea whenever I wanted!

At first I saw the transfer as rotten luck, but my promotion certainly helped my mood, as did the fact that, as you can see in the photograph, I didn't have far to look for female company. That made a very welcome change. I also ended up enjoying playing in the pantomime that had brought me there. We had a trio, consisting of myself, a drummer and bass player, and at the interval I played a couple of numbers by the jazz drummer and singer Ray Ellington, who I thought was marvellous. As it was pantomime, one of the songs I chose was 'The Three Bears'. I loved that. And a lot of people came away saying it was the best part of the show! That's my recollection, anyway.

I spent six months in Hampshire and then the RAF decided they no longer needed me. At last I was a free man.

THIS MUST HAVE BEEN taken not long after my demob, as I'm playing one of the hit songs of the moment, 'My One And Only Highland Fling' from the Fred Astaire and Ginger Rogers movie *The Barkleys of Broadway*.

By this stage in my life I was, at last, improving on the piano, having taken the opportunities offered to me in the RAF to practise. As a young boy I had been very naughty in that regard. At home we had an old German upright, an Eungblut, but I wouldn't stick with my lessons – something I have regretted for the rest of my life. Yes, I finished up being able to play, mostly by chord symbols, but I'm not a good reader of music.

I'd only begun to take the piano seriously when I was with the American Red Cross. We had a good little quartet – clarinet, drums, piano, tenor sax – and they would hold jam sessions after each show. Often some of the GIs from the audience would join in.

I used to sit up close to them, fascinated by how the piano player knew all the chord sequences, not by reading music but just from memory. I hadn't come across playing by ear previously. They were all like that. Someone would say, 'Let's do "Lady Be Good",' and everyone knew that would always be in the key of G, or that 'Honeysuckle Rose' was always in F. Then off they would go, each instrument blending seamlessly while still allowing for moments of individuality. The piano chords kept it all together while from time to time the others would play off the melody, making up lovely little phrases. That aspect of the music fascinated me then and still does. I enjoy a bit of traditional jazz, but my real love is modern jazz. Not the 'progressive' variety, however. That just sounds discordant to me and never seems to go anywhere.

In this photograph I'm modelling myself on the great Hoagy Carmichael. Isn't it obvious? Cigarette casually hanging from mouth, late-night hooded eyes adding an air of mystery. I thought I looked cool . . . until my eyes started to well up with tears! Smoke sure can sting your eyes something awful, I can tell you. Not that I was deterred. I kept on playing, kept on smoking and, of course, kept on trying to look cool.

This wasn't my first attempt at portraying myself as a louche character. Oh, no. Back when I was with Jack Jackson and His Band I was allowed a short solo spot, an impersonation of the Inkspots, plus Les Roy and I would put on a tap routine, but apart from those moments my job was playing the piano to the side of the band. Near the audience. That gave me plenty of opportunity to spot any pretty girls in the front rows and try to make eye contact in a sophisticated manner. Honestly, that was how it was. If successful, I'd turn my head and roll my eyes, which hopefully indicated that the girl in question should come round to the stage door afterwards. As you can imagine, I was hard to resist. Yet a lot of them did.

ON THE DAY I walked out of the Windmill in 1947 to join the RAF a marvellous thing happened. Anne Mitelle approached me to say that even though I had only been with them a matter of weeks, she and Vivian Van Damm had been suitably impressed with my performances. 'When your time is up with the air force, there will still be a job here for you, if you want it.' Those words kept me going during my two and a half years in the service. Not only would I have a job to go to, I would have a good job to go to. That length of time away from the business could have sounded the death knell on my not-yet-career. Without their backing I would have been forced to start again from scratch. As it was, towards the end of 1949 I was back in the theatre, a happy and grateful member of 'A Company'.

I am delighted to have unearthed a selection of photographs from my Windmill days and have included some of them overleaf to demonstrate the breadth of material in what was known as 'Revudeville'.

We put on six hour-long shows every day, each including various dance routines, duets, and what were known as 'scenas'. These were basically musical scenes, ensemble pieces with lots of different songs by individual performers that would then climax in a big full-cast number. In the third photograph here, the one where I'm wearing a fez (I have no idea why), I'm thrilled to see my great pal from Buddy Bradley's, John Shackell, wearing the white shirt in the middle. I don't think either of us could have wished for more when we first walked through the doors of Buddy's studio in Denman Street than to be onstage together at the Windmill Theatre. When I married a few years after this photograph was taken, I was very proud to have John as my best man.

Accompaniment at the Windmill consisted of two pianos and a drummer. When I returned from the RAF there was a very good resident pianist called Dennis and, whenever possible, I would arrive early so we could play together. During the shows Dennis used to love trying to improvise with a touch of jazz. Whenever he managed to slip in a sequence, he would look up at me with a twinkle in his eye and I would look back as if to say, 'Yes, Dennis, you got it, you got it.'

With six shows a day, comprising such variety, it's no wonder the Windmill required two full companies, A and B, performing on alternate days (not Sundays), which would be reversed the following week. The entire Windmill show would change every six weeks, which meant that in addition to the actual performances, each company had to rehearse on their days off. There might be a week or two with no rehearsals, but that was all.

With six shows a day, comprising such variety, it is no
wonder the Windmill required two full companies.

How did we manage to fit it all in? Easy, really. We were all very upbeat, in our twenties, with boundless energy, happy to be working and performing. We loved what we did. And the money was good. That helped. I think I was earning around thirty pounds a week when I returned.

It was a wonderful theatre and a great place to work – very well run and successful. It famously never closed during the war. It was a pleasure to walk through the doors every day. You felt like a true professional because you were treated like one. The facilities that Vivian Van Damm provided were first class. The changing rooms were much better than most I have been to (still!), and upstairs, near the rehearsal room, a canteen provided a surprisingly decent selection of food, given the country was still under rationing.

Sometimes, of course, you just wanted a change of menu and scenery, and right next to the stage door there was a big cafeteria where we would grab something to eat and play table football. And, if you wanted a beer, directly opposite there was a pub. I was never much of a drinker but I often saw the comics on the bill come offstage, head straight across the road and into the pub, where they would stay for a couple of hours before returning for their next performance.

Another great joy during my years at the Windmill was having the opportunity to go and watch a film or a show in the heart of London. If there was something we wanted to see, the members of each company would arrange to go as a group, making a day of it.

For me the biggest thrill would always be a new Fred Astaire or Bing Crosby movie, especially if it was on at the Empire, Leicester Square. That was just the best theatre to see a film. Not only could you lose yourself in the big Technicolor musical, but also, before the main event, they put on a full variety show on the stage in front of the screen, often with fairly big names and a line of dancing girls. It seems almost unbelievable now, but it's true. For the first hour we would be entertained by a full orchestra and three or four acts, followed by the main feature film. Three hours of fantastic entertainment. All just around the corner from the Windmill.

What a place to work and what a time to start out in the business.

Not long after my return Van Damm put me in charge of choreographing the tap-dancing duets – numbers like 'Baby It's Cold Outside' or 'Take a Letter Miss Smith'. I had to come up with a different routine every six weeks. A lot of pressure but excellent experience. I would teach the numbers to dancers from both companies, as we put on the same shows. For a few weeks I remember running through the steps with a young chap who had joined B Company. His name was Lionel Blair. I wonder if he ever made it in the business.

For these numbers, we interchanged the dancers, so I had to make sure that at least two other girls and two guys from each company knew the routines. I would be in five of the six shows we put on and the girls would alternate.

When I first met Penny Calvert back in 1947, she was one of the company dancers. I wasn't there long enough to get to know her. However, when I returned to the Windmill and started to produce the duets I could see she was an excellent dancer with a very appealing personality. I would arrange to work with her whenever possible.

This photo is of Penny and me doing one of the numbers I had devised. Don't ask me which one. Instead, just look at how straight my leg is! Studying it now, I'm thrilled by my posture. Penny's leg is supposed to be straight as well. Maybe this was a rehearsal . . .

Newquay in the summer of 1950, with my father and mother. I'm looking positively chipper, which is surprising, given that I have only recently had my left kidney removed.

In the weeks leading up to that moment I'd been experiencing various unpleasant symptoms – blood in my urine, that type of thing – and eventually I paid a visit to the doctor. He recommended an X-ray, which promptly revealed that one of my kidneys was twice the size of normal. Why? Because the other had packed up long ago, probably when I was around fourteen. The good one was doing the work of two. In my early teens I used to suffer terrible back pains that my mother treated with hot-water bottles. Turns out it was my malformed kidney shrivelling up.

Having undergone the operation, I joined my parents on holiday, which was the perfect start to my recovery. The Cornish air was doing me the power of good, and after a week or so I felt more than ready for a round of golf. My mother did not think this was a good idea. At all. Both she and Dad had been incredibly worried about me when I was in hospital and she was convinced that I was about to do myself a mischief. It makes me smile just thinking about how worried she was and how much she cared.

Another reason I love that particular photo is because Mum and Dad are in their bare feet. They must have been for a paddle together. They had such a happy marriage and adored each other. For me, seeing them like this, relaxed and enjoying each other's company, captures perfectly their relationship.

How about this for a song title: 'How Could You Believe Me When I Said I Loved You When You Know I've Been A Liar All My Life?' Fred Astaire performed it with Jane Powell in the film *Wedding Bells*. When I first saw it I knew it would be a great number for me and Penny.

We are performing it here in spring/summer 1951. I know it is the Windmill from the glass tiles you can see on the stage. During performances they were lit from below, creating a spectacular setting. Another indication of how good a theatre Van Damm had created. This must be a publicity shot: we wouldn't have been performing a real tap routine on the glass without first laying down a tap mat.

It can't have been long after this shot that Penny and I decided to leave the Windmill and strike out on our own. We joined a touring show called *It's A Riot*, playing (and losing money) in the variety theatres on the number-two circuit. We followed this, more successfully, thank goodness, with an overseas tour entertaining troops, with musician Tito Burns and his band, plus Tito's wife, the lovely singer Terry Devon.

HERE I AM IN Sabratha near Tripoli in 1951, and Benghazi in December of that year, where we spent Christmas Day because our plane had broken down. None of us was very happy about that. It was not the ideal location for our much-anticipated festive break!

The day before we had been due to fly home we'd been performing at the British base in Benghazi, where we were invited for a drink in the officers' mess after the show. Our host was a very well-to-do major, with a cut-glass upper-crust accent. 'Grand show. Grand show indeed, my boy,' he said to me, as we stood at the bar. 'What can I offer you to drink? Would you like a B-rrr?'

A what? I looked at him blankly.

'A B-rrr. Would you like a cold B-rrr?'

At last the penny dropped. 'Oh, a beer! Yes, please. Thank you.'

'WE'RE A COUPLE OF swells . . .' Well, we would be if Penny hadn't been cut out of the photograph. We're performing here in a cabaret club, having finished with the touring party. This was a tough time for us, trying to make it as a duo. We did pick up a few of these cabaret slots, but as a song-and-dance act in variety theatre we struggled. It seemed agents either wanted a singing act or a dancing act. Never both.

Salvation of a sort arrived in early 1953 when we were offered a four-month tour of India. We jumped at the opportunity, and decided to get married before we left. Our booking agent had suggested that if we were man and wife we could be together and would be entitled to a bigger cabin. As Penny and I had known for some time that we wanted to be married, this provided an incentive to move our plans forward.

We enjoyed a very brief four-day honeymoon and then we were off. In performing terms, the Indian tour was a success, but we found the poverty we saw, the heat and different food hard to cope with. I have heard it's different now, but back then we were not used to it. I ended up living on boiled eggs for six weeks. I'm not sure I've had one since! I lost about two stone, but it was Penny who suffered most. In Calcutta she caught a nasty flu-like virus that resulted in me having to perform solo for three or four nights, something I hadn't done since the dreadful page-boy routine at Bilston.

I was terribly, terribly nervous stepping onstage that first evening on my own. As I had been preparing in the afternoon, I remember thinking that, even though I could sing, dance, play the piano and do impersonations, I didn't *have* an act. Somehow I managed to pull something together that just about worked and the audience didn't leave. What a relief.

Later, in our room after my performance, I mentioned what I'd been thinking about to Penny.

'Well, it's about time you put that right, isn't it, Bruce?'

Then she reminded me of something the 'old man', by which she meant Vivian Van Damm, had said to her when we were leaving the Windmill.

'You know, Penny, sooner or later Bruce is going to have to go out on his own.'

We both knew Van Damm was right. If I was going to make it in the business, it was most likely as a solo performer. The harsh reality was that opportunities just did not exist for Penny and me as a double act.

BACK IN ENGLAND, HAVING attempted to make headway on my own, without much success, I decided to try the Windmill again.

Van Damm agreed to see me and, having worked out what I felt was a good solo routine, I walked into the audition feeling confident. That confidence was not dispelled after I had finished, especially when Van Damm approached me with the following words, 'Yes, Bruce, definitely . . .'

My eyes lit up. 'Yes, Mr Van Damm?'

'Yes, Bruce, definitely . . . you definitely need material. Take as long as necessary. You know I will always see you. But find better material.' I took his advice, worked on my act, and by August I was in. A solo spot meant six shows a day, six days a week. That's thirty-six shows a week!

These two brochures, reproduced on the opposite page, illustrate the

WINDMILL THEATRE
GREAT WINDMILL STREET, PICCADILLY CIRCUS, W.1
LICENSED BY THE LORD CHAMBERLAIN TO — — VIVIAN VAN DAMM

238th REVUDEVILLE EDITION
"A" COMPANY
Entirely conceived and Produced by VIVIAN VAN DAMM
In collaboration with ANNE MITELLE

This Programme is subject to alteration without notice

1 "OUR SPRING SONG" (*Bridges and Rose*)
   THE WINDMILL GIRLS

2 ADELE FRENCH

3 "ROADS TO SONG" (*Bridges and Rose*)
   Vocalist .. .. .. TONY CLARE
   Tap Trio : JUNE KENNEDY and THELMA WARD or JOBYNA MILLHOUSE and UNA DENTON, with JOHN SHACKELL
   Gigolo .. .. REG DREW or HAROLD ROBINSON
   Gigolette .. .. PAMELA LUCKETT or LENOR BARRY
   Morocco Bounders : WANDA ALPAR or HAZEL PRICE with BRUCE FORSYTH
   Veil Dancer .. .. RENEE BAXTER or IRENE KING
   Lady of the Strand : JACKIE JOY or PENNY CALVERT

4 "TARZAN'S DONE US WRONG" (*Bridges and Rose*)
   The Girls : DIANE CAMERON and PAULINE COLEGATE or PAMELA LUCKETT and JEANNE WEATHERSTONE
   Tarzan .. .. .. REG DREW

5 "GAME OF CHANCE" (*Arranged by Keith Lester*)
   The Players : GERALDINE STIDDOLPH, JOBYNA MILLHOUSE, WANDA ALPAR and IRENE KING
   The Lover .. .. .. KEITH LESTER
   Bad Fortune .. LENOR BARRY or RENEE BAXTER

6 PATRICIA D'OR

7 "DUSKY CHLOE" (*Gaila and Rose*)
   Chloe : JEANNE WEATHERSTONE or GERALDINE STIDDOLPH
   Joey .. .. BRUCE FORSYTH or JOHN SHACKELL
   Rich Lady : DIANE CAMERON or PAULINE COLEGATE
   Her Escort .. .. .. TONY CLARE
   Sailors .. JOHN SHACKELL and HAROLD ROBINSON
   The Girls .. .. WINDMILL GIRLS

8 "TANTALISING TABBY" (*Gaila and Rose*)
   JEANNE WEATHERSTONE or PAMELA LUCKETT

9 DANSE ROMANTIQUE
   Vocalists .. ROSALIE WHITHAM and TONY CLARE
   Waltz Couple : TONY CLARE or BRUCE FORSYTH, IRENE KING or WANDA ALPAR
   Tango Dancers : JUNE KENNEDY or HAZEL PRICE and REG DREW
   Tambourine Dancer : JOBYNA MILLHOUSE or DIANE CAMERON
   Merry Widow Waltz : LENOR BARRY and RENEE BAXTER

10 "THE FERRY BOAT INN"
   The Girls : PENNY CALVERT or JACKIE JOY and the WINDMILL GIRLS
   The Boy .. .. JOHN SHACKELL or BRUCE FORSYTH

11 "THE STORY OF LEDA AND THE SWAN"
   (*Arranged by Keith Lester*)
   Leda .. .. .. RENEE BAXTER
   Her Sisters : DIANE CAMERON, GERALDINE STIDDOLPH and JEANNE WEATHERSTONE
   Jupiter .. .. .. KEITH LESTER
   Mercury .. .. HAROLD ROBINSON or REG DREW

12 ALAN GARDNER

13 "THE OLDEN DAYS" (*Bridges and Rose*)
   Lady Ermyntrude : PENNY CALVERT or DIANE CAMERON
   Sir Tiltalot .. .. .. TONY CLARE
   Henchmen .. TONY CLARE and JOHN SHACKELL
   Sir Neckalot .. .. BRUCE FORSYTH
   Lady Matilda .. JUNE KENNEDY or WANDA ALPAR
   Turkish Slave .. PAMELA LUCKETT or LENOR BARRY
   Ladies .. .. .. WINDMILL GIRLS

   "NEWS GIRL" (*Ronald Bridges*) .. .. ..
   JUNE KENNEDY or GERALDINE STIDDOLPH

WINDMILL GIRLS :
   JUNE KENNEDY, RENEE BAXTER, PAMELA LUCKETT, JOBYNA MILLHOUSE, IRENE KING, JEANNE WEATHERSTONE, PENNY CALVERT, JACKIE JOY, HAZEL PRICE, PAULINE COLEGATE, GERALDINE STIDDOLPH, WANDA ALPAR, LENOR BARRY, ROSALIE WHITHAM, UNA DENTON, HELEN BARRY, ANGELA OSBORN, DIANE CAMERON, THELMA WARD.

Scenery by Ambassadors Scenic Studios. Dance producer and arranger, Mrs. M. Cryer.
Musical advisers to production department, Miss Molly Milne and K. Frensdorff.
Photography by Alfa Superspeed. Stockings by Kayser-Bondor. Cigarettes by Abdulla.
Suntan effect with Damaskin Leg Make-up Cream.

This THEATRE opens at 12 noon. LAST PERFORMANCE starts at 9 p.m.
Any additional artificial aid to vision is NOT permitted
As this Theatre is open continuously from 12 noon, the Management respectfully informs its patrons that any seat vacated for more than 15 minutes will be considered as free and therefore liable to be re-sold.

General Manager and Producer	VIVIAN VAN DAMM
General Director	ANNE MITELLE
House Manager	L. B. LESTOCQ
Stage Director	JOHNNIE GALE
Musical Director	DENNIS HEDGES
Stage Manager	R. WHITELEY
Assistant House Manager	E. HORTON
Press Representative	KENNETH BANDY

Costumes designed by Phyllis Dexter and executed by Mary Hall

239th EDITION of REVUDEVILLE
with complete change of Programme will commence here
MONDAY, APRIL 23RD, 1951
(FOR SIX WEEKS)

WINDMILL THEATRE
GREAT WINDMILL STREET. PICCADILLY CIRCUS. W.1
LICENSED BY THE LORD CHAMBERLAIN TO — — VIVIAN VAN DAMM

258th REVUDEVILLE EDITION
"A" COMPANY
Entirely conceived and Produced by VIVIAN VAN DAMM
In collaboration with ANNE MITELLE

This Programme is subject to alteration without notice

1 "HOW'S THAT" (*Bridges and Rose*)
   The Cricketers .. .. THE WINDMILL GIRLS

2 "SEC'S APPEAL !" (*Ronald Bridges*)
   The Secretaries .. LYDIA BARTON, JACKIE JOY and LESLEY WADE or LYN SHAW, JUDY BRUCE and MAUREEN O'DEA

3 "A MODERN ROMEO AND JULIET" (*Arranged by Keith Lester*)
   Juliet .. .. JANE BOWMAN, RAE BERRY or GERALDINE STIDOLPH
   Her Father .. HAROLD ROBINSON or JOHN SHACKELL
   Romeo .. .. KEITH LESTER or TEDDY HASKELL
   His Sisters .. KATHLEEN COOPER and JOBYNA MILLHOUSE or ANNETTE PHILLIPS and IRENE KING

4 VIKI EMRA

5 "MY LADY PREPARES" (*Oxley and Rose*)
   My Lady .. .. JACKIE JOY and LYDIA BARTON
   The Escort .. RAYMOND WATERS or ANTHONY BATEMAN or TONY CLARE
   My Lady's Maids .. IRENE KING and ANNETTE PHILLIPS or MAUREEN O'DEA and LESLEY WADE
   The Models .. .. LYN SHAW, RENEE BAXTER and MAUREEN CLAYTON or SALLIE DOREY, ROMA YOUNG and JANE BOWMAN
   Stole Dancer .. JOBYNA MILLHOUSE or KATHLEEN COOPER
   Fan Dancer .. GERALDINE STIDOLPH, JUDY BRUCE or MAUREEN CLAYTON

6 BILLY BAXTER

7 "FÊTE AT SEVILLE" (*Arranged by Keith Lester*)
   The Lovers .. JOBYNA MILLHOUSE or IRENE KING and KEITH LESTER or HAROLD ROBINSON
   Conchita .. JANE BOWMAN or GERALDINE STIDOLPH
   The Toreador .. TONY CLARE or RAYMOND WATERS
   The Revellers .. ANTHONY BATEMAN, WILLIAM GRAHAM and the WINDMILL GIRLS

8 "TOP HAT" (*Ronald Bridges*)
   ANNETTE PHILLIPS or MADELEINE HEARNE or RAE BERRY or JACKIE JOY

9 "THE GAMBLER" (*Arranged by Teddy Haskell*)
   The Spirit of Gambling .. .. RENEE BAXTER or GERALDINE STIDOLPH
   The Gambler .. TEDDY HASKELL or JOHN SHACKELL

10 "DING-DONG BOOGIE"
   MADELEINE HEARNE or JACKIE JOY and JOHN SHACKELL or WILLIAM GRAHAM with the WINDMILL GIRLS

11 "CHEZ MADAME" (*Arranged by Keith Lester*)
   Madame .. ROMA YOUNG or MAUREEN CLAYTON
   The Barmaid .. SALLIE DOREY or LYN SHAW
   Oriental Dancer .. RENEE BAXTER or JUDY BRUCE
   The Parasol Dancer .. .. RAE BERRY or ANNETTE PHILLIPS
   The Soubrette .. JOBYNA MILLHOUSE or KATHLEEN COOPER
   Her Protector .. TONY CLARE or RAYMOND WATERS or ANTHONY BATEMAN
   The Sailor .. KEITH LESTER or HAROLD ROBINSON or TEDDY HASKELL

12 BRUCE FORSYTH

13 "SO THIS IS HAWAII !" (*Lindon and Rose*)
   Bill .. .. JOHN SHACKELL or WILLIAM GRAHAM
   Mac .. RAYMOND WATERS or ANTHONY BATEMAN
   Dodo .. .. TONY CLARE or HAROLD ROBINSON
   Prunella .. JACKIE JOY or ANNETTE PHILLIPS
   Aloma .. JOBYNA MILLHOUSE or JANE BOWMAN
   Honolulu Lu .. MADELEINE HEARNE or LYN SHAW or GERALDINE STIDOLPH
   Flamingo Dancer .. LYDIA BARTON or ROMA YOUNG
   Hawaiian Dancers .. THE WINDMILL GIRLS
   "NEWS GIRL" (*Ronald Bridges*)
   IRENE KING or GERALDINE STIDOLPH or RAE BERRY or MADELEINE HEARNE

WINDMILL GIRLS :
   LYDIA BARTON, RENEE BAXTER, RAE BERRY, JANE BOWMAN, JUDY BRUCE, MAUREEN CLAYTON, KATHLEEN COOPER, SALLIE DOREY, MADELEINE HEARNE, JACKIE JOY, IRENE KING, JOBYNA MILLHOUSE, MAUREEN O'DEA, ANNETTE PHILLIPS, LYN SHAW, GERALDINE STIDOLPH, LESLEY WADE, IRIS WHITE, ROMA YOUNG

Scenery designed and executed by Ambassadors Scenic Studios.
Dance producer and arranger, Mrs. M. Cryer.
Musical adviser to production department, Miss Molly Milne.
Photography by Alfa Superspeed. Stockings by Kayser-Bondor. Cigarettes by Abdulla.
Suntan effect with Damaskin Leg Make-up Cream. Drinks by Appolinaris.

This THEATRE opens at 12 noon. LAST PERFORMANCE starts at 9 p.m.
Any additional artificial aid to vision is NOT permitted
As this Theatre opens continuously from 12 noon, the Management respectfully informs its patrons that any seat vacated for more than 15 minutes will be considered as free and therefore liable to be re-sold.

General Manager and Producer	VIVIAN VAN DAMM
General Director	ANNE MITELLE
Manager	L. B. LESTOCQ
Stage Director	JOHNNIE GALE
Musical Director	DENNIS HEDGES
Stage Manager	R. WHITELEY
Assistant House Manager	E. HORTON
Press Representative	KENNETH BANDY

COSTUMES DESIGNED BY MICHAEL BRONZE AND EXECUTED BY MARY HALL

259th EDITION of REVUDEVILLE
with complete change of Programme will commence here
MONDAY, AUGUST 10TH, 1953
(FOR SIX WEEKS)

difference between being in the company and being booked as a single act. As you can see from the first one, dated April 1951, my name is listed as a member of A Company, performing in scenas (the part of Joey in 'Dusky Chloe' and Sir Neckalot in 'The Olden Days'), as a dancer (Waltz Couple) and singing with Penny ('The Ferry Boat Inn').

Two years later I'm back, performing for the first time as a comedian, with comic routines such as parodying different types of golfer – for instance, the show-off, the slogger, the short-sighted player and the old man. I would often close my act with impersonations. Tommy Cooper was a favourite for a while. Even though he wasn't a very big name then, he was a regular at the Windmill where the audience loved his sense of humour and in turn responded well to my routine.

Now don't take this the wrong way, but my exit from the stage was particularly popular. Remember, this is all in Tommy's voice.

'Now for my last trick I am going to disappear. Right in front of you. I just say the magic words.

'Hocus pocus, fishbones choke us.'

Then I would impersonate Tommy shaking his hands from side to side, casting his spell.

'Ju-ju-juzz. Ju-ju-juzz.'

Having repeated this a few times, when nothing happens, I call into the wings: 'Am I standing in the right place?'

Then I try again.

'Ju-ju-juzz. Ju-ju-juzz.'

Still nothing, so I cup my hand in front of my mouth, and in a stage whisper shout. 'Pull the lever! Pull the lever!' At which point a stagehand suddenly appears with the lever in his hand.

'Pull the bloody thing yourself!' And throws it down, clattering on the stage in front of me.

Now, if you take a close look at the 1953 brochure, you will see that immediately before I come on there is something called 'Chez Madame', arranged by Keith Lester.

That spells trouble.

Keith was a highly accomplished ballet dancer, teacher and choreographer, who also put together some of the famous Windmill nude tableaux. These did involve some choreography, that's true, but that was hardly the main attraction.

Onstage, among the scantily clad dancers, there would also be a girl standing on a pedestal, totally naked. This was permitted by the Lord Chamberlain, who was responsible for such things, provided the girls did not move an inch. They had to remain completely still during the entire four- or five-minute routine. (Some wag once suggested the theatre's famous slogan 'We Never Closed' should be changed to 'We're Never Clothed'!)

As you can imagine, these tableaux were *very* popular with the predominantly male audiences. For me, however, they caused all sorts of problems. As resident comedian, I always followed the tableaux and it's fair to say the guys sitting in the front row, some of whom would have been there for four or five hours, had not come to see me.

Eventually some of these stalwarts would have to leave, which meant that just as I walked on there would be an almighty scramble as the men further back jumped over seats in their desperation to take up the vacant places in the front few rows. I'll tell you, the Grand National had nothing on the Windmill. When I walked out there it was like facing a stampede.

One final observation on these brochures. Looking at the fine print, there is a great line: 'Any additional artificial aid to vision is NOT permitted.' I think we know why.

Vivian Van Damm was a marvellous character. I liked him and I was fortunate that he liked me. This is the only photograph I have of the two of us together. It was taken on the occasion of the theatre's twenty-fifth anniversary in late 1956. Vivian is being presented with a cup to

ted Their Careers in The Theatre

MARTELL	1941	JULIA BRETTON
KENT·	1942	MICHAEL HOWARD
ON	1944	ALAN CLIVE
RD de COURCY	1946	JIMMY EDWARDS
MIAN INNES	1946	HARRY SECOMBE
E BILLINGS	1946	ALFRED MARKS
Y OSMOND	1946	MICHAEL BENTINE
D BERENS	1947	BILL KERR
GE CARDEN	1948	PETER SELLERS
E TANDY	1949	ARTHUR ENGLISH
	1947	LESLIE WELCH (THE MEMORY MAN)
	1948	TONY HANCOCK
	1948	ROBERT MORETON
	1950	GEORGE MARTIN
	1953	BILL MAYNARD
	1953	BRUCE FORSYTH

commemorate the occasion and that is me behind him, dressed as the Galloping Major. These were very happy days indeed.

This photograph demonstrates to me just what a lovely man Vivian Van Damm was. I'm standing by the stage door where he had installed this billboard listing all the big-name stars who had performed in his theatre. For some reason, for which I am for ever grateful, Van Damm decided to add me to the list, before I became at all well known. It was a truly wonderful gesture. Seeing my name up there with all those great performers gave me such a confidence boost. Thank you, Vivian.

IN THE WINTER OF 1956, having once again been touring the country's variety theatres and cabaret clubs for a couple of years, I rejoined Van Damm at the Windmill. I stayed for a happy twenty-three-week run, but when offered the opportunity to remain as resident comedian, I declined. I was at a crossroads in my career. When Penny and I returned from India in 1953 I had given myself five years to 'make it'. Time was beginning to run out and I felt I had done all that I could at the Windmill. I knew I had to take a chance and hope something happened for me.

During this period, Penny was incredibly supportive. By then we had a beautiful baby daughter, Debbie, and the three of us would often tour together, living in a caravan towed by my trusty Wolseley car. That's our car here in this photograph although, just to be confusing, it isn't our caravan! We're visiting my parents who were on holiday in a caravan park in Dymchurch, Kent. Penny is behind the camera, I think, and that's my mother and sister, along with a friend of Maisie's. Goodness knows where my father is.

During this five-year make-or-break period I must confess I began to grow quite frustrated. Take a look at this Leeds Empire Theatre poster from May 1954. No, really, look hard. My name *is* there, I promise. Way down the bill, behind the acrobatic Aerial Skylons and actress Iris 'Saucy but Nice' Sadler. My billing, just in case you don't have a magnifying glass to hand, reads as follows: 'new style comedian'.

What that really means is I was booked as 'the first comic'. In those days a dance act often opened these shows, and following on immediately from there came the poor comedian, sent out to warm up the audience for everyone else's benefit.

That was my job throughout much of those five years, stuck out there with a stone-cold audience. As my deadline of 1958 loomed, I was without doubt reaching the time where I began to wonder, Is it worth it?

THIS PHOTOGRAPH MEANS so much to me.

It wasn't all doom and gloom and audience-warming during this period of my career. I did receive some breaks along the way that in retrospect I can see helped lay the foundations for what was to come. One of these was a direct result of my appearing in this theatre, the Metropolitan, Edgware Road.

Following on from that first solo stint at the Windmill, in 1953, I was then back on the variety circuit and endured the most terrible week at the Empress Theatre, Brixton. That was such a difficult venue. There was very little atmosphere at the best of times and, to add to the 'fun', a lot of out-of-work professional entertainers lived in the area and would come along to see 'the competition'. Let's just say they were not very receptive. Anyway, having suffered the most dreadful week ever, I went to the City Varieties in Leeds, a classic old theatre, small but very nice, and had a marvellous time with exactly the same material. From there it was on to the Met, where I enjoyed another fantastic week. After my final appearance, on the Saturday, a guy called Albert Stevenson knocked on my dressing-room door. He introduced himself as the director of the BBC's *Saturday Night Music Hall* programme, broadcast from the Shepherd's Bush Empire and one of the biggest shows on TV. He went on to explain his reason for calling in on me.

'Bruce, I enjoyed your act enormously and I wondered if you'd like to appear on next week's *Music Hall*?'

He didn't need to ask twice. 'You bet I would!'

That was my first big TV break, thanks to Albert Stevenson and the Met Theatre, Edgware Road.

My *MUSIC HALL* APPEARANCE provided very welcome television exposure and hope, but it was the Summer Seasons that really laid the groundwork for what was to come in my career.

Gaytime at the Concert Hall, Babbacombe, Devon, 1955. My first Summer Season, in what was a delightful little theatre, with a capacity of around six hundred. That is what the summer shows were called back then – I don't think they would use that title today.

Those shows were devised and produced by Hedley Claxton. He was an amazing man who ran similar shows in a number of seaside locations, such as Newquay, Morecambe, Eastbourne and Weston-super-Mare. He would book himself on a succession of sleeper trains over the course of the summer so that he could visit each of his productions regularly, often passing on the funniest lines he heard from each show among the various comedians. He was extremely hard-working and dedicated. I owe him a lot.

If you look carefully at the second photograph you can just about make out '5 Complete Programmes'. That's how the Summer Seasons operated. You started off rehearsing the first show for a couple of weeks before opening. Then, while that was on, you would start to rehearse show number two. Once that was up and running, you moved on to show three, and so on. In time you would have six completely different shows ready, changing from one to the next every three days. It was hard work but a wonderful experience.

As you can see from the brochure on the next page, Summer Season shows consisted of a company of performers, rather than individual acts.

In addition to the musicians, usually a pianist and drummer, there would be a soubrette – a girl who could act and sing – a baritone, another female singer, an accordion player, a dance pair, plus maybe three dancing girls. Each performer took on different roles, which were intermingled throughout the show.

Rowena Vincent was our leading lady for my Summer Season debut in 1955. She was a very good actress and perfect for the comedy sketches, which was just as well because before then I had never really performed comic routines in this way. At the end of the season, however, I had appeared in twenty-four sketches, four per show. That was incredibly valuable in building a portfolio of material. My solo time at the Windmill had pushed me to produce a strong core of variety routines – hugely beneficial for these summer shows in which I went out on my own for

SYDNEY SNAPE

Our Baritone, has toured many thousands of miles with the "Opera for the People" series. He appeared in Opera at the Cambridge Theatre, London, and also at the Stoll Theatre. Previous Summer Seasons have been spent at Southend and Newquay. During the winter has been in big demand at Celebrity Concerts, and has also broadcast in the Light Programme.

KAY STEVENS

was born in Liverpool and is a graduate of the Royal Manchester College of Music. She then studied under Roy Henderson, singing oratorio in the North of England, and giving recitals of Lieder to music clubs. Last summer she played a summer season at Falmouth, and at Christmas was the Fairy Queen in pantomime at Leicester Palace for Prince Littler.

HEDLEY CLAXTON *presents the 1957 version of the* SPARKLING SUMMER SHOW

'GAYTIME'

Devised and produced by Hedley Claxton with the co-operation of Bruce Forsyth and Ivor Worring. Costumes by Dolly Martin. Scenery by Berre and Browne of Hastings. Draperies by John Holliday and Son, Ltd., London. Nylon Hose by Kayser. Choreography by Harry Haythorne. Special decor by Eddy Clifton.

GRAND FAREWELL PROGRAMME

OVERTURE with Ivor Worring at the Piano and Les Plested on the drums.
Revel
1. We invite you to have a GAYTIME.
2. Bruce Forsyth sets the ball rolling.
3. Make Mine Music—Kay Stevens and Sydney Snape.
4. Comedy Sketch—MEET AUNTIE—with Bryan Hartley, Sydney Snape, Gillian Wye, Elaine Clifford, Kay Stevens and Bruce Forsyth.
5. Song Scena—NEW ORLEANS—with Our Three Young Ladies, Harry Haythorne, Maureen Young and Kay Stevens.
6. Comedy Sketch—NOT YET (Robt. Rutherford), with Sydney Snape, Bryan Hartley, Elaine Clifford, Marcus Deans, Kay Stevens and Bruce Forsyth.
7. Kay Stevens will sing.
8. One of Life's Little Incidents.
9. The Modern Comedienne—Elaine Clifford.
10. Song Scena—NEW YORK, PARIS and LONDON—The Company.

INTERVAL

11. COMPOSERS' CAVALCADE, bringing you melodies that you will remember.
12. My Accordion and I—Marcus Deans.
13. A Novelty Item—OFFICE OPERA (Wilcock and Rutherford), with Kay Stevens, Elaine Clifford, Sydney Snape, Harry Haythorne, Our Three Young Ladies, Bryan Hartley and Bruce Forsyth.
14. Maureen Young and Harry Haythorne will entertain you.
15. A Trip in the Country—with Elaine Clifford and Bruce Forsyth.
16. Sydney Snape will sing.
17. Comedy Sketch — A ROOFTOP RENDEZVOUS — with Elaine Clifford, Sydney Snape, Harry Haythorne, Maureen Young, Marcus Deans, Bryan Hartley, Gillian Wye and Bruce Forsyth.
18. Song Scena—DOMINO—with Sydney Snape, Harry Haythorne, Maureen Young, and our Corps de Ballet.
19. Bruce Forsyth, the irrepressible comedian.
20. And so, with happy memories of our stay in Babbacombe, we bid you adieu.

GOD SAVE THE QUEEN

Stage Director		Ray Thorne
Wardrobe Executive	For Hedley Claxton	Dolly Martin
Manager	Productions Ltd.	Ivor Worring

HARRY HAYTHORNE

is an Australian. He was soloist in the Metropolitan and International ballets, and appeared in "Top of the Town" at Blackpool and "Ring out the Bells" at Victoria Palace, London. He appeared in "Can Can" at the London Coliseum, and played Samuel Zook in "Plain and Fancy" at Drury Lane. He has been featured in B.B.C. Television on several occasions.

MAUREEN YOUNG

started her dancing career at the age of four. Her first real engagement was in B.B.C. Television when she danced in the Ivor Novello Commemoration programme. She has played in pantomime at Theatre Royal, Newcastle, and was principal dancer last Christmas at Brighton Hippodrome. Last summer she played her first summer season at Brighton in the Ruby Murray show

the final act – and now this new experience with sketches added another dimension to what I could offer.

A further element to these Summer Seasons also proved to be critical to my career. The law at the time, thanks again to the Lord Chamberlain, stated that on Sundays you were not allowed to wear costumes. That didn't mean we all ran around naked – I'm certain that wouldn't have been his intention! No, on Sundays the girls had to wear cocktail dresses and the men dinner suits. No scenery or anything. This, of course, changed the shows entirely for that one day, especially for me. Instead of the usual singing, dance and comedy numbers, we played silly games with the audience, things such as Name That Tune or eating a doughnut without licking your lips. Up until then I had never done any audience participation.

UP UNTIL THEN I HAD NEVER DONE ANY AUDIENCE PARTICIPATION.

If the sketches had been new territory for me, this was a different world.

On my very first Sunday, Hedley Claxton was there to advise. 'One of the most important rules, Bruce,' he told me, 'one that we must never, ever break, is that the show *has* to finish by ten p.m. If we run over, we are in serious danger of being closed down by the Lord Chamberlain.' Okay, Hedley.

I absolutely loved this first experience of working onstage with members of the public. So much so that the first half of the show came down at twenty to ten, an hour and forty minutes after we opened! I was having so much fun with the contestants that I forgot the time. We were left with a ten-minute interval, and a ten-minute second half consisting of a couple of tunes from the accordion player, the whole cast appearing in what was known as a concerted number, in which everyone had a line or two to sing, followed by 'God Save The Queen'. Then at 9.59 p.m., the curtain came down.

I didn't make that mistake again. Hedley and I discussed what to do and we decided that, instead of limiting my interaction with the contestants, we would drop some of the games. That suited me perfectly. It was the laughs with the audience that I enjoyed the most.

I appeared at Babbacombe three years in a row, before moving to the Eastbourne Hippodrome for the 1958 Summer Season. I learned an incredible amount over those four summers. Without those little shows by the sea, I would never have made it to the Palladium.

Chapter Four

SUNDAY NIGHT AT THE LONDON PALLADIUM

For the Summer Season shows between 1955 and 1958, I performed with a cast that numbered eleven in total; that's not counting the orchestra, of course. By which I mean piano and drums. You can see us all in the top photograph. Now, imagine appearing in a show produced on that scale on Saturday, 13 September 1958 . . . and then on the very next evening being in a production of the magnitude you see in the photo below!

VAL PARNELL'S SUNDAY NIGHT *at the London Palladium*, with a *thirty-*piece orchestra, an audience of 2,500 in the theatre and millions watching at home. It was *the* top show on television. Nothing could touch it.

I'm standing in the middle, with the wonderful Val Parnell on my right, in the light suit. His extremely efficient secretary, Miss Wood is next to him. Woody, as we all called her, used to sit behind Val in the theatre and was like our auntie on the show, making sure everyone got a boiled sweet from the bag she always brought with her. On my left is the actor Robert Beatty and next to him is the top of the bill, singer Johnnie Ray. The chap in the cardigan is Albert Locke, one of our producers.

It was an incredible change of fortunes for me.

How on earth did it happen?

Two of the people in this photograph play a big part in the story. That's Norman Wisdom to the left, but the key couple in my tale are Joy and Manny Francois, on the right. They performed a successful comedy dance act under the stage name Francois & Zandra. We appeared on numerous bills together, and whenever possible we tried to find digs in the same place because we had so many laughs. Manny wasn't a golfer, but I didn't hold that against him. He was a great character and they were both big supporters of mine.

During my final Summer Season at Babbacombe in 1957, Manny and Joy came down to see the show – not only for the regular *Gaytime* performance during the week but also for what was known as *The Sunday Rendezvous*. That proved critical.

Manny and Joy had never seen me do the audience-participation elements of the Sunday show before, but having done so, and being suitably impressed, they spoke to their good friend Billy Marsh. Now Billy just happened to be Bernard Delfont's second-in-command at the Delfont Agency. And the Delfont Agency was responsible for booking some of the acts for *Sunday Night at the London Palladium* acts. Keeping up?

This is Billy Marsh a few years later, after he had become my agent (and what a top-rate agent he was). Having been persuaded by dear Manny and Joy to come and see me himself, Billy appreciated what I could do and tucked my name away in the back of his mind until the time was right.

Thinking about Billy now makes me smile. He had a huge influence on my career, not only the part he played in bringing me to the Palladium but also in how he guided and advised me over the years. He was a tough, straight deal-maker, who cared about his clients and always wanted the best for them. I am very grateful for everything Billy did for me.

It has often been said that the term 'legend' is overused. Perhaps so, but not in Billy's case. He was a legend in show-business. When he died in December 1995 his ashes were placed under the stage at the Palladium. There could be no more fitting tribute to the man.

Losing Billy was a blow personally, but also professionally. However, I was very fortunate as the agency was taken over by Jan Kennedy, who had worked with Billy for many years and cared for him during his illness. In the years since, until her recent retirement, Jan looked after my interests fantastically well, just as Billy did. That is the biggest compliment I can pay her.

RETURNING TO 1958, IT's then that a number of different strands of the story come together.

First there is *New Look*, a revue-style show that has just been commissioned for TV. *New Look* is to be an hour-long programme, filmed live in front of an audience at the Wood Green Empire, north London. As it is an Associated Television production, there are commercial breaks. Thank goodness. That's when the changes of costume and scenery occur.

It's quite amazing to think of it now. The stage crew were brilliant. The performers would constantly be standing in their way, but somehow they managed to move the sets around at lightning speed, knowing that in two and half minutes the show would be back on air.

New Look was the brainchild of the brilliant Brian Tesler, who also just happened to be a producer on *Sunday Night at the London Palladium*. (Which, by the way, I am now going to start calling *SNAP*, as it was known back then.) Brian was a lovely, lovely man. He believed in nurturing young talent and was determined to create this show with relative unknowns he thought were due for stardom. One of the 'rising stars' he chose was me.

Here's the *New Look* line-up. On the left is Joe Baker, who was in a double act at the time with the chap next to him, Jack Douglas. Jack, of course, went on to do very well in the *Carry On* films. Then it's me and Ronnie Stevens, a very good actor and a clever guy. The two girls in the middle are Gillian Moran and Stephanie Voss. Crouching at the front are Joyce Blair (Lionel's sister) and Roy Castle.

Now, before I continue with how I got my 'big break', I'd like to pause for a moment and reflect on dear Roy Castle.

ROY WAS ONE OF the good guys of the world, and one of the most underrated entertainers. He could do everything – sing, dance, play instruments. Such talent. He did a great solo act, but could also perform incredibly well in comic roles. In fact, he had a very inventive comedy mind, both onstage and in real life. Roy and I worked together many, many times. Here I am accompanying him onstage at the Palladium. He had a great voice. Just another of his numerous talents. What a loss it was to our industry when Roy died in his early sixties. I miss him very much. I can't help thinking of all the shows we could have done together.

RIGHT, BACK TO THE story.

So, Brian Tesler has asked me to join the *New Look* cast and Billy Marsh has seen me in Summer Season, and crucially has witnessed me interacting with the audience.

The final strand of the tale is Val Parnell.

Tommy Trinder had been compère of *SNAP* for a number of years, but in 1957 the decision was taken to use a roster of compères, each hosting for three or four weeks at a time. There had been Dickie Henderson, Bob Monkhouse, Hughie Greene, Alfred Marks, Tommy Trinder again, and my favourite, Robert Morley. Robert was wonderful, in particular when it came to the game segment of the show, Beat the Clock, in which couples from the audience participated.

You could always tell by their eyes which compère actually enjoyed

Beat the Clock, and it was obvious Robert Morley loved it. He enthused when he was explaining the games to the contestants, playing it very straight, like a kindly uncle. There was no sense of him wondering why on earth he was involved in such nonsense. I am sure some of the others did feel like that. I could see in their faces that they were wondering where the laughs would come from. Not Robert.

So, having introduced the roster of compères, for the next series Val decides he wants to revert to a single host, and is on the lookout for someone to take on the role. That is when it all comes together for me. Both Brian Tesler and Billy Marsh recommend me. According to Billy, Val is open to the idea of giving me a try, save for one concern. 'What about Beat the Clock?' Billy, having seen me at Babbacombe, is able to allay Val's fears. 'Don't worry about that, Val, this fella can do it standing on his head.'

I am in. *The* huge moment of my career. I am thirty years old.

The only downside is that I have to pull out of *New Look*. It just isn't possible to make it all work. I end up only appearing in one episode, which is a shame.

'GOOD EVENING, LADIES AND gentleman. Welcome to *Sunday Night at the London Palladium*.'

I first sang those words on 14 September 1958. They kicked off my opening number for every show, following on from the sensational dancing girls who always took to the stage first. For the rest of the song I wrote different lyrics each week, usually introducing something topical. I might mention the time of year, for instance, Hallowe'en or Easter, or perhaps the money available in the Beat the Clock jackpot. Or I might mention something memorable that had occurred in the previous week's show.

What was important from my point of view was that, with this opening number being right up to the minute, it always received an instant reaction – the perfect way to start the show off on the right footing.

In truth, moving in the blink of an eye from relative obscurity to hosting the biggest show on television was almost too much to cope with. Everything seemed to be happening at once, everything I had ever dreamed of was suddenly a reality. This really is the London Palladium. And I really am on its stage performing. Incredible.

The famous US comedian Alan King appeared on the show a few months after I'd started, and backstage he asked me, 'How long have you been in the business?'

'Sixteen years,' I replied.

'And you've just got this job?'

'Yes.'

'So it took you sixteen years to become a star overnight!'

Exactly.

I don't begrudge those sixteen years for a second. If it had not been for all that experience I would never have been offered the job, and I certainly wouldn't have kept it. Thanks to all those performances at the Windmill, all those years of touring, plus the Summer Seasons, I couldn't have been better prepared for the demands of the Palladium.

Funnily enough, the only box I couldn't tick was hosting. That is the single element I had to get used to, and fast. I understood the reality of my situation. In effect I was undergoing a six-week trial period. I had to prove I was a success in Val Parnell's eyes, or someone else would very soon be offered the job. That's show-business.

THIS 'OVERNIGHT' SUCCESS WAS to come at a personal price, however. This photo is from *SNAP* in 1961, my wife Penny and I singing our favourite 'How Could You Believe Me?' number.

Three years after this was taken, Penny and I separated, although in truth our marriage had been in trouble for some time before then. Penny was a talented performer: she danced very well and possessed a good singing voice. She would not have been on the Palladium stage if she had not earned the right to be there, that's for sure. However, our marriage felt the strain of my success. From the point of view of our relationship, it was a shame that the business suddenly shot me to incredible heights while she was somewhat left behind.

Penny had the talent to make it herself, no doubt about that, but timing was against her. She gave me three amazing, beautiful daughters – Debbie, Julie and Laura – but raising a family made travelling the country for work virtually impossible. Only one of us could do that and it happened to be me. That's how things were back then, and it eventually caused us to drift apart. In the years that followed, we did experience some difficult times, but ultimately we remained close, both of us loving and caring for our wonderful girls.

DESPITE THE ACCUMULATION OF a good-sized body of material over the years, as the end of my six-week 'trial' approached I began to worry that the well was running a little dry. In addition, many of my contemporaries were counselling me in the danger of over-exposure. 'Television eats up material, Bruce,' they would tell me. 'When the time comes to return to the variety circuit, the public will think they have seen everything you have to offer.'

Thanks, fellas.

Billy Marsh and I decided to approach Val Parnell to discuss the issue. He was having none of it, dismissing my concerns with a wave of his hand. 'What are you on about, Bruce? Don't talk such nonsense. You are a new face. Over-exposed? Ridiculous.' He then delivered a bombshell. 'You are here and you are going to stay here. What have we done now? Six weeks? So you have another thirty-four shows to do.'

Honestly, I could hardly believe my ears. The job was mine for the remainder of the series. I was stunned. And thrilled. 'If you're worried about coming up with new jokes and sketches week in week out, don't be. We can help with writers. Listen to me, Bruce, the only way to treat television is to go out there, do it, and once it's done, forget it. Then, the following week, do it all over again and forget it.'

Val was so right in what he said to me that day, and it has been my attitude to television ever since. Good, bad or indifferent, do it and forget it.

Val was as good as his word when it came to the writers, first linking me up with Jimmy Grafton, who wrote for Dickie Henderson, and then the two very clever guys, Sid Green and Dick Hills, pictured on the previous page. The three of us ended up working together a lot and, more importantly, we became great mates. We enjoyed many laughs together.

WITH THE SUPPORT OF Sid and Dick, my fears about having to come up with ideas on my own quickly evaporated. One of the most successful gags we devised, certainly one of the best received, concerned the newly launched drip-dry shirts.

I thought these were a marvellous invention. When touring I did all my own laundry and those new-fangled garments proved to be a godsend. In fact, I still hand-wash my shirts. I like to make sure they dry on the hanger in a certain way, pressing in the collar with my thumbs and straightening the cuffs. Mad? Well, I've been doing it like that for years. It's a little late to change now.

For the Palladium sketch I arranged for a clothesline to be held tight across the stage, with a hanger in the middle and below it a large tin bath. I then produced a soaking shirt from the tub and hung it up. 'Ladies,' I announced, 'I know ironing shirts is a chore to many of you. Well, I have some wonderful news. With these marvellous drip-dry shirts, your days with the iron are numbered, as I can demonstrate for you right now.' I then pointed to my own shirt. 'I washed this one only two hours ago. And look at it, it's perfectly dry. The only trouble is, my shoes are full of water!'

That one joke launched an incredible avalanche of mail. It arrived at the Palladium in sacks, from all over the country, offering very helpful advice such as, 'Why didn't you wear drainpipe trousers?' and 'Next time you do that, Bruce, you should wear pumps.' It went on and on. The press latched on to it as well, staging photographs of me with the shirts. And, as you can see, a member of the public even sent in a little model they had made for me. I was proud to hang that in my dressing room, as a reminder of just how effective television could be in reaching people.

The overwhelming response to that one short routine was the first time that the astonishing power of television properly struck me. The Beat the Clock segment of *SNAP* offered further examples.

As I mentioned, this was an audience participation game, in the middle section of the show, ahead of the top of the bill. I chose the contestants at the beginning of the evening, just before we started. I would step out in front of the curtain, crack a couple of silly jokes, then randomly pick couples from the stalls, upper and dress circles. They were brought backstage where we discovered a little about them and made sure they had no health issues that might prevent them from participating. The games were a mix of physical and mental challenges, all played against the clock, with a prize jackpot on offer, which increased each week by £100 if it was not won. When the sum reached £1,000 the money was donated to charity and the amount reset at £100.

Beat the Clock was what is known as a 'buffer' – that is, we could tailor its length as required. Very handy if, for instance, we learned that the headline performance wasn't as long as we thought it would be and the other acts had been a bit short. The longest Beat the Clock I ever did was twenty minutes and the shortest was eight. Jack Matthews, the stage manager, would tell me just before we started how long I had. Depending on the length of the segment we might be on to our second or third couple when the bell sounded to stop the game. This led to one of the first famous lines from the show, when I would ask the pair, 'Can you come back next week?' More often than not they could, and they reappeared the following Sunday to finish their game.

THIS PHOTOGRAPH IS A classic Beat the Clock game, with the contestants required to bounce a certain number of tennis balls over two drums and

on to the cymbals before the time ran out. In this second picture, I'm clearly introducing myself to the couple before we begin. Tucked away in the corner you can see some milk bottles. These must have formed part of whatever game was to come. Goodness knows what it would have been. One thing's for sure, though, it would have been great fun. The games always were.

The undoubted star of Beat the Clock in my first season was a sweet lady called Beattie.

Beattie was so excited to be there that she wouldn't stop talking. Not for a second. 'Oh, Bruce, it's marvellous to meet you. I never thought in all my life that I'd be here. And here I am. Meeting you. Onstage. Absolutely marvellous. Who would have thought . . .'

Initially I was trying to help her and her husband win a television set, but she just wouldn't pay attention. She kept on talking and talking and talking. Same thing when we reached the jackpot round. 'This is so exciting, Bruce, it really is. I'm having so much fun. Thank you . . .'

'Beattie, hold on a second, my love. Beattie! *Beattie!* BEATTIE!'

The audience loved Beattie and so did I. She was real character.

The following afternoon I was appearing in the Palladium pantomime, *Sleeping Beauty*. This was a big deal, a real thrill. There was a scene in which the witch comes flying across the stage screeching, 'I'm going to get that Sleeping Beauty! Soon she'll be in my power for ever! No one can stop me . . .' She went on and on, so just for the boys in the band, I said, 'Listen to her. She's worse than Beattie!' It got one of the biggest laughs in the show. Needless to say, we kept it in from then on.

It never entered my head that everyone in the audience would get the joke. It was just meant as a little laugh for the lads but, of course, the people in that matinée crowd had watched the television the night before. Again, the power of television amazed me.

BEAT THE CLOCK GAVE birth to my first fully fledged catchphrase. I was trying to show a couple how to play one of our games, a tricky one. The challenge was to keep a table-top balanced on a trestle by throwing plates on to each end. Our two contestants were getting into such a pickle that I had to intervene.

'Stop the clock. Stop the clock. Goodness, what a mess you're making of this. Let me show you . . .' I demonstrated what they were meant to do, and was about to start the game again when the woman was suddenly off on her own, throwing the plates!

'Hold on! Hold on! I haven't started the clock yet. It's my game, after all. I'm in charge.'

Next day I was chatting with a friend who worked in radio. He commented, 'Bruce, that was a very good line you came up with last night.' I looked at him quizzically. 'The "I'm in charge". It really worked well.'

It had been one hundred per cent ad-lib, but that comment, from someone in the business, started me thinking. It was a fun phrase and I decided to try it again. In no time it took on a life of its own. People on the street would shout it out and I even saw it scribbled in the dust on the back of lorries.

THE GREAT JOY OF Beat the Clock was that no one ever knew what was going to happen next. That's why it was so popular. Critical to this were the games, which provided the framework around which the fun and laughs were created. They had to be visually interesting and possible to complete. Otherwise people would quite rightly have felt cheated, both the contestants and the public. We spent a lot of time rehearsing and fine-tuning the games with stagehands and some of the dancers standing in as contestants.

Jim Smith is the chap here with the gorilla arm (don't ask why, I have no idea) - he devised many of

the challenges. Opposite him is Angela Bracewell, Beat the Clock's hostess, who introduced the contestants and assisted with the games. Angela was a talented dancer with excellent comic timing. She also appeared with me in my Summer Revue shows, *Every Night at the London Palladium*. In 1967 she married the American actor and singer Stubby Kaye (perhaps best known for his rendition of 'Sit Down, You're Rockin' The Boat' in *Guys and Dolls*).

ANGELA AND THE FOUR regular Beat the Clock assistants were all members of the George Carden dancers who, alternating weekly with the Tiller Girls, performed the show's opening routine. Now that really was a spectacular way to kick off *Sunday Night at the London Palladium* – quite literally. Glamour, razzmatazz and wonderful dancing that set the tone for the evening's entertainment. Both dance troupes were excellent to work with and featured in a variety of numbers throughout each show.

ONE OF THE MOST famous broadcasts of *SNAP* featured only two performers – Norman Wisdom and myself. There is a myth about this particular show that I want to put straight. The reason that Norman and I appeared on our own was not because of an actors' strike. Yes, there was an Equity dispute on at the time, December 1961, but it had no impact on our plans for that show. In those days, there were two show-business unions, Equity and the Variety Artists Federation. Norman and I were members of the latter, as were the dancers/assistants who featured in Beat the Clock. So the strike didn't affect us. All the talk of having to put the show together at the last minute was a load of nonsense. It had been planned weeks in advance.

It wasn't even the first time we'd done it. When Norman and I filmed a TV promotional piece for the initial two-hander, which was a couple of years earlier, we were sitting back-to-back in the Palladium stalls, pretending to be exhausted.

'Well,' begins the interviewer, 'here we are at the London Palladium and we're looking forward to the show. Bruce, who is on tonight?'

I turn and point at Norman. 'He is.'

'And, Norman, who else is in the show?'

'Eh, oh, eh, him . . . and me.'

We thought this was funny, until a note came round from Val Parnell requesting (instructing) that we do it again. 'This time don't sit there saying it's just the two of you. Instead say, "Him and me and an all-star cast."' Seems Val wasn't a hundred per cent convinced that Norman and I alone could pull in an audience!

Unfortunately that first show was not saved. Norman had requested a recording but it wasn't done, based on cost. He was livid. It's a great shame. I think the earlier performance was the better of the two, and was certainly very well received. So much so that when we were preparing the promo for the second show, word came down from on high: 'Don't forget to say it's just the two of you.' Val had changed his tune completely!

Now, I like to rehearse, to know exactly what I'm doing, but no more than that. I like to feel there's a degree of spontaneity.

MY WAY, HOWEVER, WAS NOT NORMAN WISDOM'S WAY.

My way, however, was not Norman Wisdom's way. He was meticulous in his preparation, but for me it felt more like over-rehearsing. Take the famous wallpaper sketch from our second performance. This was pure slapstick, no words, so, yes, timing was critical. I understood that. For Norman, however, it wasn't merely practising exactly when to duck or spin round: for him, every glance, every gesture had to be nailed down precisely. 'When you walk over to me at that point, don't look at me straight away, only after you pick up the bucket.' And we did it again and again and again and again. Not just for that routine, but for the whole show.

To be fair, I was very much the straight man throughout the performance. I did get a few laughs but mainly I was there to set up his gags. No one can feed a comic better than another comic, but at the same time I did understand that the pressure lay more on him than me. I was happy to go along with how he wanted to prepare, as it was right for him to work in that way.

Beat the Clock went ahead in both those shows, and for the second Norman received permission to make an unprecedented intrusion into the game.

Norman and I were having lunch with the show's producers and writers in Verrey's restaurant, Regent Street, next door to the Delfont Agency. Throughout the meal, as we were discussing the various sketches and routines, Norman kept insisting that he wanted to come back on after the wallpaper scene, still covered in slush, and dance with the female contestant on Beat the Clock.

'Val has very strong feelings about Beat the Clock,' I told him. 'It's sacrosanct and he won't allow you to interfere.'

Norman kept on asking and I kept on repeating that Val would not permit it.

'What if I went to see Val, right now?'

'You can try, but it'll do you no good.'

How wrong I was. Norman kept going on and on and on, until Val eventually crumbled. I'm certain Val thought it was a lousy idea but Norman wore him down; he was a little devil at getting things the way he wanted.

And, of course, the dance with the lady contestant was such a big laugh. We spoke to her in advance, offering to buy her a dress if she agreed to the plan. She was over the moon. 'I get to dance with Norman Wisdom, on the Palladium stage, and receive a new outfit? Of course I'll do it.'

> 'I GET TO DANCE WITH NORMAN WISDOM… OF COURSE I'LL DO IT.'

That earlier photo of the wallpaper sketch is actually from a 1968 performance we did for a charity event. I've included it because it gives a sense of what the original sketch was all about.

Sunday Night at the London Palladium kept the public in touch with so many big names – from Hollywood, other parts of the world, plus our home-grown star entertainers and actors. As a show it helped people stay in tune with the times. When I announced who was going to be top of the bill for the following week, it was a big deal.

I introduced so many stellar performers on to the Palladium stage that it would be impossible for me to talk about them all. So I'm not going to try. Instead, here is a selection of my favourite stories. It was a truly amazing time in my life. It really was.

Lena Horne, October 1959.

I love this photograph. I know exactly what's happening and what I'm saying. First, though, there are a couple of things worth noting.

This was taken right at the end of the show. You can see the revolving stage and the letters that spelled out *Sunday Night at the London Palladium*. The entire cast would gather there to wave goodbye, including the top of the bill, as the stage slowly circled round. People used to write in regularly asking how that worked, so Sid and Dick produced a little sketch for me to explain.

'One of our stagehands, a lovely guy called Fred, who would do anything for me, is underneath the stage right now as I speak,' the routine began. 'Next to Fred there are two big, big cogs, attached to a thick steel wire, which goes all the way around the entire stage. Now when I stamp my foot like this . . .' Stomp! Stomp! '. . . and shout out, "Fred!", that's Fred's cue to start operating all that heavy-duty, complex machinery below us. By turning a handle! And it's not easy.'

I then mimed what Fred would be doing, straining to operate the mechanism.

Back to Lena Horne. Just as Lena and I came round to facing the audience on the revolving stage I stamped my foot again, Stomp! Stomp! and shouted out, 'Hold on, Fred!'

Earlier in the day Val Parnell and I had been talking. Now, I've said a couple of times already that *SNAP* was *the* show on television, and that is true. Even so, to find a big star forty weeks in a row was not always possible. The week following Lena's appearance was one of those rare occasions when Val had no one lined up. He had a solution, however.

'I've spoken to Lena, Bruce, and asked her if she'll do next week's show as well. She said she's happy to.'

The audience knew nothing of this. So, with Fred having stopped the stage on my signal, I ushered Lena forward. I remember to this day standing next to her, just as you see here. She had only moments ago finished her act and she was glowing, beads of perspiration still trickling down her beautiful face. It was a very special moment.

'Lena, can you come back next week?' I asked her, which is exactly what I said to the Beat the Clock contestants every week. This got a big laugh.

Then I called out to the auditorium, which is what I am doing in the photo. 'Would you like to see her again next week?' It was unheard of to have a moment like that with such a big star, using a catchphrase normally associated with a daft game.

The response was incredibly enthusiastic. The audience wanted Lena to come back as much as we did and, of course, she agreed. 'Really, you can come back? Well, that's marvellous because we'd all love to hear you perform three more songs.'

Having made the announcement, I then guided Lena back to the revolving stage, banged my foot, 'Fred!' and the show came to a close.

NAT KING COLE, SUNDAY, 15 May 1960.

On the Saturday I had been playing variety in a theatre up north and returned home at around 2 a.m. Next morning, while I was still in bed, Glyn Jones telephoned. Glyn worked for the Delfont Agency, looking after the American artists who came over to perform. He also looked after me a lot. He was one of my favourite people.

So, Glyn called. 'Bruce, you know we have Nat King Cole on the show tonight.'

I idolized that man, his piano-playing and his singing. I had all his old 78 records and listened to them endlessly, trying to copy some of the things he did on the piano. 'Yes, Glyn, I know. I'm so looking forward to meeting him later.'

'Well, better than that, he's arrived early. He's here at the Palladium right now

and there are two pianos set up backstage. Nat says he's up for doing a number with you. If you can make it here during lunch-hour, you can both talk it over and we can work it into the show.'

I couldn't believe it. The possibility of doing a number with Nat King Cole!

I was there in a flash, and at lunchtime, with the auditorium deserted, I went backstage to talk to Nat.

In that wonderful rough voice of his, he said to me, 'Now, what kind of number could we do, Bruce?'

'Well, I have so many of your records I know practically everything you've ever done. But perhaps a good one would be "Paper Moon"?'

'Right, "Paper Moon". Yeah. Now, what key do I do that in?'

'Well, I do it in F . . . so you'll have to do it in F!'

'Okay, let's try that.'

We arranged the routine in five minutes, rehearsed it through a couple of times and then (*this* is the amazing bit) Nat King Cole spent the rest of the lunch-hour in the empty Palladium playing and singing me songs from his new LP. It's hard to believe he would do that. He was perhaps the nicest, warmest big star I ever met.

SUNDAY, 10 SEPTEMBER 1960. Bob Hope is top of the bill. What a treat for those sitting in the front row, to be close to a show-business legend.

Sadly this was not to be the case. In fact, there was no one sitting there at all. Lining the entire front row of the Palladium, about thirty-two seats, there is a series of large cue cards.

That's what Bob Hope always used for his act – and it wasn't merely prompts written on the cards. This was his script. I don't mean any of this in a negative way. It was just how he worked. He was a very professional entertainer, who used the cards all the time, working on what he was going to say, and even taking them back to his dressing room as he continued to hone his act. Then, before the show opened, they were placed on the seats. No one in the audience could see them and the director just had to be very careful with his camera angles!

SUNDAY, 1 OCTOBER 1961, was the first time I performed with 'Mr Wonderful' himself, Sammy Davis Jr. Sammy will make at least a couple of further appearances in the book, so I'll keep this *SNAP* memory brief.

The first time Sammy and I actually worked together on this straw-hats number was at the band call on the Sunday morning of the actual show. Lionel Blair had choreographed the routine but unfortunately for him I was appearing in a northern variety show in the week leading up to the performance. That meant poor Lionel had to travel to see me, run through the number, listen to my feedback, then jump on a train back down to London, go through it with Sammy, work with him on his suggestions, then up to see me, another run-through, more ideas, then once again he would be on the London-bound train to catch up with Sammy. This went on all week. I'm exhausted just writing all that down. Goodness knows how Lionel felt.

THE BEATLES APPEARED TWICE on *SNAP*, in a short space of time – 13 October 1963 and 12 January 1964. In between those dates, 'I Want To Hold Your Hand' was released and spent five weeks at number one in the charts. Beatlemania had truly gripped the nation.

As they said themselves, when talking about that first appearance: 'In October the big one was *Sunday Night at the London Palladium*. There was nothing bigger in the world than making it to the Palladium. And we were on the roundabout and it was dynamite!'

For the Beatles' second show, pictured overleaf, Val Parnell wanted more than three straight numbers. He was convinced there was something else we could do. In search of ideas, our producer, Jon Scofield, and I went along to see them in the preceding week at the Finsbury Park Astoria. The noise was deafening. That was one thing Val wanted desperately to avoid, all the screaming girls in the Palladium. It proved impossible. The moment the Beatles appeared on the *SNAP* stage, the theatre erupted.

We'd known this would happen, of course, so we decided to create a special opening to the whole show. As the curtains were raised the audience saw four male silhouettes sitting around a table. As anticipated, the screaming started instantly, the girls in the audience going absolutely crazy at this first glimpse of their heroes. Then, as the lights came up, all was revealed. Me and three stagehands playing cards!

As the screams quickly turned to laughter I glanced at my watch, 'Oh, the show's started already. We'll finish the game later, lads.' Then walking towards the audience I said, 'Don't worry, they're here. You'll just have to wait a little bit.' The whole thing was a big tease, but the audience loved it.

It was the perfect way to introduce the biggest band in the world. I'm getting ahead of myself. Back to Finsbury.

As Jon and I watched the concert it became apparent that if we tried to do anything extra with the band, anything that involved them speaking, no one would hear a word. Then an idea struck me. The audience might not be able to hear a word, but they could still see. So why don't I hold a visual conversation with the boys? Between their second and last song each of them could run on- and offstage to grab different cue cards, introducing themselves and responding to questions.

The routine was a big success. The Beatles had that fantastic attitude of being willing to give anything a go to inject some fun. I wish I'd worked with them on more than just those two occasions. I would have enjoyed that.

One final thing to note on the Beatles. As you can see in this photograph, my left wrist is in a cast. A few days before the show I was involved in quite a nasty car accident, involving a very icy road and a very solid tree. I had to tell the boys that, even though their single was riding high, they couldn't hold my hand that evening!

THESE PAST FEW PHOTOGRAPHS have all featured top-of-the-bill acts . . . and here is another, Zsa Zsa Gabor. Not that she was actually booked in that capacity. This was another of those occasions when Val struggled to find a big name.

'Ladies and gentlemen,' I had announced the previous week, 'I'm sure you will all join me in looking forward to welcoming the star act in our next show . . .'

No, not Zsa Zsa. Top of the bill was a comedy music act called the Wiere Brothers.

To be fair, they were an excellent trio, who put on a great performance. They had started out in vaudeville in the 1920s, appeared in the 1951 *Royal Variety* and featured in numerous films and television shows over the years. However, by 1964 they had become less well known in Britain. Nonetheless, they still deserved top billing, which, of course, brought with it the added bonus of the No. 1 dressing room.

Then Zsa Zsa turns up. 'Surely, darling, that is for *me*!'

She was quite unbelievable, a force of nature who was almost impossible to resist. The brothers were out of the room and Zsa Zsa was in.

Now, don't get me wrong, Zsa Zsa Gabor was a star, no question about that. And rightly so. She was a delightfully larger than life actress with a big personality, even though she didn't really seem to sing or dance. I think you can see from my face that I'm a bit worried about what's going to happen!

One thing I can say categorically is that Zsa Zsa was great fun to be around, with a terrific sense of humour. We rehearsed together at the Hilton Hotel, in a massive suite of rooms filled with countless staff running around after her. It was during those rehearsals that I was privileged to experience one of those classic, unexpected and unforgettable moments.

> SHE WAS QUITE UNBELIEVABLE, A FORCE OF NATURE WHO WAS ALMOST IMPOSSIBLE TO RESIST.

We are sitting having tea together in one of the reception rooms when I hear a door open and there, emerging from the back of the suite, is none other than George Sanders. Yes, the star of *All About Eve* and countless other films, the voice of the sinister Shere Khan in *The Jungle Book* and . . . and Zsa Zsa's ex-husband by some ten years.

'Goodbye, my dear.' His only words, as he tips his hat and walks out.

'Was - was that George Sanders?' I stutter.

'Oh, yes, darling,' replies Zsa Zsa, with not the slightest hint of awkwardness. 'Georgie comes to see me quite often.'

FROM SEPTEMBER 1958 TO June 1964, with a couple of years out through a combination of illness and other theatrical commitments, I compèred something approaching 120 *Sunday Night at the London Palladium* shows. My final broadcast as host was on 28 June 1964. Norman Vaughan took over my duties after that, followed by Jimmy Tarbuck and then an assortment of compères, including Bob Monkhouse and Des O'Connor.

In 1967 the decision was taken to bring *SNAP* (or *The London*

Palladium Show, as it was then called) to an end. Why? Viewing figures, I assume. In my opinion, a fateful decision had earlier been taken when Beat the Clock was dropped. For a while the press had been on and on about it, saying it was a silly game to have in the middle of a variety show. The powers-that-be responded accordingly and the ratings fell. I think people saw Beat the Clock as something of a lynchpin in the show. Audiences were used to it, regarding it as integral to the running order. When it disappeared, it was as though they were watching a different show: one the public no longer loved.

The date here is 11 June 1967. It's true to say there were subsequent one-offs and later revivals, but this moment marks Jimmy, Bob, myself and Norman Vaughan, all hosts at one point in the show's history, saying our farewells to *SNAP* in the best way we knew how, with a musical tribute. 'Dearie, do you remember when we . . .'

I most certainly do remember. Thank you, *Sunday Night at the London Palladium.* You were responsible for putting me in the Big Time!

Doors that had not merely been
closed to me, but locked tight,
were suddenly open.

A VARIETY OF
PERFORMANCES

S unday Night at the London Palladium most certainly did put me in
the Big Time. My face gained widespread public recognition almost
overnight. In time it even found its way onto a bubble-gum card, for
goodness' sake.

THIS PARTICULAR CARD IS from A&BC's 'Fotostars' collection of 1961.
Here I am alongside Hughie Green and Patrick McGoohan. Please forgive
me, but I just *have* to quote a little of what they say about me on the back.
Here goes: 'Bruce has a wonderful sense of audience participation and has
the knack of making everyone feel perfectly at ease, and his clean, rhythmic
brand of comedy appeals to all ages.'

How lovely.

A bubble-gum card was the least of the changes I faced in the years
after I first walked out on the Palladium stage as host of the biggest show
on television. Nothing was ever the same again. Doors that had not merely
been closed to me, but locked tight, were suddenly open.

Less than a year earlier I had been thrilled to be offered a five-minute
solo spot on the Associated Television show *Sunday Night at the Prince of
Wales*. The next day, a critic writes the following review: 'I like the look of this
new boy with the original appeal. Note the name: George Forsyth.' George?

Then *SNAP*! Everything changes.

One year on and I am presented to Her Majesty the Queen, backstage at the Coliseum Theatre, following *The Royal Variety Performance*. In the line-up with me are, from right to left, Charlie Drake, Eartha Kitt (whom I remember as being very quiet-spoken and really delightful), the fabulous Spanish dancer Antonio, Pat Boone, and talented comedian Ron Parry. Ron and I worked on many bills together over the years, but never one quite as grand as this!

Within twelve months I have gone from 'new boy' George Forsyth to performing in front of the Queen. It still astonishes me.

Two years after my first appearance on *SNAP* I receive an even greater honour: not only am I invited to appear in the 1960 *Royal Variety Performance* at the Victoria Palace Theatre, I am asked to compère it.

The date of the performance is Monday, 16 May. If you were able to travel back in time from there, only twenty-four hours or so, where would you find me? Sitting in a deserted London Palladium listening to Nat King Cole play songs from his new LP.

As soon as Nat finishes his final big number on the Sunday night and we've waved farewell to the audience, I find myself in a taxi heading to late-night rehearsals at the Victoria Palace, wedged between two of the biggest names in the business – Nat King Cole and Sammy Davis Jr, both of whom are appearing in the *Royal Variety* the following evening. Sammy joined us at the Palladium to enjoy Nat's performance, then travel with us to the rehearsals. At one point in our journey, Nat turns towards me and says, in his gravelly voice, 'Bruce, you should do a book show.' He's using the American term for a musical, a song-and-dance show. I can tell he's serious about it. It's an incredible compliment coming from someone of his stature and ability.

NAT AND SAMMY AT the rehearsals, with Adam Faith.

And here's me helping Sammy run through his routine. Or am I merely fiddling with a piece of string while he gets on with it? Hard to tell.

A YEAR ON FROM there, the 1961 *Royal Variety Performance* took place at the Prince of Wales Theatre in November and once again I was invited to compère. One element of that particular show immediately springs to mind, when I think back on it now, and that is a sense of disappointment. I know that sounds strange and it will sound even stranger when I say that the source of the disappointment was Sammy Davis Jr.

Everyone was, of course, thrilled that Sammy had agreed to join us for the second year in a row, but when he announced that he was going to do only one number, we all felt a little deflated. The act he performed, a dance routine with Lionel Blair based around trying on hats in a shop, was, of course, fabulous; it was just that we wanted Sammy to do more, some solo material.

WHILE WE'RE ON THE subject of the *Royal Variety*, I'm going to stick with it for a couple more performances.

This next sequence is from the Palladium in 1980 and includes a photograph I've always loved. Once again it was taken backstage, during the presentation line-up.

Here's the build-up.

IN THIS CONTACT SHEET you can just about make out the fabulous jazz saxophonist Johnny Dankworth and his wife, singer Cleo Laine, plus Sammy, comedian Arthur Askey, then next to me Broadway star Mary Martin and her son JR – sorry, Larry Hagman.

THE PHOTO I PARTICULARLY like comes here in the sequence. The Queen Mother has obviously spotted someone she's a fan of, and starts to laugh and wave at him or her, much to everyone else's clear delight.

I've enjoyed looking at this photograph many times over the years, but for the life of me I could never remember who the mystery person next in line was. Well, now I know, having come across a view from a different angle.

Drum roll . . . Danny Kaye!

FINALLY FOR THE *ROYAL Variety Performance*, we've moved into 1988, the year in which Ronnie Corbett and I compèred together. A double act like that hadn't been done before and I thoroughly enjoyed the experience. Ronnie is always a delight to work with.

I BEGAN THIS CHAPTER discussing the contrast between my career before *SNAP*, and what subsequently happened in my professional life after I had appeared on the show. Well, my work in cabaret is another good example of that seismic shift.

Let's take a step back in time for a moment, to 1955.

THIS IS THE CABARET world I inhabited then. Glamorous, isn't it?

I do hope that young couple are looking up, thinking, *That's not how you spell his name.* I doubt it somehow. More likely, *Who's he?*

As I mentioned previously, before returning to the Windmill in 1956, I spent a couple of years trying to make a name for myself (without an extra *e*) performing up and down the country in variety theatres and on the cabaret circuit. It was tough going on occasions, certainly, but at the same time I learned a huge amount.

There is a considerable difference between performing in front of rows of seats in a theatre and entertaining in the more intimate cabaret setting. Frankly, give me the rows of seats any time. In the smaller cabaret clubs in which I was appearing during this period, the audience would be seated at individual tables on three sides of you, perhaps still eating and drinking, with the band behind. This creates a very different atmosphere to that in a theatre. People feel more isolated round tables, less a part of a collective experience. That makes it much harder to engage everyone in what you are doing. So you have to learn to adapt.

Then there is the length of your act. When I started out in variety, the first thing I always did on arrival at the venue was to check the running order. Everyone on the bill would have a number listed against their name, indicating *exactly* the length of their act. Thirty seconds over and you were in trouble. As the first comic, eight minutes was my norm.

The challenge set by cabaret, however, was altogether different. Instead of eight minutes I suddenly had to fill an hour, something I had never done before. Thank goodness for all those days and nights at the Windmill. They provided me with the basis on which I began to build and adapt my act. That's why I view these cabaret years as an education *and* a transition. Had I not taken those early cabaret bookings, I would never have been forced to develop sixty minutes of entertainment and, without that, the one-man shows I embarked on from the 1970s onwards, right through to today, might never have happened.

The cabaret scene might have been hard work back then, but it paved the way for me. I am forever grateful to it.

I MENTIONED HOW VITAL the Windmill was in developing my body of material, well, here is a perfect example. I'm obviously working through the golfers' routine I first developed around 1953 – the amateur, the slogger, etc. With that stance, I can only hope I've reached the 'old man' section of the act. You can also see just how close the audience could be in cabaret. Very different from a theatre setting.

Some of the clubs in which I performed were awful. Take the Benelux, which you can see opposite, for instance: it's hardly salubrious, is it? What you were faced with was a mixed bag. Sometimes I would discover that I had been booked into a delightful spot in an unlikely location – Wakefield, for example, had a marvellous club – while on another night, even later in my career when I was better known, the venue might prove unexpectedly challenging. The Golden Garter in Wythenshawe, near Manchester, was one example.

This had originally been a bowling alley, with a very low ceiling. I appeared there on the opening night after its conversion into a cabaret club. That was a lesson learned. Never perform somewhere new until it has been tried and tested. You don't know what can go wrong. At the Golden Garter it turned out to be the extractor fans. Performing as the clouds of smelly, oily smoke emanating from the kitchen swirled revoltingly just above head height did not make for a bundle of laughs.

There were no such problems at my favourite cabaret venue of all time – The Talk of the Town. Even appearing on a bubble-gum card couldn't match the thrill of performing at the country's premier nightclub in London's Leicester Square. I genuinely did feel I'd made it then. It's no exaggeration to say that The Talk of the Town was beautiful. It emerged out of the old London Hippodrome following an extensive conversion in

1958. What a concept. Let me quote from the programme produced for the grand opening: 'The policy of The Talk of the Town is to provide three forms of entertainment under one roof; here patrons may wine and dine satisfyingly, and elegantly dance to the music of famous orchestras, and, in the course of the evening, enjoy the two contrasted stage presentations that form the theatre-entertainment. Whether you are relaxing or celebrating, you can have a complete night at The Talk of the Town from cocktail-time to the small hours.'

The wining and dining by the 'patrons' took place at tables around the dance floor, which then, at the appropriate hour, magically raised itself by three feet for the 'two contrasted stage presentations'. The first of these would be a floor-show – dancing girls, high kicks, dazzling costumes, the works. Then around 11 p.m., the main act appeared, up on the stage and clearly visible to every member of the audience. Truly wonderful.

I MADE MY DEBUT there on 4 May 1964. Here I am backstage on that very night, with the Beverley Sisters who had come along to celebrate their birthdays. *All* of their birthdays, not just the twins, Babs (on the left) and Teddie (on the right). Yes, Joy, who was three years older, shares the same birthday as her sisters – 5 May.

I tried to schedule a run of performances at The Talk of the Town once a year, at least. I loved playing there as much as I enjoyed appearing at the Palladium. That tells you something.

I felt a great sadness when the venue closed down in 1982. Part of the reason for the closure was certainly because tastes in entertainment naturally change – cabaret slipped out of fashion. That's not the whole story, however. I believe that the allure of cabaret began to fade because some audience members were becoming too drunk during the shows. This never applied to The Talk of the Town, but it was certainly true for many other venues up and down the country. It doesn't take many noisy individuals to ruin the evening for everyone else, resulting in cabaret acquiring an unwanted reputation.

I often wonder if this would have been avoided had

Robert Nesbitt, the highly successful theatre producer, been able to realize his dream of reproducing the wonder of The Talk of the Town in all the British major cities. That would have been absolutely marvellous, in my opinion. Performers in London could have enjoyed a run at The Talk of the Town, then taken their show on the road, to all those venues of equivalent quality. As it was, some of the clubs we performed in, through to the 1970s, became pretty dreadful.

Unfortunately Robert's idea was not taken up by Bernard Delfont, one of the founders of The Talk of the Town. If it had been, access to high-quality cabaret in clubs that would never permit drunken behaviour would have been open to many more people, and as an entertainment form it would have remained popular for much longer.

The Talk of the Town's demise means that Frankie Vaughan and I will for ever jointly hold the record for number of appearances. I can think of no one I would rather share that accolade with.

I worked on bills with Frankie many, many times, first in the early days when he was sitting on the top and I was one of the smaller acts, then later at the Palladium and on television.

This is the two of us together on *SNAP* in 1961. You will note that we both have our eyes closed. I suspect we were worried that if we kept them open we would be too distracted even to clap!

Frankie and I became good pals. He was a lovely performer and great to work with because, as top of the bill, he would be responsible for the type of audience who turned up. Different entertainers draw different people. With Frankie it was always a very good-natured, enthusiastic family crowd – dads who felt he would be a laugh to have a beer with, and mums and daughters who fancied him. Lucky devil.

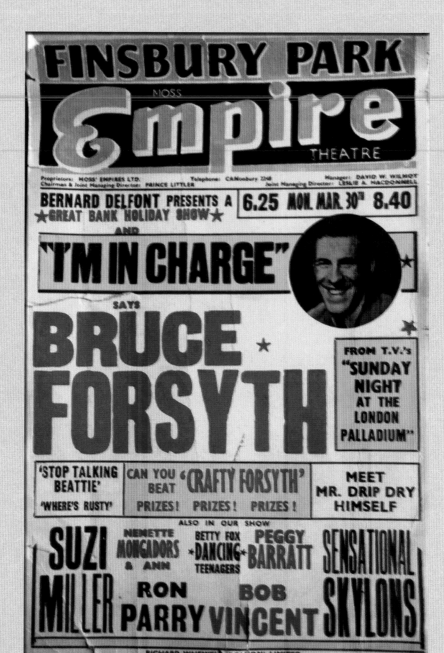

Chapter Six

IN CHARGE

For the first time in my life I am top of the bill and there could be no more appropriate venue – the Finsbury Park Empire, the theatre my parents took me to every week when I was growing up. Now I'm back, and in charge. Quite incredible.

I know I have already made it abundantly clear that *Sunday Night at the London Palladium* changed everything for me and I promise not to go on about it too much longer. This poster, however, captures better than anything just how quickly the show catapulted me to stardom.

It's from March 1959, towards the end of my first season on *SNAP*. Not only have I been elevated to the headline act but, as you can see, the bill matter clearly reflects the aspects of the TV show that caught the public's imagination: 'I'm in Charge', Beattie, Rusty, Beat the Clock, drip-dry shirts. All those unforeseen, unscripted, impromptu moments that were miraculously embraced by the audiences and viewers over the previous seven months of Sundays are encapsulated in this one poster. The power of television.

Oh, and if you're wondering who 'Rusty' is, he was my absolutely wonderful dog, who used to appear with me on the Palladium stage from time to time. I'll tell you all about dear Rusty a little later on.

LESS THAN EIGHTEEN MONTHS prior to that Finsbury Park Empire show, I was also on a stage, but in a very different capacity: panto at the King's Theatre, Southsea. *Puss in Boots* starring Charlie Drake.

Pantomime, especially in prominent theatres such as Southsea's King's, was a big deal. The length and breadth of the country, the biggest stars of the day would feature and the audiences flocked to see them. The productions ran for months, from Christmas through to the spring. This was big show-business.

So, you would think *Puss in Boots* was an excellent booking for someone of my standing in 1957, and you would be correct. Up to a point. You see, I wasn't so much *in* the pantomime, as *in front of* it. Charlie Drake and I never actually met onstage. All my scenes, four or five pieces, were what we call 'front cloth', meaning little routines I performed to keep the audience entertained, while behind me and the closed curtain the scenery for Charlie's next sketch was frantically being set up.

YES, ONE OF MY routines was that old favourite featuring the different types of golfer, while another involved me taking off a great pantomime tradition – I'm playing a boy, playing the principal boy, who is normally played by a girl. I think I've got that right.

In fact, that last sketch very nearly put me in hot water. And, let me tell you, hot water was in short supply where the incident occurred.

I arrived back at my digs after an evening performance to find my landlady waiting. She had been to the show and wanted to tell me what she thought. 'I enjoyed myself very much,' she said. I was delighted. Then came the bombshell. 'Mr Forsyth, I must say, you have *very* nice legs.' I locked my door that night! And, frankly, given the level of accommodation I could afford back then, I was lucky it had a lock. I'd have been up all night in terror otherwise.

IN 1958 I WAS once again appearing in pantomime with Charlie Drake – but this is very different from Southsea. It's The Big One. The Palladium. Top of the Christmas tree for panto season. And I'm very much onstage, not 'front cloth', and we're doing *Sleeping Beauty*.

I'm fourth on the bill, as you can see, and, honestly, that was beyond my wildest dreams. Finally, at the biggest theatre of all, my name really was up in lights.

We performed twice a day, six days a week, right through to April. And on the seventh day? I was on the same stage, compèring *SNAP*. It should have been an exhausting schedule, but with the adrenalin that was

*'Mr Forsyth,
I must say, you have
very nice legs.'*

coursing through my body then, I hardly noticed.

I never really got to know Charlie Drake in either of the shows in which we appeared, but Bernard Bresslaw and I were assigned dressing rooms next to each other at the Palladium and that proximity led to a great friendship. He was a delightful man who, of course, went on to star in many of the classic *Carry On* films. It was so sad that he died before he even turned sixty. He had so much potential, so much still to give, and suddenly it was all over. I think about that sometimes and it just doesn't make any sense.

I PLAYED PRESTO THE Jester. Now I bet you're thinking, *Sleeping Beauty*? Presto the Jester? I don't remember him. Well, you would be correct, because the part was written specifically for that production.

The producer of the show was Robert Nesbitt, whom I mentioned

earlier. A lot of the professionals regarded Robert as the 'Prince of Darkness'. He was a tough taskmaster, for sure, and wielded a lot of power in London's theatre district for a long time, but I thought he was great guy. I first met Robert when I went to discuss my role in the pantomime. I knew then I had the part, and also that it had not yet not been fully scripted, so a couple of days beforehand I had decided to compose a song for possible inclusion in the show.

Once we'd settled into our meeting, I made my move. 'Mr Nesbitt, I've written a song I would like to play for you. I think it would be great for my character, Presto.' He looked at me and raised an eyebrow. 'Really? Phil Park is doing the music. He's very experienced, you know. But go ahead, let's hear what you have.'

I played it and he liked it. 'Yes, we'll put that in the show.' Simple as that.

I had hoped, but I had not expected. 'Really? Thanks!' It was another one of those 'I can't believe this' moments that seemed to be coming at me thick and fast in the second half of 1958.

STICKING WITH PANTOMIME, HERE I am appearing in *Turn Again, Whittington* in 1962 at the Hippodrome, Bristol. My wife Penny played the Queen of Catland, a role described as follows by a local reviewer: 'Penny Calvert, acting as guide, mentor, counsellor, comforter and friend in her built-up role'. That's a lot to take on at the best of times, but as Penny had given birth to our third daughter, Laura, barely a month before we opened her performance was extraordinary.

Oh, let me briefly quote further from that review: 'Is it possible to have too much of a good thing? In the case of Bruce Forsyth, the answer is emphatically "No."'

I just thought you might be interested…

IT'S TIME FOR A confession. I don't particularly like pantomime. Never have. It's because there is no single audience to gear the show towards. We played to both children and adults, and without the more sophisticated scripts they have today, which appeal to all age groups, I found there was just too much time-filling waffle! And my views on pantomime were certainly not improved by my experience in a 1967 production of *Aladdin*. To be fair, that wasn't really the fault of the show. Let me explain.

It all started at the Windmill in 1953. Yes, way back then. I know this sounds like it's going to be a long tale, but don't worry. I'm going to make it as short as I possibly can. You'll understand why in a moment.

SO THERE I WAS, appearing solo at the Windmill for the first time, with one of my routines involving the Tommy Cooper impersonation. This caught the attention of Tommy's agent, a musician called Miff Ferrie, who came along to check whether I was pinching any of his client's material (I wasn't). At the time I was looking for an agent myself, and as they were not exactly beating down my dressing-room door, when Miff introduced himself I decided to give him a go. Bad mistake. You see, Miff wasn't really an agent at all: he had fallen into the role by accident. He was really no more than a band leader; he knew virtually nothing about how the wider business operated. Not that I realized this at the time.

I signed a contract with Miff. It was registered by the London County Council, so was absolutely legitimate. And, to be fair, Miff did ask me to read it carefully before signing. I took only a cursory glance. I was too excited about finally having an agent to focus on details. Surely all contracts were basically the same. Another mistake.

It didn't take me long to see that Miff and I were not exactly a match made in Heaven. Without going into great detail, he would book me into theatres at which I didn't want to appear, and would tell directors and producers I would have been very interested to work with that I was already committed for a year in advance. 'It will make you sound more popular and in demand, Bruce.' What it actually meant was that I missed out on some big opportunities.

After about five years I'd had enough and told Miff I was ending our relationship. I was happy to work out any notice period, but that was it. Miff then explained. The contract I had signed was for five years, which he could renew but I could not terminate. Oh, and in addition I was paying fifteen per cent commission when the industry norm was ten.

THAT IS THE BACKGROUND, which explains why you see me here on 5 June 1962, outside the High Court, attempting to have the dastardly contract set aside. Miff is on my right, my solicitor, Alan Lazarus, on my left, and dear Jimmy Lee – my old golfing partner, sometimes minder, driver, roadie, fellow performer and one of the funniest guys I have ever known – offering his support behind. I am smiling. I shouldn't be. I'm quoted as saying to the press at the time, 'Now we're both in charge.' Rubbish. I lost the case. As the judge said in his summing up, 'It appears that it is far easier for one to get rid of one's wife than one's agent.'

The contract was extended for a seven-year period and I had to pay Miff a lump sum of £7,000 to secure that privilege. *Seven thousand pounds!* A huge amount of money then, and now. Seven years! A lifetime in show-business. I had no choice, though.

Fast forward five years (which is skipping a lot of unpleasant scenes between Miff and myself), and I place a phone call to Frankie Howerd. His sister answers. I know her well and we chat.

'Hello, Bruce, how are you?'

'Just fine, my dear, thank you. And you?'

'No problems at all, I'm happy to say. I guess you're looking for Frankie?'

'Is he around?'

'I'm afraid not, but I'll let him know you called.'

'That's great, thanks.'

'My pleasure. Oh, and by the way, I hope it all goes well with the panto in Wimbledon.'

'Excuse me?'

'Yes, I saw it in the papers. You know, *Aladdin*. With Tommy Trinder.'

I won't repeat what I said next. Suffice to say, I was not best pleased. This was the first I had heard of the booking, for a show I knew I wouldn't even enjoy. And, worse, I was appearing with Tommy Trinder. Now, I had nothing against the man, but I very much suspected the same did not apply the other way around. He regarded me as the person responsible for robbing him of the compère gig on *SNAP*. Miff knew that was how Tommy felt.

It was the last straw. I called my solicitor and demanded he get me away from Miff, whatever the cost. It turned out to be an awful lot – an additional £20,000 for Miff to walk away. Best money I ever spent.

As for the panto, well, I appeared but arranged with the producer that Tommy and I were never onstage at the same time. It wasn't worth the risk. We only ever met at the curtain call.

So, no, that experience did not change my views on pantomimes.

A final word on Miff and then I'm done. Looking at that photograph of us outside court reminds me of how dreadful he was. Honestly. He knew nothing about comedy but he thought he did. That made it so much worse. Here's one awful example.

Miff signed up a comic called Alec Pleon, a very funny man who had made a name for himself in the forties as second on the bill to Sid Field in the show *Strike a New Note* at the Prince of Wales Theatre. Alec and I were appearing on the same TV show, and in the run-up I knew he had been spending hours with Miff working on his routine. I remember Alec saying to me, 'Isn't Miff marvellous? He's helped me so much with my act.' I feared the worst and those fears were realized at the rehearsals on the day of broadcast. It was dreadful. I wanted to stop Alec going on but of course I couldn't: it was too late. He bombed and I later heard, although I can't say for certain it's true, that the poor guy suffered a nervous breakdown. Awful. Enough Miff, back to stage appearances in the sixties.

A PRODUCTION CALLED *SHOWTIME* at the Wellington Pier Pavilion, Great Yarmouth, in the summer of 1961. As you can see, I'm appearing once again with Penny, who not only has a number with me and Gary Miller but also a solo slot. That gives another indication of how talented she was. Seeing

 **PROGRAMME**

BRUCE FORSYTH
Well known as a resident compère of Sunday Night at the London Palladium. Chosen to appear before Royalty at the Royal Variety Performance in 1958. Has consistently broken all Box Office Records wherever he has appeared.

1. " SHOWTIME "   JACK RANKIN
   and the Pavilion Orchestra

2. " YOU GOTTA HAVE PACE "
   PENNY CALVERT,
   The Pavilion Lovelies & the Boys

3. " HERE HE IS "—**BRUCE FORSYTH**
   with GARY MILLER and PENNY CALVERT

4. " A JUGGLING COCKTAIL "
   unusually unique entertaining by EDDIE ROSE and MARION

5. **BRUCE FORSYTH** says " I'm In Charge "

6. " MY TIME IS YOUR TIME "
   GARY MILLER, The Lovelies and The Boys

7. " CRAFTY **FORSYTH !** "   Himself!

INTERMISSION

THE PAVILION GIRLS
   Janice Galton, Sue Addams, Gabrielle Murrow, Rena Jarvis, Valerie Kemp, Diane Langton, Jill Parsons, Jenny Bannister
THE BOYS
   Richard Fox, Basil Patton

8. " ON WITH THE SHOW "
   JACK RANKIN & the Orchestra

9. " LET YOURSELF GO!"
   The Pavilion Lovelies
   and Dancing Boys

10. RHYTHMIC MOMENTS "   PENNY CALVERT

11. DAISY MAY and her friends . . . assisted by SAVEEN

12. "THE DOLL SELLER "   The Doll Seller—Richard Fox
   Teddy Bear—Basil Patton   Dancing Dolls—Our Girls
   introducing The MORLIDOR TRIO in a Continental Surprise-packet

13. IT'S **BRUCE AGAIN!**

14. " SHOWTIME "   Finale   THE FULL COMPANY

GOD SAVE THE QUEEN

Costumes by the Bernard Delfont Wardrobe Dept. and St. John Roper.
Tights and Shoes by Gamba.   Scenery by Bernard Delfont Production Dept.

Productions and Variety Acts being copyright, photographing in the Theatre is forbidden.
The Management reserve the right to change, vary or omit any of the items of the programme rendered necessary by illness or other unavoidable cause without any previous notice.

After the Show is over . . .

 Visit  **MERRIVALE**  **MODEL VILLAGE AND RAILWAY**

Wellington Pier Gardens

Entrance from this Pier

✳ Fascinating scale model of the English countryside with its old world villages and modern town centre.

✳ Over an acre of beautiful landscape garden, with lake, waterfalls and rockeries. 1000 feet of 2¼" gauge railway.

✳ Refreshments available on terrace overlooking gardens.

✳ A paradise for young and old.

Gary's name there brings back very happy memories. Gary, his wife Joy and their boys meant a great deal to Penny and me. Our two families often got together during those Summer Seasons when we were performing on the same bill, and enjoyed ourselves enormously.

This brochure also offers a fascinating sense of time and place. The sixties were not yet swinging and that is reflected in the old-fashioned innocence of some of the descriptions. There is 'unusually unique entertaining' offered by the husband-and-wife juggling duo of Eddie and Marion Rose, while the rag-doll act, the Morlidor Trio, are a 'Continental Surprise-packet'. As for 'The Pavilion Lovelies and Dancing Boys', you would never see that today. And, of course, we closed the show with 'God Save the Queen'.

HERE IS THE PAVILION. They must have been giving away free ice cream that day!

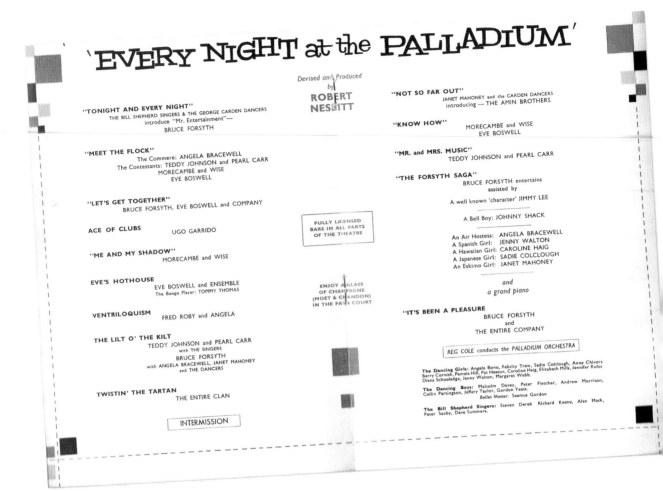

'EVERY NIGHT at the PALLADIUM'

Devised and Produced
by
ROBERT NESBITT

"TONIGHT AND EVERY NIGHT"
THE BILL SHEPHERD SINGERS & THE GEORGE CARDEN DANCERS
introduce "Mr. Entertainment"—
BRUCE FORSYTH

"MEET THE FLOCK"
The Commere: ANGELA BRACEWELL
The Contestants: TEDDY JOHNSON and PEARL CARR
MORECAMBE and WISE
EVE BOSWELL

"LET'S GET TOGETHER"
BRUCE FORSYTH, EVE BOSWELL and COMPANY

ACE OF CLUBS   UGO GARRIDO

"ME AND MY SHADOW"
MORECAMBE and WISE

EVE'S HOTHOUSE
EVE BOSWELL and ENSEMBLE
The Bongo Player: TOMMY THOMAS

VENTRILOQUISM   FRED ROBY and ANGELA

THE LILT O' THE KILT
TEDDY JOHNSON and PEARL CARR
with THE SINGERS
BRUCE FORSYTH
with ANGELA BRACEWELL, JANET MAHONEY
and THE DANCERS

TWISTIN' THE TARTAN
THE ENTIRE CLAN

INTERMISSION

FULLY LICENSED
BARS IN ALL PARTS
OF THE THEATRE

ENJOY A GLASS
OF CHAMPAGNE
(MOET & CHANDON)
IN THE PALM COURT

"NOT SO FAR OUT"
JANET MAHONEY and the CARDEN DANCERS
introducing — THE AMIN BROTHERS

"KNOW HOW"   MORECAMBE and WISE
EVE BOSWELL

"MR. and MRS. MUSIC"
TEDDY JOHNSON and PEARL CARR

"THE FORSYTH SAGA"
BRUCE FORSYTH entertains
assisted by

A well known 'character' JIMMY LEE

A Bell Boy: JOHNNY SHACK

An Air Hostess: ANGELA BRACEWELL
A Spanish Girl: JENNY WALTON
A Hawaiian Girl: CAROLINE HAIG
A Japanese Girl: SADIE COLCLOUGH
An Eskimo Girl: JANET MAHONEY

and
a grand piano

"IT'S BEEN A PLEASURE"
BRUCE FORSYTH
and
THE ENTIRE COMPANY

REG COLE conducts the PALLADIUM ORCHESTRA

The Dancing Girls: Angela Bono, Felicity Trew, Sadie Colclough, Anne Chivers
Berry Cornish, Pamela Hill, Pat Heaton, Caroline Haig, Elizabeth Mills, Jennifer Rufus
Diana Schooledge, Jenny Walton, Margaret Webb.

The Dancing Boys: Malcolm Davey, Peter Fletcher, Andrew Morrison,
Collin Partington, Jeffery Taylor, Gordon Yeats.
Ballet Master: Seamus Gordon

The Bill Shepherd Singers: Steven Derek Richard Keene, Alan Mack,
Peter Saxby, Dave Summers.

JUNE 1962, *EVERY NIGHT at the London Palladium*. A summer revue show with a brilliant cast, including Morecambe and Wise (whatever became of them?), singers Eve Boswell, Pearl Carr and Teddy Johnson, and the lovely Angela Bracewell from Beat the Clock. This was the show that could have had as big an impact on my career as *SNAP*. Could have, but didn't.

Backstage before one performance there was a huge buzz in the air. Word had come through that US TV host and star-marker Ed Sullivan would be in the audience. This was the man whose eponymous variety programme had helped to bring Elvis to the masses and which, a couple of years later, would introduce the Beatles to America. Make no mistake, Ed Sullivan was big news, especially when it was confirmed he was looking for new British talent to appear on his show.

Now, as is clear from the brochure, much of the second half is dedicated to 'The Forsyth Saga' in which I am the all-round entertainer, ably assisted by members of the cast. Surely the perfect vehicle for me to demonstrate my talents to Mr Sullivan. Yes, had he stuck around to see it. Sure, he sat through the first half and went on to book Eve, juggler Ugo Garrido, and Eric and Ernie for his show. Then he left. A prior engagement, I was told. How very odd.

IN JUNE 1964 I decided to step away from *SNAP* for good. Why? One reason was that I felt stretched too thin, worn out by appearing seven days a week for virtually the entire year, travelling back and forth to London from cabaret, variety shows, Summer Seasons. It was affecting my health and I knew I needed a break, a change of routine. I also felt that the time had come for me to branch out again. I'd been at the Palladium for a long time and had enjoyed such wonderful experiences, but niggling away at the back of my mind was the belief that I had to find a new challenge. In that summer of 1964 the perfect opportunity came along.

Val Parnell couldn't believe it when I told him of my decision, but I was determined. It was time for new stimulus. Did this turn out to be a good decision? Well, I would categorize the following fifteen months as being the best of times, the worst of times. Here's what happened.

An American producer called Arthur Lewis, based in London, approached me with an idea. Would I be interested in starring in the West End version of a musical that was currently running in Detroit? Yes, I was interested. This might be the 'book show' Nat King Cole had recommended I find.

'It's called *Little Me*, written by Neil Simon. Cy Coleman has done the music and Carolyn Leigh the lyrics,' Arthur told me. 'It's perfect for you, Bruce. Go over and take a look. See what you think.'

Off I went to the States to do just that. Sid Caesar played the lead – well, the seven leads, actually: that was what the part entailed, twenty-nine costume changes for seven characters of varying ages and accents, all of whom had a connection with the leading lady. Now, Sid Caesar was a hugely talented comic actor, but this was not a role for him. He seemed to be suffering from some kind of affliction that caused him to cough after every line. This gave the impression that he wasn't really trying. And yet I was still enjoying it.

I came away convinced this would be marvellous for me. I said yes.

I was in Summer Season at Bournemouth, and because the decision had been taken to anglicize the script for the British audience, Neil Simon himself came over to work with me on the changes. Incredible, really, to think of it, but that was how much the show meant to him.

I learned the entire script in one week, while appearing in two shows a night at the Pavilion and working with Neil during the day. Fortunately for me, the poetic quality of Neil's writing made the words easy to learn – every syllable meant something. So, at the end of the Bournemouth run, I moved straight into four weeks of rehearsal before opening at the Bristol Hippodrome on 29 October for ten nights. From there we transferred to the West End, the Cambridge Theatre. That, I felt at the time, was a mistake. It was an old converted cinema, there were no boxes and it was cold. It's very hard to connect with an audience when they are shivering in their seats.

And yet we were a smash.

LITTLE ME IS WITHOUT doubt the best straight performance that I have ever done. The photo montage opposite gives a good indication of the challenge I faced in playing such a range of characters. I loved it.

'This show will run for as long as Bruce wants it to.' That was the overriding tone of our reviews. I could not have wished for more.

Then out of the blue, ten months into our successful run, it was announced we were to close. I couldn't understand it then, and I still don't today. The critics had been positive – 'The best reviews we've had since *Annie Get Your Gun*,' Bernard Delfont, who was involved in the production of the show, told me, when he announced we were shutting down – and the box office continued to be very healthy. I was devastated. Overnight we were being written up as a failure, which just wasn't true.

So, what on earth happened?

I wish I could say, but I don't know. The reasons behind the closure were never explained to me. It still upsets me to think of it.

THE PHOTOGRAPH ON THE following page is from the fabulous *Five Past Eight Show* from the Starlight Room of the Glasgow Alhambra. I was top of the bill there in the summer of 1966. Now this really was some show. The word 'lavish' doesn't do it justice. It rivalled the Palladium variety performances in every aspect, from the set design, scenery, costumes and dancers to the stars who appeared there.

All the big names headlined the *Five Past Eight Show* until the theatre closed in 1969 – Ricki Fulton, Jimmy Logan, Kenneth McKellar, Stanley Baxter, Ronnie Corbett, Max Bygraves, Shirley Bassey, Norman Wisdom, Harry Secombe, Lena Martell, Moira Anderson . . . The list goes on and on. They say the word 'fabulous' became part of the show's unofficial title. I wouldn't argue with that.

THIS PHOTOGRAPH SHOWS ME in the opening number and I can't say for sure whether it was that white suit or something else that riled an audience member, but riled he most certainly was. At the interval the guy came to the stage door, demanding to see me. I was busy preparing for my next big entrance so I sent word that I would happily have a chat with him after the show and thought no more of it. All too quickly it became clear this had not been an adequate response.

During my long solo spot in the second half, just two notes into my Liberace impersonation, while wearing my dinner jacket inside out to reveal a lining of glittering sequins, a beer bottle flew down from the upper circle, shattering on the glass stage. It could have killed someone. It could have killed me!

One of the stagehands went belting up there to grab the offender while the police were called. Having been escorted from the theatre, he was held overnight at the station and later appeared in court, even though I was never interested in pressing charges. He was fined fifty pounds and, after the hearing, the press wanted me to meet with him to shake hands. They seemed to think a photo op was just what I wanted. My response? 'You've got to be joking!'

I don't think my beer-bottle-throwing friend ever fully explained exactly what it was that prompted his moment of madness, but he did tell the judge why he had the offending item with him in the first place. Apparently it was because he knew all the public houses would be closed by the time the show finished. Surely he could have found a less dramatic way to leave early if he really felt that desperate for another drink!

THIS IS A STILL from one of my TV shows in the late sixties, with the German entertainers the Kessler Twins, who were very popular performers in Europe during the 1950s and 1960s and are still popular to this day. The reason I have included it is because they play a part in one of the biggest theatrical mistakes of my career.

The Italian film producer Carlo Ponti, Sophia Loren's husband no less, and the man behind *Doctor Zhivago*, was staging a musical in Rome and approached me with the idea of bringing an anglicized version to London. Would I be interested in starring in it? You bet I would.

I took myself off to Italy to have a look at the show – which featured the Kessler Twins – and I loved it. This could be huge, I thought.

It would have been around spring 1969. Unfortunately, the wheels of show-business can sometimes turn rather slowly, and as the weeks and months dragged on I began to feel anxious that it wasn't going to happen. So when I was offered a part in a comedy play called *Birds on the Wing*, at the Piccadilly Theatre, I took it. Inevitably, once I had said yes, the possibility of the Carlo Ponti show re-emerged, just too late for me to reverse my decision. I was committed to *Birds on the Wing* and never considered pulling out. It would have been totally unprofessional to do so. Carlo was not prepared to wait and the opportunity was lost.

HERE I AM WITH my co-stars in *Birds on the Wing*, June Barry and Julia Lockwood (whose mother was the actress Margaret Lockwood). They were both fantastic to work with and we enjoyed a pretty good run with the play, but I think back on it now with some regret. It cost me my chance to work with one of the world's most highly regarded movie producers.

Chapter Seven

TELEVISION TIMES

I n the sixties – and I think you'll agree it would be difficult to look more classically sixties than this I do in this photo – I was lucky enough to host two television series, imaginatively entitled *Bruce's Show* (in 1962) and *The Bruce Forsyth Show* (1966–9). Both shared a basic format: a mixture of conversation, dance routines, songs and comic sketches, with a variety of guests joining me each week. It's those guests I'm going to concentrate on now, many of whom were or became great pals.

THE TALENTED MUSICIAN AND singer Ray Ellington. I was very much a fan. When I was in the RAF, Ted Heath (the band leader, not the politician) used to put on Sunday concerts at the Palladium, with Canadian actor Paul Carpenter as MC, accompanied by singers Lita Roza, Dennis Lotis and Dickie Valentine. And as if that line-up wasn't enough, in the second half we were treated to the Ray Ellington Quartet. I went as often as I possibly could to see Ray as much as Ted Heath.

So, you can imagine how delighted I was when I learned that Ray's son Lance was joining the *Strictly Come Dancing* band as a singer. Lance and I were given the chance to duet on one of his father's most famous numbers, 'The Three Bears', with one of *Strictly's* professional dancers, Ola Jordan, accompanying us as a lovely Goldilocks. It was a song I knew well, of course, from playing it near enough sixty years previously at the RAF panto in Andover. Lance is a marvellous singer, and being onstage with him brought back many happy memories of his father.

Douglas Fairbanks Jr. Doesn't he look fabulous in this photograph? You can imagine the impact he had when he came into the studio. There were women swooning left, right and centre. I can assure you that *never* happened when I was around.

Douglas was, without doubt, one of my favourite guests of all time. He was great fun, extremely pleasant and courteous, with the ability to out-Cooper Tommy Cooper! That's right, the swashbuckling, dashing hero of so many Hollywood adventure films was an amateur magician. And hilarious with it.

In those days, for programmes such as this, we would rehearse a couple of shows at a time over a two-to three-week period, similar to what we did in Summer Seasons. We all looked forward to the days Douglas was due in because we knew he would bring a new conjuring trick every time. He would act it out for the whole cast and production team, deliberately making a mess of it and playing himself up wonderfully. We'd be in stitches. What a man.

Two dear friends, Dudley Moore and Tommy Cooper.

This was a sketch based on our relative heights – Tommy stood six feet four inches, while Dudley was more than a foot shorter. I am somewhere in the middle. The skit began with Dudley complaining that he looked far smaller on the screen than Tommy and me, so we agree to pacify the little chap by standing in a line, Dudley at the front, me four paces behind and Tommy another few steps further back.

This, of course, makes any conversation rather awkward. 'What's he saying about me?' Tommy would ask me. I then call out to Dudley, 'Did you say anything about him?' This carries on up and down the line until eventually Tommy can't take it any longer. 'I've had enough of this. I've got an idea. Follow me, Bruce.' And together we walk up to Dudley and lift him up, so we are all the same size. 'Do you feel better?' says Tommy. 'Now, what were you saying?'

Honestly, it was funny at the time!

Tommy Cooper was one of those people who are the same offstage as on it – he loved to laugh and joke all the time. If we were in a bar after rehearsals, for instance, and someone approached him with a gag, Tommy would listen attentively, duly laugh when the punch line was delivered, then say in that voice of his, 'That's funny. That really is very funny.' Then he'd attract someone else's attention. 'Excuse me. Excuse me. Come here a moment, would you? This gentleman here, he has a lovely joke. Go on, tell him it.' He would do this half a dozen times to the poor guy until everyone in the bar was crowded around them. It was one of his favourites and always hilarious.

Tommy had this marvellous ability to build up the simplest of things into something incredibly funny. He wasn't doing it to show off or impress anyone: that wasn't what it was about for him. Tommy only wanted to bring some happiness into people's lives.

I don't think Tommy Cooper knew how funny he actually was. I used to come across him occasionally outside Hamleys toy store in Regent Street. He went there regularly to see if they had any new tricks he could use in his act. On seeing me, he would say, 'Hold on a second, would you, Bruce? I want to show you something. Do you think this is funny? Do you?' Then he would put on this little performance in the street.

Was it funny? Of course it was. Tommy was always funny.

As for Dudley, well, we did many, many shows together. He was a joy to work with.

This was taken at his home in LA, before he fell ill. It was just awful what happened to him, suffering for a number of years with a degenerative palsy before he eventually died. So desperately sad.

Dudley was perhaps one of the most multi-talented person I ever worked with. He was well known for his comedy, of course, but he was also a fine straight actor and a hugely talented pianist. Technically brilliant, he could play just about anything, and play it very well.

In the early nineties Dudley was performing at the Royal Albert Hall, backed by a full symphony orchestra. My wife Winnie and I decided to go along. On the day of the concert we received a phone call from Howard Keel, with whom I had become very friendly over the years. Howard was in town and hoping to meet up.

'What are you doing this evening, Howard? Winnie and I have a box at the Albert Hall to see Dudley Moore. There's plenty of room if you're interested.'

Howard was not convinced. 'Will he be doing all that ooby-dooby-dooby scat music?'

'WILL HE BE DOING ALL THAT OOBY-DOOBY-DOOBY SCAT MUSIC?'

I had to laugh. 'No, Howard, he won't be doing ooby-dooby-dooby. He's not that kind of performer. He's got a concert orchestra.'

Howard joined us and loved it. I hadn't told Dudley we were coming as I wanted to surprise him, so, afterwards, we made our way backstage to say hello and let him know how much we had enjoyed the show. There were lots of people milling around, who I presumed were friends and family. As we were chatting and congratulating Dudley I mentioned that we were going out for dinner at Langan's Brasserie and asked if he wanted to join us. It was an off-the-cuff remark. With all those other people there, I was certain he must have prior plans. He thanked me for the invitation but said he wasn't sure whether he could make it.

'No problem at all, Dudley. You know where we'll be.'

At the restaurant, just as the three of us were beginning to order, a cab pulled up outside and out jumped Dudley. We were absolutely thrilled he had decided to join us after all, and we enjoyed a delightful evening with lot of laughs.

At one point during the meal I remember saying to Dudley, 'Well, you've it made now. You can play any city you want. All you need to do is have your musical director go a day in advance to rehearse the orchestra and you turn up the following day to run through it, and there you are. It would be wonderful. You could be a concert performer for the rest of your life.'

I don't know if Dudley took what I had said to heart, but I am convinced that if he had wanted a new career, it was there for him: he had more than enough ability.

THE GORGEOUS KATHY KIRBY. This is from a show broadcast on 28 August 1966, three years after Kathy's big hit 'Secret Love'. I don't think that's what we're singing here, but if it had been it would certainly have been appropriate. You see, I was Kathy's secret love for a short period in the early sixties. That's all I'm saying!

I BET YOU DIDN'T think Frankie Howerd could dance, did you?

Well, that's correct, he couldn't!

For this number, featuring the singer Julie Rogers and our lead dancer from the show, the marvellous Aleta Morrison, I had to teach Frankie the slightly tricky step-over move you can see here.

In rehearsals I showed him it a few times, then asked, 'Have you got it?'

Frankie looked at me, raised his eyebrows and, in a deadpan voice, replied, 'Do I look as though I've got it?'

Frankie and I developed a very close association and recorded a number of TV specials together that were hugely enjoyable. You never quite knew what Frankie was going to do, except when I had a singing number. At the end of the song, when the camera cut to Frankie he would always look straight into it, straight at the viewers, and say, 'Wasn't that rotten? Absolute rubbish.'

Frankie was hospitalized in April 1992, but was discharged in time to be home for Easter. I went to visit him, bringing a box of chocolates. He took one look at them and said, 'Thank God, you brought chocolates. When I woke up in hospital and opened my eyes the first thing I saw was dozens and dozens of bouquets of flowers. I thought I was in the funeral parlour.'

That was his sense of humour, even when he was so ill.

As we were chatting he mentioned he had something to ask me. 'Listen, Bruce, I've had so many lovely cards and messages and calls that it would be impossible to answer everyone. It means so much to me that so many people have taken the trouble to send me their best wishes. It's been overwhelming. So I was hoping you can do me a favour.'

'Of course, Frankie. Just say the word. From tomorrow I'm away for a couple of weeks, but when I'm back, anything you want.'

'Great. What I was thinking is that if I could arrange a little interview on television, I could then thank everyone for their kindness. I'd like you to do the interview with me.'

'Of course I will, Frankie. I'd love to. Thank you for asking me.'

Frankie died suddenly three days before I returned from my break. I was so sad, so very sad.

WE'VE MOVED INTO 1969.

I suspect it won't surprise anyone that Cilla Black was great fun to work with. You can see here how I'm trying desperately to keep a straight face, and failing. That is what it was like whenever we did a show together – laughter all the time.

For this one, Lionel Blair and I persuaded Cilla to perform her first piece of scripted dialogue. We went to see her in a cottage in the countryside while she was taking a few days off. It was just a page of dialogue but she was still very dubious and nervous about it, repeatedly reminding us that she was a singer, not an actress. Lionel and I calmed her down by reassuring her that we would rehearse properly, and finally she agreed to do it.

Cilla was an amazing person – a fantastic lady.

Finally, in a fitting close to this trip down Memory Lane, in the company of old friends from my television shows of the sixties, I arrive at the delightful Harry Secombe.

Harry and I were pals, and would often golf or go out for meals together when we were on the same bill. In truth, Harry wasn't much of a golfer but that didn't worry him in the least. He went out there to enjoy himself and he always did. In between shots, and Harry had a lot of shots, he would burst into song. I swear if we were playing a course in the country, the cows in the neighbouring field would start to look around and prick up their ears at that big, big Secombe voice. Maybe they were scared, maybe they were enjoying it, I'm not sure.

During my days touring the variety theatres and living out of the caravan, one week in 1955 found me playing Cleethorpes alongside Harry. I say 'alongside' but way, way below him would be a more accurate description. Harry was very much top of the bill and I was very near the bottom.

On arrival at the theatre on the Monday morning I went to the stage door to find out which dressing room I had been allocated; and who I would be sharing with. It turned out to be me . . . and the dog act Duncan's Collies! Me sharing a dressing room with a dog act! You have got to be kidding.

This is never going to work, I thought. Every time I bend over to tie my shoelace there'll be a dog sniffing around! It's too ridiculous! I decided the best thing to do would be to get dressed in my caravan, walk over to the stage door in normal shoes, and put on my tap shoes in the stage-doorkeeper's office.

So there I am on the first night, standing in my socks, in a tiny, cramped space, when Harry walks by.

'Hello, Bruce. What are you doing?'

'I'm just putting my shoes on.'

'Why here?'

'Well, I'm sharing a dressing room with Duncan's Collies!'

Harry is unable to contain himself, booming out that unique, hysterical laugh of his, until eventually he manages to say, 'You can't do that. Come in with me.'

He then leads me to his dressing room. 'Pick any corner you like,' he says. 'It's yours for the rest of the week. I'll tell the stage manager to give you a key so you can use the room whenever you need to. We're all in this together. Duncan's Collies!' He shakes his head and the laughter starts all over again.

There was no one nicer than Harry Secombe.

HOSTING YOUR OWN SHOW is tremendously rewarding, but it can also be exhausting. In the build-up to every programme you're under constant pressure to come up with ideas, while during the recordings the spotlight is relentlessly focused on you to ensure everything runs as planned.

It can often be a very welcome relief and great fun, therefore, sometimes to relax as a guest on someone else's show; let them do all the worrying for a change.

The photo opposite is from a 1968 Millicent Martin series called *Piccadilly Palace*. I appeared on three occasions during the show's run, enjoying myself thoroughly each time. These were great shows to be involved in, not least because they were aimed primarily at a US audience (even though they were filmed at Elstree Studios – as was a popular Tom Jones series, also produced for US television, and later in the seventies *The Muppet Show*), with American production values. Everything was always very well organized and professional.

LOOKING AT THIS PHOTO of me dancing with Millicent, I must say I'm really rather envious of my younger self. It's many years since I've had that rather stylish, cool look about me!

Millicent was a wonderful artist whom I always enjoyed working with. We appeared together on numerous occasions, including a full Summer Season in Blackpool in 1967 and I was thrilled when much later she found a whole new audience for her talents, playing Daphne's mother in the hit US sitcom *Frasier*.

JUST AS I'M THINKING about Elstree Studios, I'm going to leap forward briefly to the mid-1970s when I found myself back there in perhaps the most 'sensational, inspirational, celebrational' show of my life.

Yes, I was a guest in the first ever series of *The Muppet Show*, one of only three British entertainers to appear in that debut season (Peter Ustinov and Twiggy were the other two). Bearing in mind that the primary market for the show was the US, where I wasn't particularly well known, why was I included? Well, the Muppets' vaudeville theatre setting demanded considerable versatility from the guests: acting, singing, dancing. In the eyes of the producers I fitted the bill. I cannot tell you how pleased I am that they gave me the opportunity.

*I found the way
in which they
managed to create
and maintain that
atmosphere absolutely
astonishing.*

As with *Piccadilly Palace*, everything about the show was so slick. On my arrival I was given a glossy folder with the Muppets logo emblazoned on it, and inside my scripts were neatly laid out. The rehearsals for each number were beautifully planned and executed, some of the most enjoyable I've ever done.

As for the actual recording, I became so immersed in the world they had created, that I forgot there wasn't an audience in the 'theatre'. I didn't think of the characters I was talking to as puppets: they were human, with their own personalities.

TAKE A LOOK AT this photo, for instance. You can see in my face that I honestly felt I'd built up a special relationship with Kermit. I was actually talking to *him*, not the legendary Jim Henson underneath the set who was manipulating rods and putting on the voice. To me it was an actual person, I mean frog, in front of me. I found the way in which they managed to create and maintain that atmosphere absolutely astonishing.

DEAR NORMAN MAEN WAS the choreographer for my dance number with these two huge birds! At one point in the routine I was standing facing the 'audience', unsure where one of my bird friends had got to, when suddenly he put his long neck right between my legs, scaring the life out of me. It looked very funny but it was cut, deemed too suggestive for the American audience. Back then they were really rather prudish, which is hard to believe these days, when you watch some of the American TV shows.

I made one mistake during my extraordinary visit. As I was leaving, the guy who was showing me out asked, 'Would you like to see where we keep them?'

'Oh, yes, I'd love to. I've had such an enjoyable day.'

He took me to a room where all these characters that I now regarded as friends and fellow performers were hanging upside down on pegs. I had become so attached to them – we had just done a show together for goodness' sake – and now here they were, cast aside. I'd wanted to celebrate with them, but instead I left feeling terribly, terribly sad.

RIGHT, BACK TO THE sixties where I am again enjoying my role as a guest, this time on Juliet Prowse's *Showtime* in July 1968.

Now, I know I have referred to many of the entertainers who have featured so far in this book as being hugely talented, but I make no apologies for doing so once again – Juliet Prowse was a big, big talent who led a big life, which was cruelly cut short by cancer. I was devastated when I heard the news.

Juliet was a one-time fiancée of Frank Sinatra, had a brief affair with Elvis while they were starring in the movie *GI Blues*, and appeared in a musical-movie called *Can-Can* that was described by Russian premier Khrushchev as 'immoral'. She could dance, sing, act, was gorgeous, with famously long legs, and enjoyed an extremely successful stage career, starring in hits such as *Mame* and winning awards for *Sweet Charity*, which she brought to London in 1967. That was when I first got to know her well. She also featured in the same series of *The Muppet Show* as me, as their first ever guest. As I said, a big life.

Juliet was also incredibly good fun to be around, as I think this photo of us fooling about ably demonstrates. Laughter was never far away in Juliet's company.

As YOU CAN SEE opposite, I'll do anything for a laugh!

These shots come from two different *Showtime* sketches and illustrate how varied the programmes were back then. You had to be adaptable – that's the key word.

I've always known I was adaptable, able to fit in with whomever I was working with in order to get over to the public what we were trying to achieve. For me, I think that has been a vital ingredient for my success and longevity. I feel I can work with anybody – whether in a play, a musical number, dancing – and shape my performance so that it gels with the people I'm working alongside.

Take, for example, my appearance in Noël Coward's short play *Red Peppers*, broadcast on the BBC in December 1969. Consider the cast – Dora Bryan, Dame Edith Evans, Cyril Cusack, Anthony Quayle: some of

On the verge
of a Brucie
tantrum?

'Me Tarzan, you
. . . Joan.' Joan
Carlyle, that is, the
opera singer. I hope
this sketch didn't
damage her career at
Covent Garden and
La Scala.

the very best actors of their generation. And me. What a privilege (and mildly terrifying experience) to be in the company of such a fine cast.

It was a black comedy about an awful double act, George and Lily Pepper, struggling on the variety-theatre circuit. It was a wonderful piece, which reflected real life. The characters Dora and I played, the Peppers, were so beautifully observed by Coward because he based them on people he knew when the music halls were flourishing. It was a big departure for me from what I was known for, and I loved every moment of it.

VITUALLY THE WHOLE PLAY takes place in our dressing room as we change into our costumes for our second number after a disastrous opening song. Cyril Cusack is the musical director, whom we are always arguing with, Anthony Quayle the house manager, who eventually sacks us, and Dame Edith Evans plays the top of the bill who complains about all the noise from our dressing room.

The producer of the show was Michael Mills, a very clever and ingenious man. He had the scenery constructed in two halves, so that sections could be removed, allowing him to shoot the entire first take from one angle, and then from an entirely different perspective for the second run-through. That way he could intercut between the two in the editing. I'd never seen anything like that before. I thought it was brilliant.

DURING MY CAREER IN the sixties, television studios were not the only places I found myself recording. Between 1960 and 1969 I released half a dozen singles, plus the cast recording of *Little Me*, and also appeared on a charity compilation album entitled *No One's Gonna Change Our World* in support of the World Wildlife Fund.

That last one is a particular favourite as I'm listed on the cover alongside the likes of the Beatles, Cilla, the Hollies, Lulu and the Bee Gees. My contribution, appropriately enough, was 'When I See An Elephant Fly'. Back at the Express Theatre, Brixton, in the mid-fifties, I would undoubtedly have said that was a more likely occurrence than me featuring on a record alongside some of the biggest ever names in popular music.

No One's Gonna Change Our World was not the only stellar ensemble in which I found myself in the sixties. In 1965 I took part in a rather bizarre but brilliant recording of *Alice in Wonderland*, with a cast including Dorothy Squires, Dirk Bogarde, Kenneth Connor, Peggy Mount and Harry H. Corbett.

I played the March Hare and sang on the track 'The Mad Hatter's Tea Party' with Tommy Cooper and the young girl you can see here, Karen Dotrice. Recognize her? From a film that had been released the previous year? That's right. She played Jane Banks in *Mary Poppins*.

Next to Karen is another cast member, Fenella Fielding, who many people will know best from *Carry on Screaming*, which is very appropriate because Fenella was an absolute scream herself. She really was. During rehearsals one day she was growing a little concerned that she didn't fully understand when she was meant to come in on her track (as the Dormouse). Young Karen, playing Alice, was sitting right next to Fenella. Most definitely in earshot. She would have been barely ten years old. Fenella and the producer, Norman Newell, were discussing how it was all going to work.

'Norman,' Fenella said, in her very breathy and upmarket voice, 'will you please tell me exactly where I come in? You see, it is a little confusing with everyone singing at the same time. And I don't want to be the only one who is fucking the whole thing up.'

Priceless.

This was taken at our house in Mill Hill in the early sixties. That's Rusty on the left, with my daughter Julie, and Pepi on the right with Debbie. They were both wonderful companions. The dogs, I mean! Not the girls. They are much more than wonderful companions: they are wonderful daughters.

Chapter Eight

MAN'S BEST FRIEND

Dogs have played a big part in my life for as long as I can remember. They have given me so much pleasure for so many years. Of course, they can also bring terrible heartache. The trouble is, we can love them too much.

I grew up with dogs in our house in Edmonton, but the first one I ever owned was while I was touring with the American Red Cross. He was a beautiful big Alsatian. Tarzan, I called him. I loved that dog. He had such a calm, friendly nature. We were staying at a hotel in Romsey, near Southampton, putting on a show nearby, when one morning I took Tarzan out for a quick run. He was still a pup, full of life - I'd only had him six months. He was bouncing around, excited to be in the fresh air. As I bent down to attach his lead, he had other things on his mind. He wanted to explore, to enjoy his freedom. He darted across the road. It had been deserted seconds before, but out of nowhere a truck appeared. It was impossible for the driver to avoid the collision. Tarzan died there, right in front of me.

He was my dog. My responsibility. I have never truly got over that moment.

THE GOOD TIMES FAR outweighed the bad, however. Here you can see little Pepi, who is in the photo opposite, enjoying a spot of fishing with me. Mind you, the fish were not swimming scared when we had rods in hand and paw. Still, if you're going to fail you may as well look good doing it – and Pepi certainly wears his rain hat with considerable aplomb.

RUSTY WAS NOT MUCH of a fisherdog, but that was about all he couldn't do. He was a truly lovely fellow who performed all sorts of fantastic tricks. His favourite was to flip a biscuit off his nose and catch it in his mouth. I'm teasing him here with a pebble instead of a treat, and by the expression on his face he isn't in the least bit fooled. He was smart was Rusty, clearly a lot smarter than me.

Rusty became such a master of the biscuit routine that I decided to try him out onstage, first at Babbacombe, where he grew used to having an audience, and then, *SNAP*! He was performing at the London Palladium.

AND THERE HE IS on that very stage. Rusty! At the Palladium! With me!

It was amazing that Rusty was able to do anything, given what happened to him. Penny and I had him while we were touring in our caravan. He had been a happy dog, running around full of life, until one day he just couldn't walk. His back legs gave up on him. Penny and I were distraught. We had no idea what had caused this sudden disability. We called the vet, who explained that Rusty was suffering from suppressed distemper. 'He will never again have the use of his back legs,' we were told.

The situation became very distressing, watching our Rusty drag himself around the caravan. It was awful to witness – almost overnight he had become this pathetic, helpless animal. The only way I could take him outside for at least some limited exercise was to grab hold of his tail and lift his back legs up, allowing him to walk on his front legs with his back end sort of gliding along. This didn't hurt him at all and he loved to be outside, but people in the street would give me filthy looks.

Neither Penny nor I was prepared to give up on him. There was no chance of that. On advice we began to massage his legs, trying to ease them back into action. I did what I could when not rehearsing or performing,

but it was Penny who really took on the responsibility. She was determined to bring our boy back to his old self. This went on for some weeks, with pressure growing from various vets we visited to have him put down. Penny refused to give up hope.

One day while we were in the caravan, Rusty knocked over his bowl of water. 'Oh, Rusty, you bad dog!' I exclaimed. 'Look what you've done! Come here!'

Then, very gradually, Rusty rose on all four legs and walked towards me. We could not believe it.

Now, he was never one hundred per cent after that, but he got around and went on to enjoy a good few more happy years with us. Rusty eventually died in 1962 and, although he was irreplaceable, we decided we wanted another dog in our lives. Enter Brutus, the Great Dane. With the emphasis on 'Great'.

TAKE A LOOK AT him dancing with me in this photograph. (I'm certain his posture would have gone down a storm with Len Goodman and Bruno Tonioli!) That is one big dog. And one big softy. He really was. So gentle and so good with children and people in general. If there was a party on, you'd be sure to find Brutus mingling with the guests, a habit that ended up causing him a rather nasty mischief.

By 1964 Penny and I had separated and I was living in an apartment in Kensington. One day my eldest, Debbie, telephoned. The moment I picked up I knew she was very upset.

'Daddy, Daddy, can you come home right now?'

'Of course, darling, I'll come immediately. What's wrong?'

Through her sobs I managed to work out that Brutus was lying on the floor, foaming at the mouth. They didn't know what was wrong or what to do.

'I'll be there as soon as I can. And in the meantime, call the vet.'

It was about a forty-five-minute drive to Totteridge, where the girls and Penny were living. When I arrived the vet was already there tending Brutus, who was lying just as Debbie had described, helpless, eyes streaming, mouth foaming. He looked like he was knocking at Death's door.

Now, Brutus was way too heavy for one person to lift. On my arrival the vet suggested that the two of us attempt to get him to his feet. Straining between us, we managed to haul him up, then tried to encourage him to move. That seemed beyond him and he stood there shakily, still foaming and looking extremely poorly. All of a sudden, he sneezed. And from out of one of his nostrils, flying like a dart . . . a toothpick!

'How on earth . . . ?'

Debbie came up with the answer. 'Well, a couple of nights ago we did have a *bit* of a party and there *was* food . . . with toothpicks.'

Brutus was such a large dog that he could easily rest his head on any normal table. You can see the proof in the picture with my daughter Laura, while she's trying to have a meal. This must have been what he was doing when he hoovered up that toothpick.

Brutus made a full recovery, I'm glad to report.

ANOTHER MARVELLOUS DOG WHO shared my life was Bothwell, a Yorkshire Terrier I gave to my second wife Anthea when we first got together in the early seventies. We called him Bothwell because of the character, the 4th Earl of Bothwell, played by Nigel Davenport in the film *Mary Queen of Scots*. We thought it was a very classy name.

Unfortunately I don't have any photographs of bossy Bothwell, but he most definitely deserves to be included here. Bothwell was incredible. He loved to join me on the golf course, which initially did not go down well with the other members. But it wasn't long before they'd changed their minds. Bothwell would never, ever walk through a bunker or run on to a green. If he went into the bushes, when he came out he would look around for me and as soon as he saw me he would cock his head inquisitively, asking if it was okay to come across the fairway. If one of my partners was about to take his shot I would motion for him to sit and wait. He always did.

On the way home to our apartment near Ascot racecourse, with Bothwell on my lap, we'd enjoy a singsong together. 'We're going *hoooome*! We're going *hoooome*!' I would sing, while he howled along with me. I don't think you could call it a descant. You should have seen the looks we received whenever we stopped at traffic lights. They thought we were mad. Bothwell and I didn't care.

Bothwell at home, however, was a completely different creature. He was Anthea's dog through and through. He wouldn't listen to a single thing I said. 'Here, boy!' would receive a dismissive flick of his tail as he wandered in the opposite direction. I must confess that I found this all very entertaining and would tease Bothwell quite a bit, crawling on my hands and knees towards his food as if I was about to steal it from him. He would defend his bowl manfully, growling and barking madly. I loved that little dog even though he once went for me while I was wearing a towelling robe, sinking his teeth into it and hanging there, refusing to let go. I probably deserved it.

He was a brave little soul, was Bothwell. He might have looked like a Yorkshire Terrier but in his mind he was a Great Dane.

As I mentioned at the beginning of this chapter, though, the joy that comes with having such wonderful companions always seems to be tempered with sadness. That is life all over, of course.

Anthea and I had two dogs: Bothwell and, a little later, Monty, a more timid Yorkshire Terrier but just as lovely. In 1975 Anthea and I moved to Wentworth in Surrey and it was there that Monty decided to go exploring and never returned. He was run over and killed at the bottom of our drive by a car being driven far too fast. Anthea was devastated. She couldn't face the idea of Monty no longer being with us so we decided to erect a small tombstone in his memory in the garden. It's still there.

Years later, in the mid-eighties, there was another dreadful occurrence. One that still saddens and angers me.

I was married to Wilnelia by then and we had two Cavalier King Charles Spaniels, Tess and Dakin, mother and son. Tess had given birth to a litter of puppies and one of them always looked so sad that we had to keep him. We were living in the house in Wentworth when both beautiful dogs were stolen during one of the golf tournaments. Dear Tess had a heart condition and required medication all the time. Whoever took her wouldn't have known how to look after her.

I just cannot understand why anyone would do such a dreadful thing.

To THE PRESENT DAY. Well, almost. This is a year or so ago.

It's our little Yorkshire Terrier Lulu and Alsatian Mace, with the indomitable Cora, who runs our house for us. Lulu was given to me by my wife, Winnie, for my eightieth birthday.

I enjoy training dogs - I'd even say I was good at it - and felt I was coming along just fine with Lulu. Until Winnie and I were due to spend three months in Puerto Rico, where Winnie grew up.

'Bring Lulu with us,' she suggested. 'We can organize it, and you can finish your training there.'

Foolishly, I didn't think this was a good idea. 'I'm not taking her all the way over there. I'll be constantly worried about her. She's just a puppy and might run off, or bark the place down and upset the neighbours.'

We leave Lulu with Cora. Three months later we return, and Lulu is no longer my dog. Lulu is now besotted with Cora. Lulu does absolutely nothing I tell her. Nothing. The only concession Lulu has made since then is to play one particular game with me. She loves to come up to our bedroom in search of my old slipper.

'Where's the slipper, Lulu? Who's got the slipper?' She'll sit there, stock still, watching my every move. She knows I'm going to find that slipper, and when I do . . .

'Ah, there's the slipper,' I'll grandly announce, producing it with a flourish from its hiding place. 'I found it and it belongs to me!' This drives Lulu crazy. She'll go for the slipper and when she gets her teeth into it there's no way she'll let go. She pulls and pulls until it's hers, at which point she darts out of the room, slipper in mouth, while I scream after her, 'Bring back my slipper! Bring back my slipper, you naughty dog!' She loves that game. And so do I.

And then there's my Mace, a lovely, lovely boy who was once trained by the police but was just too good-natured for that line of work. How Mace joined our family is rather shocking. Being a big golf fan, in July 2002 I was staying with Ronnie Corbett and his wife Annie at Muirfield for the Open Golf Championship and while I was absent our house was burgled, with Winnie, my son JJ and Cora inside. Cora was badly injured during the incident. I cannot tell you how traumatic this was to us as a family. I was determined to take action and decided we needed a big dog to help protect our property. We were so lucky when we found Mace. He was perfect. In every way.

Through his partial police training, Mace had become the most impeccably behaved and obedient dog I have ever owned. He was remarkable. All I had to say was 'Talk to me,' and he would reply, 'Hello, Bruce!' Something like that, anyway. Mace even gave Rusty a run for his money when it came to the biscuit trick. I used to tease him a little when I took his treat out of the tin, pretending it was for me. He used to whimper and give me a look as if to say, 'Isn't that biscuit mine?' And of course it always was. He was such a good friend to me.

Mace died last year in 2014. I adored him and miss him every day.

This was my main scene, a
song-and-dance routine with
Beryl Reid and Julie Andrews.

Chapter Nine

THE SILVER SCREEN

'*Bruce Forsyth, movie star!*'

Unfortunately that is not an accurate description of my career on the silver screen, even though I had once hoped it might be. There were a couple of occasions, which I will come to in a moment, when big, meaty roles seemed to be within my grasp, only for Fate to take a hand and the opportunities pass me by. Looking back, it is a regret – not a big one as I've enjoyed the most marvellous career, I really have – nevertheless there is a mild sense of 'What if . . .?'

Not that I'm giving up hope, not a bit of it. I still harbour ambitions for a really good cameo part in a great film. I hope you're reading this, Mr Spielberg.

I VERY MUCH ENJOYED my first excursion into the world of movies, in a 1968 film that never quite lived up to expectations even though it had impeccable credentials. The film was *Star!*, a biopic of music-hall legend Gertrude Lawrence, directed by Robert Wise (Oscar-winning director of *West Side Story* and *The Sound of Music*) and featuring Julie Andrews at the height of her popularity in the lead role. I played Gertrude Lawrence's father, Arthur.

In the routine opposite with Beryl and Julie, Beryl plays a woman I eventually run off with. We performed in an old-fashioned West End theatre, reproduced in Hollywood. The authenticity of the set was astonishing: you really were transported back to the London of the 1920s. The same applied to our 'audience'. Everyone was in full make-up and costume, and in between takes members of the production team rushed up and down the aisles to make sure every single person looked impeccable, in case the camera moved in for a close-up.

The attention to detail impressed me hugely, although always in the back of my mind was the thought, How much is this all costing? I was used to very different television budgets!

I started rehearsing our big number a few days before Beryl arrived. It was one of those routines that required a lot of jumping about, meaning we were constantly on the balls of our feet. Even for experienced hoofers, that style of dancing can result in a few days of aching calf muscles. By the time Beryl arrived I had been suffering the agonies of a gruelling workout, eased somewhat by icing my muscles after each rehearsal, and had come through the other side.

I warned Beryl that the number was very much 'on your toes', and would give her calves a bit of a going-over.

'Oh,' says she, 'don't worry about that, dear. I was a dancer when I was eleven years old. You can't teach me anything about that sort of thing.'

'Okay. I was just meaning that it's a good idea to work yourself into the routine gradually. I wish I had.'

'Don't worry about me, Bruce. I'll be fine.'

You can guess what happened.

After the first rehearsal I telephoned her at the hotel to see how she was.

'OH, BRUCE! OH DEAR! OH DEAR, OH DEAR!'

'Oh, Bruce! Oh dear! Oh dear, oh dear!'

'What's wrong?' As if I didn't know.

'I got out of bed and I fell over! My legs are killing me!'

I couldn't help laughing. 'You wouldn't listen, would you, my love? If you'd taken a nice hot bath when you got back last night, with Epsom salts, you'd be right as rain today.'

Beryl was laughing now. 'I'm sure that's true. I don't know *what* I was thinking, not packing my Epsoms! But it doesn't change the fact that I still can't come in today. I can barely walk, let alone dance!'

When I relayed this conversation to Julie later that morning, she thought it was hilarious. Poor Beryl missed the rehearsal, bless her heart, but she made it in the following day and everything worked out fine.

As I mentioned, the film proved less successful than anticipated, mainly, I think, because the songs weren't strong enough – they couldn't carry a film that found itself out of sync with the times. The late sixties was such a vibrant period, with everyone looking forward – the Age of

Aquarius and all that – that nostalgia for the old-fashioned world of music hall just didn't resonate. Perhaps it would have been better if they had focused more on Gertrude Lawrence's private, rather than stage, life; easy to say in hindsight.

It is a great shame that *Star!* struggled to make an impact because it put paid to the next big musical movie Robert Wise had in mind. It had been Robert himself who had suggested me for the role of Arthur Lawrence, and although I can't say for sure that I would have been involved in the production that never was, I certainly believe I would have been considered.

Can Heironymus Merkin Ever Forget Mercy Humppe and Find True Happiness? How about that as a film title? Released in 1969, it was directed by and starred Anthony Newley, with his then wife Joan Collins.

DURING EDITING TONY, WHO you can see rehearsing with me here, had to cut some of my character's song, 'On The Boards'. Tony had the courtesy to call me himself to explain. I thought that was very decent of him. Many directors wouldn't have bothered but that wasn't Tony's style. He was a good man who went on to become a dear friend, right through to his death in 1999.

How did it do at the box-office? Well, I think the publicity tag-line offers a pretty good indication: 'A motion picture that is definitely not for everyone.' How right they were.

THIS IS MY FIRST straight movie role, playing the sinister spiv Swinburne in Disney's 1971 *Bedknobs and Broomsticks*, alongside the truly fabulous Angela Lansbury and David Tomlinson.

I had no idea at the time what an impression this character would leave on young minds. But I found out in a most curious way.

IN 2009 AMY WINEHOUSE joined us on *Strictly* to sing with her goddaughter Dionne Bromfield. I thought it was a gorgeous, generous thing for Amy to do, to support Dionne like that, given that Amy was by then an absolute superstar with constant demands on her time. I find it almost impossible to believe that she is now gone. It is so sad. She was such a talented singer.

Back in the *Strictly* studio in 2009, my wife Winnie knew how keen I was to meet Amy, and went to find her in the audience after they had completed Dionne's number.

'Bruce would love to say hello, Amy. Would you like to come back to his dressing room after they've finished recording?'

'I'd love to, thank you,' Amy replied.

I was delighted to find the two of them waiting for me after the show. However, I was in for a shock when Amy spoke.

'Oh, Bruce Forsyth, you frightened me. You really did.'

I was quite taken aback. And confused. 'Oh dear. I'm so sorry. What – what did I do?'

'In *Bedknobs and Broomsticks*! You were that awful man with the knife. You really, really terrified me. Whenever we watched the film at home I had to jump on to my father's lap when your bit came on! It was the look in your eyes. You are a very scary man!'

I thought initially she was saying it as a joke, but I quickly sensed that

she was being absolutely genuine. That was the moment I discovered the power of my acting. If only it had been recognized earlier! What a leading man I could have been! What roles I could have played! Heathcliff! Mr Darcy! They were made for me!

LOOKING AT THIS AGAIN, Amy did have a point.

Now for the two that got away.

I first met Lionel Bart, the creator of *Oliver!*, at one of Alma Cogan's parties. Now before I go any further with this sorry tale I'm going to take a brief moment to tell you a little about Alma.

This is Alma in Blackpool, August 1960, with Harry Secombe and myself, judging the Miss UK competition. Being invited to participate in such events was certainly one of the perks I most enjoyed after making my breakthrough on *Sunday Night at the London Palladium*! As I look at this photograph now, that cheque we're about to present to the winner must have been for a large amount – shockingly large by the look of my hair!

Similar to Harry, Alma, bless her heart, was one of the nicest people you could hope to meet, the only one of us in those days who tried to keep all the show-business people together as mates. She threw fantastic parties at her flat in Kensington High Street. The likes of Roger Moore, Tommy Steele and Stanley Baker would be in the card room, while the rest of us partied the night away.

The police were also regular visitors to that flat. Alma would invite the big-name pop groups of the day who, at the height of their powers, would think nothing of blasting out their songs at maximum volume. It was hardly a surprise the neighbours complained.

Alma had a very inventive streak, when it came to her parties. Back to Lionel Bart, I remember one particular do that she organized for Lionel's birthday, in which she had us all sitting down to watch a Punch and Judy show. Within seconds all these well-known show-business men and women were shouting at the puppets like a bunch of kids. So much fun.

ALMA HAD A VERY INVENTIVE STREAK, WHEN IT CAME TO HER PARTIES.

Anyway, I'd got to know Lionel fairly well through Alma, so receiving a phone call from him was not that unusual, but what he had to say on this particular occasion most certainly was.

'Bruce, you've heard we're about to start filming *Oliver!*, haven't you?'

I had. It was all over the press. I loved the musical and I was certain the film was going to be a smash.

'Well, we have a problem. Ron Moody played Fagin in the stage version, as you know, and he's meant to be taking on the role in the movie. Only he's got himself into some contractual dispute with the backers. I don't know the full details, but we're due to start filming in just over a week, and, well, I was wondering. Would you like to play Fagin, Bruce?'

Unbeknown to me, Lionel had come along to the Cambridge Theatre while I was in *Little Me* and had enjoyed what he saw.

'I think you'd be perfect. Would you consider it?'

'Would I! Oh, Lionel, I'd *love* to play Fagin.'

'Well, this is just a sounding-out call for now, to see if you were interested.'

'Well, I can assure you I am.'

He phoned me every night that week to keep me informed of progress. Then on the Friday he hit me with the news: 'I'm sorry, Bruce, they've settled whatever the problem was with Ron. He's decided to do it, so I'm afraid you're out.'

What I wish I'd said next was something clever, like, 'I totally understand that the film no longer needs me, now that Ron has completed reviewing the situation.'

What I actually said was, 'Thank you for thinking of me, Lionel.'

Ron went on to receive an Oscar nomination. I wished him well, but you can imagine how I felt.

Almost ten years later, a similar situation unfolds. It's 1977, and I'm on a golfing trip in Spain when my agent calls.

'Bruce, you're not going to believe this. I'm just off the phone with the casting director of a Disney film called *Candleshoe*. Jodie Foster is playing the child star and they want you as the adult lead! It seems David Niven was pencilled in but he's pulled out for family reasons. You're top of their list to take over. It's virtually a done deal. You just need to get back here as soon as you can.'

A couple of days later I'm on a flight home. Jodie Foster is one of the hottest names around, having recently received an Oscar nomination for *Taxi Driver*, and the rest of the cast is equally strong – the fabulous multiple-award-winning stage actress Helen Hayes (who also appeared in Disney's *Herbie Rides Again*) and Rumpole himself, Leo McKern. I'm incredibly excited as I settle into my seat.

I've looked into the part and I know it will be perfect. I'll be playing the butler to a lady of the manor who has very bad eyesight and whose estate is in financial difficulties. The butler adopts various roles – chauffeur, gardener, estate manager – in an attempt to hide the fact that the real staff have all been let go. In among all this, a baddie is seeking buried treasure.

I hope they finalize everything quickly so we can get started. I can't wait. I am so excited. I pick up my paper to distract myself.

Everything is indeed finalized quickly – before we've even touched down in London. I read an article that reports David Niven has changed his mind and signed up for the role. On arrival home the casting director calls. She is very upset and apologetic.

'I'm so sorry to tell you this, Bruce, having dragged you back from Spain, but David Niven's had a change of heart.'

I tell her I already know and she's even more upset. 'I feel awful. I wanted to tell you myself.' I don't blame her, of course, these things happen. But I am disappointed. Very disappointed indeed.

Now to a movie I did actually appear in, an Anglo-Russian 1983 film called *Anna Pavlova*, which told the life story of the famous ballerina.

I played Alfred Butt, the manager of the Palace Theatre in Shaftesbury Avenue, where Pavlova performed – on a variety bill! I know that sounds strange, but short ballet segments or actors reading serious prose and poetry did sometimes constitute variety acts in the twenties.

On the day I received my script, four or five pages, I was hosting the TV gameshow *Play Your Cards Right* and only returned home from the studio at around eleven o'clock at night. It probably took me until two a.m. to learn the part and, as I had to be on set by six the following morning, I didn't manage much sleep that night. That didn't worry me in the least. Far more important was to nail my lines, especially as the co-director of the film was the acclaimed Michael Powell. I wanted to impress him with my professionalism and readiness.

My sequence took place in the office of the Palace Theatre, although it was actually filmed in a beautiful room overlooking Parliament Square. I duly arrived at the appointed hour to be met by Michael, who quietly ushered me into a corner. 'Bruce, I'd better explain that for this film we have a Russian crew and a Russian director, who, by the way, doesn't speak a word of English, not a word.'

'Not a word?'

'But don't worry, he has a French secretary who speaks some English and she can help.'

'Well, I'm sure it will be fine. I've learned the script.'

'Excellent. Good luck.'

Soon after the secretary approached me. 'Ah, Monsieur Forsyth, I am here to tell you that the director does not like this scene.'

'Oh, yes . . . ?'

'He feels that the dialogue, it is too much. Too . . . staged. He wants you to make it up. Ad-lib. Can you do that?'

'I can give it a try.'

'This is how he sees the moment. You are sitting reading your newspaper when there is a knock on the door. That will be Mademoiselle Pavlova. She will come in. You will get up, rush over to her and tell her how marvellous she is. How the audiences love her. How she cannot leave England now. How the press reviews are all so good. How she must stay at the Palace Theatre. He wants to see passion. Can you do passion?'

'I can give it a try.'

'HE WANTS YOU TO MAKE IT UP. AD-LIB. CAN YOU DO THAT?'

I DID THE SCENE as requested, producing something like a three-minute impassioned monologue in front of a beautiful young Russian actress . . . who just stood there, impassive. Right at the end I got down on my knees to beg.

'My dear Pavlova, please promise me you will stay at the Palace Theatre for ever!'

She looked down at me and said, '*Nyet*.'

Nothing more. It was only then I realized she hadn't understood a single word I had said.

We repeated the scene a couple more times. She said, '*Nyet*,' a couple more times. And I was on my way home.

Just before I left, I asked her, 'Did you enjoy working on the scene?'

'*Nyet*.'

Now I realize that my Alfred Butt may not go down in cinematic history as a classic performance, but it clearly made an impression on some people in the industry. . .

TAKE A LOOK AT this. For the US market the film was adapted into a TV series, in which I'm billed above Martin Scorsese!

My film career may not have delivered everything I had once hoped, but for one production at least I will always know that I was seen as a bigger draw than the award-winning director of *Taxi Driver* and *Raging Bull,* Martin Scorsese. That's not too bad at all.

Starring
Galina Beliayeva as Anna Pavlova
James Fox as Victor Dandre
and
Bruce Forsyth
Martin Scorsese
Sergei Shakurov
V. Larionov

Written and Directed by
Michael Powell and Emil Lotianou

Produced by Frixos Constantine
Production Supervisor Gary Kurtz producer of 'Star Wars'
Executive Producers Peter Cary and Jean Cary

Chapter Ten

THE NAME OF THE GAME

I n the spring of 1971 I found myself in the office of Bill Cotton, the BBC's head of Light Entertainment. I thought I was there to discuss the possibility of hosting a talk show. Bill had other ideas.

'Bruce,' he said, 'make yourself comfortable. There's a video I'd like you to watch.' He put the tape into the machine and Bill, my agent Billy Marsh, and I viewed a Dutch television programme called *One Out of Eight*, a mix of gameshow and variety acts. It ran for two hours and at the closing credits, Bill turned to me. 'Bruce, if we just use the games, do you think we could do that in forty-five minutes?'

I thought about it. There were so many good aspects to the show. I liked the games in which experts demonstrated their particular skills, and pairs of family members a generation apart had to try to copy them. I liked the basic stage set, with the eight contestants sitting on stools and the big scoreboard. I liked the element of spontaneity that came with the host talking to the contestants. And I liked the gimmick at the end, when the winner had forty-five seconds seated in front of a conveyor-belt of prizes (a vase, a torch, a fan heater, a Teasmade, heated rollers . . .) and then had to remember as many as possible in a given time to win them. Yes, there was a lot to like, but that did not include the singers and dancers who came on between the games. I couldn't see the point. To me, they were nothing more than interruptions serving only to stretch the show out. Bill obviously agreed.

'Even if we cut out the acts,' I eventually replied, 'I think forty-five minutes would be pushing it, Bill. But fifty-five minutes, yes, I think that's possible.'

'And would you be interested in presenting the show for the BBC?'

Again I thought for a moment. The Dutch host was a popular female presenter called Mies Bouwman. She was very good indeed, clearly central to the show's success. And she wore a dress.

'Bill, if you expect me to appear in drag then I will have to say no. You'd better contact Danny La Rue. Otherwise, I'm in. Are you going to stick with the Dutch title?'

Bill shook his head. 'No, I was thinking of *The Generation Game*.'

In that moment, the highest-rated gameshow in British television history was conceived. But its delivery was not without complications.

> IN THAT MOMENT, THE HIGHEST-RATED GAMESHOW IN BRITISH TELEVISION HISTORY WAS CONCEIVED.

WE RECORDED A PILOT in May, for which I wrote the theme song. 'Life is the name of the game, and I wanna play the game with you. Life can be terribly tame, if you don't play the game with two.' I was pleased with the words, they seemed to convey what the show was all about. Or what the show *should* have been all about, to be more precise. In truth, we knew we hadn't entirely got it right. Yes, it had gone okay, it had a sense of fun about it, but it was ragged and overlong.

At least, however, we had gone out on a big finish. The final game had involved eggs placed on a wooden board, with glass tumblers underneath. The idea being that the board would be whipped away, resulting in the eggs dropping neatly into the tumblers. When our expert, a juggler, demonstrated this he succeeded with all but one egg. Then the first contestant stepped up. Broken eggs everywhere. Had we messed up? Was it too difficult? The second contestant stepped up. Perfect. Every egg intact in its tumbler. I could have kissed him.

The green light was given for a series, but our first episode, well, that was a disaster. We had taken a step backwards in terms of the feel we wanted to project. In the weeks between the two shows, in our excitement and enthusiasm we had somehow managed to over-complicate things. Whereas in the pilot stagehands were clearly visible to viewers as they moved the props for the various games, in that first episode the decision had been taken to keep such practicalities off-screen. That meant we were stopping and starting all the time. It killed the rhythm of the show.

With two days to go before the scheduled transmission on 2 October

1971, we knew we were in trouble. Bill Cotton had put his head on the block for this show – it had been his idea to bring it over from Holland – and somehow we had contrived to mess it up. A post-mortem was hastily convened, with Paul Fox, the controller of the BBC, Bill, the producers, director and myself. There was only one thing on everyone's mind: could we raise the show from the dead?

I made a suggestion. 'I think we should forget this recording altogether. Why don't we put the pilot out instead?'

There were things wrong with the pilot, we knew that, not the least of which was it overran the time allotted for broadcast. With only two days to fix it in the editing suite, it was going to be incredibly tight, but everyone agreed that was the only option. The editing team produced a miracle, hitting the deadline by the skin of their teeth, and the first *Generation Game* went out at 17.45, directly after *The Partridge Family* and a brief news update, and before the film *Carry On Jack*.

I asked our producers, the very talented Jim Moir and Colin Charman, what the normal size of audience at this time on a Saturday evening would be. Jim and Colin told me they would be delighted with six million viewers. In fact we drew in seven million, and from there the ratings steadily climbed. After eight weeks we were reaching fourteen million viewers.

I think there were two critical decisions we made between the pilot and our first series that contributed significantly to this success.

Initially, Bill Cotton had thought it would be a good idea to have one singing guest star in each programme, but all that did was hold up the show. Bill and I discussed this and agreed to cut the acts, concentrating instead on a purer *Generation Game*, executed as if we were a live show. To help with this I told the crew to forget this was television and instead think of it as theatre. 'It's got to look live.'

That is one of the key reasons why we were so successful. People responded to watching a show that naturally flowed. It was authentic.

The second major decision we took was to introduce a hostess, at first just to streamline the entrance of each pair of contestants. About fifty candidates were interviewed, but no one seemed quite right. Then I remembered a fellow judge I had met at a Lovely Legs competition earlier that year. She had a super personality, looked gorgeous and might just have

the magic ingredient we were looking for. Unfortunately I couldn't remember her name.

Eventually some investigative work from our production team tracked down Anthea Redfern, a former Miss London, and she was invited in for a chat. We had no idea whether presenting was something Anthea had ever contemplated, but the moment she arrived for her interview with the producers, they knew she was perfect.

ANTHEA QUICKLY BECAME A firm favourite with the viewers, growing into her role and taking on a more active part in the show as she gained experience and confidence. There is no question that she was another key reason that *The Generation Game* proved so popular for so long.

It wasn't only on *The Generation Game* that Anthea made a huge impact. She did the same for me on a personal level. By the early seventies Penny and I had been separated for many years but it was not until the summer of 1973 that we formally divorced. By then Anthea and I had been a couple for eighteen months or so, and on Christmas Eve 1973 we married. Three years later, we were blessed with our beautiful daughter Charlotte; and the following year we had gorgeous Louisa.

LOOK AT THEM. AREN'T they amazing? Both Charlotte and Louisa proved to be lovely daughters, who have turned into two beautiful, hard-working women. Both Anthea and I are immensely proud of them.

Unfortunately my marriage to Anthea did not survive. Over time the pressures of the industry – the travelling, the relentless recording schedules – took their toll as we came to realize we were looking for different things to make us happy. We formally separated in July 1979, still loving each other but no longer *in* love in the sense of a married couple.

It was the right decision for us both and we have remained close ever since, continuing to share time together with our daughters and my wider family.

My one regret is that because of the circumstances I did not see as much of Charlotte and Louisa growing up as I would have wished. I used to pick them up on Friday from school and we would spend weekends together. Of course, that was never as much as any of us wanted, but I'm glad to say there has been no ill-effect on the strong, loving bonds we enjoy to this day.

IN ADDITION TO ANTHEA, and our drive to maintain the pace of the show, what else made *The Generation Game* such a success? Well, the games themselves for one thing. When you think that we required five per show, two sets of elimination rounds and the final game, it was quite a task coming up with new ideas. The games had to be simple – if they required too much explanation it was wasted time – and they had to be safe, naturally.

It was a joint effort devising the games – everyone involved in the show pitched in. Not all of our ideas were a runaway success, though. Sometimes they fell a little flat, and on those occasions, even though I knew it was a bit of a cheat, to gee up the audience and generate applause, I would turn to them and say, 'Good game! Good game!' I was always looking for ways to keep the show as upbeat as possible.

THIS IS A PARTICULAR favourite photograph of mine, taken at rehearsals with an RAF troop. I love the flight sergeant's inscription: 'Thank you Corporal Forsyth'. I hadn't been called that in a very long time. Happy memories of Padgate, Carlisle, Andover . . .

For the first rehearsal I always sat with the producer in the stalls, while the stage manager took my place and stand-ins played the games. This meant I could see what was going on, what was working or not, and assess whether we could increase the fun by approaching the games in a different manner.

FOR THE DRESS REHEARSAL, as in this photograph here, I would step in and see closely what was involved, again with stand-ins for contestants. As you can see, Anthea loved this aspect of the programme!

The contestants, of course, saw none of this. They were never given any indication in advance of what they were going to be asked to do, so when the games were wheeled on the looks on their faces could be priceless. Their shock at what they were about to attempt was absolutely genuine.

CATCHPHRASES ALSO PLAYED THEIR part in the success of *The Generation Game*. They helped to build an instant rapport with the studio audience, generating a positive, fun atmosphere, while also connecting to the millions of viewers at home. They felt involved in the show right there in their living rooms.

Just as 'I'm in charge' in the sixties grew out of a throwaway remark, the new batch in the seventies were also largely unplanned and unrehearsed.

FIRST, HOWEVER, THERE CAME 'the pose'. This I did create, although once again luck played a major part. It evolved in the planning stages, out of a discussion I had with Jim Moir concerning how we were going to open the show. I asked him what I was supposed to do for an entrance.

'The plan is for the stage to be dark with you standing silhouetted on some steps at the back, right in the middle of the frame. Then a spotlight will suddenly illuminate you, you'll keep still for a second or two to make

There's the Sodastream, but I wonder if he'll remember there's a cuddly toy on the way?

sure we have a good shot, then come to life and walk down towards the audience. What do you think?'

I nodded at Jim, but I felt a little uncomfortable. I thought I might look a bit daft, just standing there. I wanted something more lively. The only trouble was, I couldn't think of anything.

At our first full rehearsal, with all the lights and stage design in place, I still didn't have any good ideas. 'Something will come to me,' I told myself. 'Until it does, I'm just going to mess around to give the crew a bit of a laugh.'

I walked out, stood sideways and slipped into 'the thinker pose'. I have no idea where it came from. I held it as requested, then gave a little kick with my leg and walked downstage. I didn't think about it again until Jim and I were chatting afterwards.

'By the way, Bruce, that opening, it was great.'

'What do you mean? I was only mucking around.'

'Well, whatever you were doing, it works. It created a really nice atmosphere, with you standing there in profile then suddenly bursting into life. Let's go with it.'

Now, I KNOW I'VE indicated all along that catchphrases just happen, and in the main that is true. There is one, however, that I did manufacture, although it wasn't me who was responsible for it catching on.

'Nice to see you . . . to see you . . . nice!' Most people, I'm sure, associate that grammatical muddle with *The Generation Game*. That's understandable, given the popularity of the show. But it wasn't where it originated. The seed of that particular phrase was planted during the late sixties, when I used it at the beginning of *The Bruce Forsyth Show*. And I always made sure to rehearse the response with the studio audience beforehand.

Now whether the general public would have picked up on it without additional help is impossible to say, because additional help was on hand in the form of a TV advert. In the weeks leading up to the transmission of my final *Bruce Forsyth Show* series in 1969 I appeared in an advert for the *TV Times* in which someone else uttered the phrase, having spotted me reading the listings magazine in a pub. It was that other actor who really made the phrase popular . . . although it's me who's been using it ever since!

EVERY WEEK ANTHEA WORE a different dress, which became a recurring theme, with me mentioning how fantastic she looked at the beginning of each show. During the first series, the BBC's budget was so tight that Anthea bought her dresses off the peg, but by the second series, as the show grew in popularity, so did the budget. Anthea's dresses were put into the hands of the fantastic BBC costume designer Linda Martin, and, boy, did she rise to the occasion.

Anthea's entrance was eagerly awaited each week, the studio audience gasping in delight or bursting into spontaneous applause when she walked on, while the fan mail increased after every creation. One week when she appeared she looked so incredibly stunning that all I could do was marvel at her. 'Anthea, you look amazing. That dress really is lovely. You *must* let the viewers see the back. Come on, give us a twirl.'

The rest is history.

It's a phrase that even today crops up in so many different shows. And I never get any royalties!

THIS LAST CATCHPHRASE AGAIN happened by chance. One morning during rehearsals for the first series, Jim Moir asked me to come up with something to say as a cue for the production team. They needed to know when to cut from one camera to another directly after the winning contestant had recalled the prizes on the conveyor-belt.

'Fine, Jim, I'll have a think.' I then completely forgot about it.

Just prior to the show itself, Jim came to my dressing room to ask about the cue. Ah.

'I have no idea, Jim.' Then, fumbling for words, I said, 'If the winner is female I'll say, "Didn't she do well?" and if he's male, "Didn't he do well?" It may not be the best line in the world, but it will have to do.'

There you have it.

One of my best-known catchphrases came about because I couldn't think of anything to say.

'IF THE WINNER IS FEMALE I'LL SAY, "DIDN'T SHE DO WELL?" AND IF MALE, "DIDN'T HE DO WELL?"'

As I HOPE I have explained, there were a number of elements in *The Generation Game* mix that contributed to its phenomenal success. There is one ingredient, however, that I have not yet touched on and it's the most important of all.

The contestants.

On the day of recording 'the *eight* who are going to *generate*' would arrive at the studio at around 6.30 p.m., an hour and a half before the show began. They would be given a cup of tea while the production team made sure their clothes would be okay for television – chequered jackets, for instance, could look very odd on screen in those days. Fifteen or twenty minutes later, after a touch of make-up, it was time for a pep talk from Jim Moir, who would explain how the evening was set to unfold, where the cameras were positioned, how the microphones worked . . . This was followed by a tour of the studio to calm nerves, keep minds occupied and allow the contestants to familiarize themselves with the set. After that we settled them on their stools, ready for the show.

Up to that point I would only have popped my head in to say hello. This was deliberate. I didn't want to meet them properly beforehand. Spontaneity was key. Prior to all this, a researcher would have conducted an interview with each contestant, to learn the basics about them, make sure there were no medical issues, and to see if they had any funny stories that I could feed off. This was all written down on cards a couple of days before the recording but, again, in order to keep it fresh, I did not re-read these again until about fifteen minutes before the recording.

During the contestant interviews before the games, my number-one rule was never to cause anyone embarrassment. I was transported right back to those Sunday-night shows during the Summer Seasons in the late fifties; that had been my rule then and it remained the same for *The Generation Game.* The contestants were not stooges: they were equal partners in producing the entertainment. When someone was particularly vocal, I was always happy to play the straight man so that they received the laughs. I would feign outrage, or shock, or hurt at what they were saying. The audience was quite rightly always on the side of the contestants, with the biggest laughs inevitably arriving when the joke was on me.

THE AUDIENCE WAS QUITE RIGHTLY ALWAYS ON THE SIDE OF THE CONTESTANTS

provided me with a golden opportunity to have some fun during our chat when she informed our researcher that she was a housewife, enjoyed cooking, flower-arranging, sewing ... and that she looked after her deaf cat.

'A deaf cat?' I said to her. 'It must be very difficult to get him to come in at night, dear.' Then stepping forward towards the audience, I cupped my hand to my mouth, and bellowed, 'H-e-r-e, KITTY, KITTY! H-E-R-E, KITTY, KITTY! I bet the neighbours love that, dear?'

This became a favourite expression up and down the country for a long time and Jean's cat became something of a celebrity.

One of the best-remembered contestants, and a personal favourite of mine, has to be Daphne Cox from sunny Bognor Regis. She and her son Harvey appeared in our fourth show and made it through to the final round.

It was the first time we had ever done a play. During one of our production meetings to discuss possible games I had suggested we could have some fun acting out little scenes with the contestants. Everyone agreed, and the show's writers went off to produce a script, which they presented a few days later ... and I wasn't in it! 'I've got to be part of it,' I explained. 'I have to be there among the contestants so I can help them out. That's where the humour will come from.' Their second attempt was much better, and that was the version we used with Daphne and Harvey.

In her previous two games Daphne had been great fun, but there had been no indication of what was to come.

Picture the scene. It's a classic farce, with Daphne playing the part of Fifi, the French maid. I start to explain to Daphne and Harvey what is going to happen.

'So, Fifi, when you come in, dear, your first line is written on the back of the door and when you get your cigarette your next line is written on that.'

As I'm indicating how small the cigarette will be, her son reaches into his pocket and produces a pair of spectacles. He hands them to Daphne. 'Mother, you'll need these.'

'What?' I exclaim. 'A French maid with glasses on?'

We can barely be heard above the audience laughter.

'All right, wear your glasses, dear.'

'No, I only need them to read. I wouldn't see anything if I put them on now!'

The penny drops. She can't move around the set with her glasses on and she can't read her lines without them. I turn to the wings in exasperation. 'Have we really got researchers on this show?'

Then, addressing the audience: 'A French maid, called Daphne, who's blind as a bat!'

By this point the audience are in uproar, which continues all the way through the sketch. Daphne's role requires a French accent and every time she speaks a line, such as 'Oh, Monsieur, you are so *naughty*,' she has to fumble first to get her specs on.

You can't write this kind of stuff, it just happens.

'A FRENCH MAID, CALLED DAPHNE, WHO'S BLIND AS A BAT!'

TIME TO WRAP UP my *Generation Game* story.

I decided to leave the show at the end of the seventh series, in 1977. I felt, not unlike I had in 1964 with *SNAP*, that the time was right to move on. Despite the huge success, I sensed that we were beginning to go through the motions, the games were feeling a little tired and repetitive. In short, *The Generation Game* required new blood and I needed new challenges.

Boy, did we go out on a high, though. My final appearance came in a show transmitted at 7.15 p.m. on Christmas Day, which pulled in a viewing figure of – and I can still hardly believe this number – twenty-six million!

By 8.55 p.m. Eric and Ernie had topped our figure with their legendary and hilarious *Christmas Special*, which had more than half the population watching – twenty-eight million viewers. Of course, the boys were helped out by Angela Rippon, plus a host of other BBC newscasters, weather men and sports presenters tumbling on to a South Pacific beach looking for a dame, while we had members of the public eating doughnuts without licking their lips.

It worked at Babbacombe in 1955 and *twenty-two years later* it worked again!

AFTER A TWELVE-YEAR BREAK, a regeneration occurred.

In early 1990 Jim Moir invited Billy Marsh and me to lunch. By then it had been announced that I was leaving the ITV show *You Bet!*, which I had been hosting for a couple of years. Jim wondered what I was planning on doing next and I mentioned I was still keen on a chat show. Jim nodded attentively. Then over coffee he threw in an apparently off-the-cuff remark: 'Any thoughts of doing *The Generation Game* again?'

'It's never entered my head, Jim. But now that you mention it, perhaps I'll go home and have a look at some of the old VHS tapes. It'll be interesting to see how they stand up.'

In fact, they stood up very well. Watching the videos, I found myself laughing out loud. I called Jim to say that, yes, I did think it could work again, but only as long as we updated the show for the nineties. Jim agreed with my assessment, but surprised me with his solution. 'It's those little plays. I think they have to go. It was fine performing them three times per show back in the seventies, but that won't work for today's viewers. It's too repetitive.'

I understood what he meant. Performing the plays once with the stars and then again with each set of contestants would be too much. The overall pace of television shows had increased and it was essential we respond to that. I just wasn't sure that dropping them entirely was a good idea. They generated so many laughs and I was convinced viewers saw them as an integral part of *The Generation Game*. To cut them completely would be a mistake. And yet Jim had a point . . .

'How about this, Jim? Say we only do two versions, with each set of contestants? We give them a brief idea of the plot before they go on and then they read their lines off the autocue. It might even be more fun.'

Jim still wasn't a hundred per cent convinced but agreed to give it a go, once we were up and running. As it turned out, the plays proved to be very popular still with the viewers and the decision was taken to continue with them, in monthly rotation with the dance numbers, the marching routines and the skill-based games, such as hat-making.

We put as much, if not more, effort into the games in the 1990s version of the show as we had back in the seventies, refining and perfecting in rehearsals in much the same way, except there was often one difference for me. If our filming schedule coincided with school half-term I could guarantee I would receive a phone call from home in Wentworth. 'Daddy, Daddy, can we come and play at the rehearsals?' Who could refuse?

On my way to work I would take a detour to Anthea's house, pick up Charlotte and Louisa and bring them into the studio with me. They *loved* acting as stand-ins for the games. They both still talk about their *Generation Game* holidays, with huge smiles on their faces. It makes me very happy.

I REMAINED ON THE new *Generation Game* for five series and thoroughly enjoyed every moment. Not only was I once again interacting with people, putting them at their ease and having fun, but I also had the great pleasure of appearing alongside a new hostess, Rosemarie Ford.

Rosemarie was an all-round performer, which was particularly wonderful when we put on the plays. If we needed a dancer, she could do that. If we needed an actor, she could do that. If we needed a comedian, she could do that. Whatever was required, Rosemarie could do it. We never needed to bring in anyone else. She was a delight to work with, and the quality of her dancing brought an exciting new dimension to the show, which I adored. In addition, her presence offered me the opportunity to notch up another catchphrase when referring to the scores.

'What's on the board, Miss Ford?'

That was an unexpected Brucie Bonus.

Who's that great
ape onstage?
Yes, the one next
to the gorilla!

Chapter Eleven

BIG NIGHTS

The top photo here is from the launch of my new ITV venture in 1978. Can you spot the difference between this shot and those seventies photographs from *The Generation Game* featured in the previous chapter? It's my moustache, and would you believe it was once a major news story?

IN 1976 ANTHEA AND I went on holiday to Barbados and on a whim I decided to grow a moustache. On our return home this 'story' was apparently the most important piece of news for the British public in four out of the nation's six tabloids! They were positive about it ('Didn't it grow well!' was a popular line), but I was still astonished that the press felt this was something worth reporting. My new look did not last long, however. Bill Cotton was not impressed. You didn't sport a moustache on the BBC. He had words with Billy Marsh and I was persuaded, rather reluctantly, to remove it for the next series of *The Generation Game*. After that final Christmas show, though, it was back. It has been part of me ever since.

> 'DIDN'T IT GROW WELL!' WAS A POPULAR LINE.

YOU CAN SEE MY moustache clearly in this shot from the Leslie Bricusse and Tony Newley musical *The Travelling Music Show* in which I played the lead role of Fred Limelight in spring 1978 at Her Majesty's Theatre, Haymarket. Tony obviously liked to cast me with characters of that name, which was not the only thing this production and his *Heironymous Merkin* had in common – they were also both very odd.

BIG NIGHTS   163

You see, the thing with *The Travelling Music Show* was that it didn't really have a plot or a script, just a series of songs very loosely linked around a family attempting to put on a vaudeville-style show. At the rehearsals we were told to make it up as we went along. Not the most straightforward instruction I have received from a director and I found myself having to add in sections of my solo material to try to patch it all together. Surprisingly, the show did quite well. We opened at the Billingham Forum, near Middlesbrough, and from there went to Brighton and Manchester before a four-month run at Her Majesty's. Not a disaster by any means, but the press latched on to the fact we closed early. Following the phenomenal success of *The Generation Game*, I should perhaps have anticipated that some negative media attention was likely to come my way. Worse was soon to follow.

> AT THE REHEARSALS WE WERE TOLD TO MAKE IT UP AS WE WENT ALONG.

The ITV venture I mentioned was *Bruce Forsyth's Big Night*. This was a new concept in Saturday-night television, a single programme incorporating a variety of elements that virtually dominated the prime-time schedule. If you take a closer look at that launch photograph you'll get a good idea of what I mean – there's Anthea once again as hostess, with comedians Cannon and Ball, Jimmy Edwards (who featured as Mr Glum in sketches based on his radio show *Take it From Here*), Charlie Drake and Henry McGee (reprising the 1960s sitcom *The Worker*) plus the dance troupe Thirty Two Feet, to name just a few. Add to that all the games, interviews and guest stars, and you can see this was a packed show, one, I think, that was ahead of its time. Unlike today, when hugely popular programmes, such as *Strictly Come Dancing* and *The X-Factor*, can run for as much as two hours or more, back in the late seventies audiences were not prepared for that type of entertainment. It was either half-hour or one-hour shows. That was it.

Big Night was Michael Grade's idea. Michael (son of theatrical agent Leslie Grade and nephew of agents and producers Lew Grade and Bernard Delfont) was head of London Weekend Television programming and he came to me with his vision shortly after *The Travelling Music Show* closed. I thought it was a fabulous idea at the time and I still think so today.

Yes, we made mistakes. Perhaps having the sitcom in the middle broke the flow, and the games didn't really feature the contestant interaction that had made *The Generation Game* so successful. In addition, we set ourselves up for a fall. *Big Night* was over-hyped before it had even started. Honestly, if we had unveiled Buddy Holly, Elvis Presley and the re-formed Beatles for that first programme it would have been seen as a let-down.

That said, whatever we might have done, I think the press would still have had their knives out. I had been portrayed as abandoning the BBC and the nation's favourite gameshow for a commercial rival. Evidently that just wasn't acceptable.

I never felt the show was given a fair hearing. It's true the ratings dropped from a high of almost fifteen million for our first programme, a huge number for ITV, down to nine and a half million, but that was hardly a disaster for such an innovative concept. And we were addressing the slide. In fact, we realized very early on that we didn't have the mix quite right. Poor Cannon and Ball never made it on to a broadcast! They had recorded a series of sketches, which were dropped before the first programme aired. It wasn't that they weren't funny: they were. The segments just didn't fit.

There is a happy ending here, of course. The producers at LWT recognized the quality and ability of the comic duo based on what they had recorded and, within a year or so, duly gave them their own show. I was delighted and they have become massive TV stars as a result.

By our seventh broadcast we had been rescheduled to earlier in the evening, cutting a lot of the superfluous material, which gave me more time to have some fun with the studio audience. Towards the end of the run, the viewing figures had climbed back up to fourteen million.

As I have said, I don't feel the press were fair in their criticism of *Big Night* and I even took to the air live on one of the shows to say so. I knew it wouldn't endear me to the tabloids, but I thought it was important that I let the public know how I felt. So many people had worked so hard for *Big Night* and they weren't being given a chance.

Despite all the difficulties, I look back on *Big Night* with great affection. Of course I do: we attracted some of the biggest stars in the business – Dolly Parton, Sammy Davis Jr, Jack Jones, Demis Roussos and the Carpenters to name just a handful. They were all a joy to work with.

The guest on my first show in October was less well known to a British audience, but that didn't matter in the least. She was clearly going to be a major star and we were very confident she would be a big hit with the viewing public. We were absolutely correct. American singer and comic firecracker Bette Midler was a smash.

BETTE WAS PERFORMING IN London for the first time, at the Palladium in her Trash with Flash tour, and our excellent producer David Bell, with whom I worked for many years, suggested I go to see her the week before she was due on *Big Night*.

I was at the Palladium on the Friday night of the run and she was marvellous. All the way through her act she kept falling to the floor and talking to the audience from where she was lying. It was very funny indeed. And, boy, could she sing. At the end of the performance, when she came out to take her applause, some of her fans in the dress circle unfurled a huge banner, about eight foot long.

Bette noticed it as she was thanking the audience for their reception. 'Just a moment, please,' she said. 'Someone has a banner. I can't quite see what it says.' Then she turned to the lighting booth. 'Can you take the spotlight off me for a moment?'

They did and she started to read it out. 'Bette . . . Show us your tits!' This received a huge laugh from the audience. Then, after a long pause, she continued. 'Oh, what the hell? It's Friday night.' With that she pulled her top down and walked off the stage.

For a second there was silence in the auditorium, and then the biggest shock laugh I have ever heard in my life.

'OH, WHAT THE HELL? IT'S FRIDAY NIGHT.'

A couple of days later I had a meeting with David Bell and the writers of *Big Night*, to discuss what we should do when Bette came on the show. I suggested that as Bette had done so much of her act lying on the floor, we should do the interview lying on the floor. 'We could also have a cup of tea served to us,' I added.

David and the writers thought this was an excellent idea and it went very well on the night. Bette loved it. As we were chatting she asked me whether I had seen her Palladium show.

'Oh, yes, I have,' I told her. 'I was there on "Big Friday"!'

'Big Friday! Oh, God! My manager gave me hell about that.'

I REMEMBER EXACTLY WHAT'S going on in this second photograph, why Bette and I are laughing so uproariously. Bette was wearing skin-tight satin leggings and when she stood up from our interview, I put my hand out to help her and accidentally touched her bottom. 'I am so sorry,' I said. 'No hard feelings.' I hadn't realized what I'd just come out with, but Bette cottoned on immediately and almost collapsed with laughter.

WITH THE DEMISE OF *Big Night* I decided to take myself off for a while, out of the country, and use the opportunity to fulfil one of my lifelong dreams – to appear on Broadway in a one-man show.

By then I knew I had the material, built up over so many years. All my experience in variety – the Windmill, *Sunday Night at the London Palladium*, *Royal Variety Performance*s, The Talk of the Town and TV shows – had combined to give me the confidence that I could perform for more than two hours on my own.

Not that my debut was on Broadway. Do you think I'm daft?

No, I tried out my one-man show at the Gaumont in Southampton in 1975. At that point I wasn't absolutely certain I could pull off a two-hour stint – coming up with a full second half was going to be a big stretch compared with my normal hour in a club or a theatre.

To work out whether I really did have sufficiently good material I set down two pieces of paper in front of me. On the first I wrote what I thought would be the best running order for the first half; then I turned to the second. If I struggled with the second hour I would know I didn't have enough quality left to make a success of the show. At the end of the exercise, thankfully, both sheets were full.

I made sure to book two nights at the Gaumont. If the first hadn't gone well, I'd use the second show to tighten the sections that had sagged, and rework routines as required. As it was, I needn't have worried. The first night went very well indeed, leaving me with the happy task of aiming to make the second just as good, if not better.

THE NEXT STEP WAS TO BRING THE SHOW TO LONDON.

The next step was to bring the show to London. That is one big step and I was advised by many trusted people in the business not to do so.

'You must remember, Bruce,' they all told me, 'there's such a choice available in the city that you might be lost in the crowd. There's a big difference between the West End and the provinces.'

I took no notice, although I did make sure to drum up some business. Not just drum it up, but mouth-organ it up, cymbal it up, the works, as you can see opposite. This is outside the New London Theatre, where the show was booked for a two-week run. It looks like my Rolls-Royce Corniche is about to get a ticket! I think I hoped my one-man-band routine would charm the traffic warden into letting me off! No chance.

The New London shows went terrifically well. They were packed out and I was thrilled with the reaction. Full of confidence, the following year I took the show on to the biggest stage of all, the Palladium, where I enjoyed two extended runs, in the spring and then the autumn. It was a great experience, to be on that stage of all stages, with a packed theatre, performing on my own. Honestly, I felt like I'd come home.

My sister Maisie was at one of the performances and was clearly very excited about something when she came backstage. 'What's the matter, Maisie?'

'Oh, Bruce, just as I was approaching the Palladium a tout offered me money for my ticket! Much more than I paid for it. Imagine that!'

I thought her reaction was lovely, and I must admit I was rather pleased to hear that the touts were looking to buy tickets instead of offloading them on the cheap. I was also rather relieved that Maisie decided not to sell!

So, as I mentioned, I decided to take a year out from the UK in 1979 to tour with my one-man show. I began with twenty-one dates in New Zealand, performing in front of wonderful audiences each night. They made me feel very much at home. From there, in early summer I arrived in New York for the big one – the fifteen-hundred-seat Winter Garden Theatre, Broadway, opening night Tuesday, 12 June.

Now, there is a specific reason I mention that the opening night was on the Tuesday. That is important in terms of what happened subsequently. I will explain in a moment.

On the Monday we put on a preview performance, for the US critics and, importantly, a very normal New York theatre audience. If you think of the preview night as being a little less grand, a little less of an 'event' than the opening night, you'll get the picture.

Standing in the wings on that preview night I was obviously very nervous, but at the same time I felt confident that my act would appeal to the US audience. After all, I had gained plenty of experience from back in

the days of the American Red Cross. The GIs had enjoyed my performances and I was sure the New York audience would as well.

There was very little difference between my regular UK one-man show and this Broadway debut. The odd word or phrase, just to make sure I was understood, but that was it. I did, however, introduce a new song into the act. I had first heard it sung by a female artist who was a friend of my pal the brilliant songwriter Leslie Bricusse, when I was visiting Leslie in LA. It was from a movie, I was told, but as I hadn't seen the film, I didn't recognize the song. I loved it, though, and decided it would be perfect for the Broadway show, adapted into a song-and-dance number.

The title of the song? 'New York, New York'. Later that year a certain Frank Sinatra recorded it. He did okay with it, as I remember . . .

Back to the preview night. It was a smash. I received a standing ovation at the end. I couldn't have been more delighted. My dream really was coming true.

Unfortunately, the official opening night on the Tuesday wasn't quite as successful. I don't kid myself about this: it's true and I don't pretend otherwise. There were a number of reasons. Part of it was down to me, of course, and I'll explain why.

As I mentioned, the preview crowd were normal, everyday New York theatregoers, looking to enjoy themselves, but those who make a point of attending opening nights are far more cynical. There was a sense of them thinking, Who is this guy? And, even more negatively, Go on, try to make us laugh, but we've seen it all before. To counter this I probably tried too hard, feeling I had to prove myself.

In addition, and this will sound harsh when I don't mean it to, Sammy Davis Jr and Tony Newley were there to support me. Now, don't get me wrong, I was thrilled that they made the effort – it meant the world to me. The problem arose, however, when they decided they wanted to join me onstage. Again, this was done out of pure friendship, a supportive gesture, and it would have been great if we had rehearsed something. As it was, I knew they were going to make an appearance, I just didn't know exactly when. They chose a bad time, appearing just before my impersonation of Sammy, which was a highlight in the show. It broke my rhythm and confused the audience.

I loved the fact they were there. I just wish they'd let me finish the show and then come up.

The reviews from the New York critics, based on Monday's successful preview, hit the newsstands in the first editions very early on Wednesday morning. They were generally extremely positive. The infamous Clive Barnes of the *New York Post*, widely known as 'The Butcher of Broadway', gave the show an incredibly good write-up. Here's how he opened his review: 'Do you remember how many times you have been invited to a party you never expected to enjoy, but felt you ought, for some reason, to go anyway? I felt precisely that about Bruce Forsyth on Broadway. It was, in the event, funny, lovely, heart-warming, terrific – pick your adjective.' As you can imagine, I was delighted. Most of the others were similarly upbeat, although, of course, there were some negative comments among the positives. That's to be expected. You can't please everyone all the time.

I came away from reading those early notices more than happy. I knew the Tuesday night had been no more than a blip and looked forward to the remaining shows with excitement and confidence.

New York is five hours behind the UK, which meant that the first newspapers to pick up on the reviews back home were the London evening editions – the *Evening News* and the *Evening Standard*. Just take a look at how they reported on what they were picking up. Honestly, this is a real photograph, not doctored in any way.

I STILL FIND IT very amusing.

What was less entertaining, however, was how the British dailies decided to react when they appeared the next day.

My manager Ian Wilson (who, as an aside, has been with me since the 1970s) started to receive calls from the UK asking if he and I were all right, while at the same time people in New

York were congratulating us. It was bizarre. We couldn't understand what was going on. Until we saw what the British press had written.

It was pretty much a universal slating. Now, I accept that some of the UK critics may have phoned in their copy after attending the Tuesday night performance but, even so, there was no balance whatsoever.

I remember one journalist later apologized to Ian for what he had written about the show. 'I wasn't able to print what I had seen,' the journalist explained, 'because my editor wanted me to tell a negative story.' That's what was happening at the time. The press had decided it was time for my comeuppance.

The show ran for a further five nights, through to the Sunday. This was reported as 'Bruce's Broadway Flop Folds After a Week', which was absolute nonsense. We had only booked the theatre for a week. In retrospect that was a mistake. Ideally we would have agreed an open-ended contract with the theatre. If we had, I'm sure it would have been extended. The box-office takings were very healthy.

It was a great shame, as I have no doubt we would have ended up with a big success. The momentum and word of mouth in New York was very strong, and all of a sudden we just disappeared. It was another lesson learned.

Anyway, enough of New York. I'm now going to take you briefly to the west coast of the States, a few months later, where at the prestigious Huntingdon Hartford venue in Hollywood I once again performed my one-man show to a US audience. Despite what had been written back home, I knew that the reaction from the American audiences had been very positive and so it proved again in Los Angeles.

Here's what one reviewer said: 'With a marvellous, captivating charm and personality, he endears himself to the audience immediately, and then captures them completely.'

How lovely.

THIS PHOTOGRAPH WAS TAKEN at the after-show party following the first of my two performances. Here, I am thoroughly enjoying the company of three of the many

'WITH A MARVELLOUS, CAPTIVATING CHARM AND PERSONALITY, HE ENDEARS HIMSELF TO THE AUDIENCE IMMEDIATELY, AND THEN CAPTURES THEM COMPLETELY.'

Hollywood stars who generously came along to support the show – actor Gene Barry, the fabulous actress and dancer Cyd Charisse, who featured in *Singin' in the Rain* and many other movies, and *I Love Jeannie*'s Barbara Eden.

Also in the audience that night was my old pal Archie Leach – better known as Cary Grant. Now, this may surprise you, but I knew Cary from way back. He saw me play Dick Whittington at the Bristol Hippodrome in 1962, when he was over visiting his mother. After the show he came backstage to say hello and we stayed in touch. In fact, when Anthea and I were in LA with Charlotte and Louisa, Cary treated us all to a behind-the-scenes visit to the Hollywood Park racetrack where he was a member of the board. He took us to the stables and we met the jockeys. At that time the girls were horse crazy and they loved it. So did I.

FINALLY, TO TIE UP this whistle-stop tour of my career in the seventies, I am going to intrude briefly into the next decade and the return of my one-man show to the UK, at the Fairfield Halls in Croydon in January 1980.

Still aggrieved at how my Broadway shows had been misrepresented, I decided once and for all to put the record straight by printing what you will see overleaf in the middle two pages of the programme.

ON THE NIGHT OF the Croydon performance a number of journalists tried to get in to see the show but were refused entry: it was a sell-out. They had to remain outside.

What a shame.

SOME REVIEWS YOU MA[...]

NEW YORK POST

Clive Barnes

Do you remember how many times you have been invited to a party you never expected to enjoy, but felt you ought, for some reason, to go anyway? I felt precisely that way about way about Bruce Forsyth on Broadway, a one-man show that officially opened at the Winter Garden Theater last night, and which I caught the night before at its preview.

It was, in the event, funny, lovely, heartwarming, terrific—pick your adjectives. It was simply a happy evening in the theater.

I expected much less. Bruce Forsyth is a lanky, cheerful British performer who does almost something of almost everything. In Britain he is the equivalent of Johnny Carson—the indisputable No. One superstar. A TV idol. Here he is unknown.

For myself—and here is where this notice has to become personal—I happen to have watched the unknown Forsyth for years. His later eruptions in British televison have not amused me. And I wondered where all the talent had gone.

I recall this happily crazy man, from when I first caught him 30 years ago when he was a song and dance chorus boy at London's Windmill Theater. It was a burlesque house—and the only theater in my experience where the patrons would be subject to a periodic exhortation: "Gentlemen are requested not to climb over the seats."The theater was that rough.

Forsyth's career prospered. After dancing and singing, he started to tell jokes. He moved onto television and became famous. He came from a tradition of English comics, such as Max Miller and Tommy Trinder, totally irreverent, mildly blue, and ferociously in charge of the audience.

The playwright John Osbourne caught the type perfectly when he created the role of Archie Rice for Laurence Olivier in The Entertainer. Bruce Forsyth is the new Archie Rice—although, transfigured by television he has survived.

I first became aware of Forsyth's true talents when he appeared in London in the Cy Colemen/Neil Simon musical Little me. He was playing the role given on Broadway by the great Sid Ceasar.

I opined the view that he was better than Ceasar the Great, but as no one in London had ever heard of Ceasar—anymore than anyone in New York has nowadays heard of Forysth—the praise went a little damp. But now Forsyth needs no apology, and need

brook no comparison. The idiot man is tremendous, and a true original.

He sings, he dances, he tells jokes, he plays host, he even plays the piano. And everything he does is achieved with a sort of grinning, self-deprecatory grace.

His English comic lineage is the music-hall, from Joey Grimaldi on, but he is that first British generation—World War II kids—to have been influenced by Bob Hope and Jack Benny, Fred Astaire and Gene Kelly. He is an Anglo-American comedian.

This one-man show—he is backed up by nothing other than an orchestra and a perky musical director, Don Hunt—is an exercise in pure arrogance and charming aggression.

Forsyth plays with the audience—he brings them up on stage and subjects his victims to painlessly naughty effronteries. He sings—surprisingly well—dances a soft shoe shuffle, plays the paino, and tells irrespressible jokes.

Most of all he manipulates. Here he is in this enormous theater and he is working it like a cabaret room. It is desperately dangerous—a high-wire walk across the Niagara. The audience is a lion, and he is the lion tamer. They can hate him or love him, they are not going to ignore him.

It is odd that Forsyth has never played New York before. Odd, beause in a very real sense he is coming home. His style has always been distinctively American, for all its English overtones, and now he is nervily risking it on its home ground. And not in Las Vegas, where the climate might be easier, but here in New York.

The man amuses and charms. He is only scheduled here for a week. Take a look at him.

Jack O'Brian
The Voice of Broadway

NEW YORK - Bruce Forsyth is at least as phenomenal a total entertainment as Milton Berle in his early TV invasions; perhaps more. He has many muted and merry British switches on Berle's personality and brashness, Forsyth less insolent in demeanor than Berle's varied comic equipment: Forsyth is a protean clown with a comic's personality and physical contributions.

*One simple [...]
his opening of [...]
way's most halle[...]
Garden, proves [...]
comedy mosaic [...]
emerges into an [...]*

*He is a cons[...]
he plays far mo[...]
his virtuosity ca[...]
by insistence, as [...]
on being kitten[...]
sionally Forsyth[...]
earnest tinkling [...]
better than B[...]
superlatively, ta[...]
from shrewdly [...]
And with it all [...]
best European [...]
energized by a p[...]
It is a One Man[...]
class and impac[...]*

*In Britain, [...]
of Sunday Nigh[...]
specials and se[...]
musicals, notab[...]
Me', in which [...]
equipped than i[...]*

*Over there, [...]
on his delighte[...]
repeat here.*

*Betimes, he [...]
clowns.*

New York
Jay Sharbu[...]

Armed with [...]
hoofing talent, [...]
game - show sk[...]
England but un[...]
Broadway.

His one-man [...]
band, premiere[...]
Garden. It's onl[...]
displays bits of [...]
entertaining in [...]

He's worked [...]
shows and hos[...]
"Sunday Night [...]
where his catc[...]
trouper was, "I[...]

After a prev[...]
yes regarding F[...]
man who boun[...]
mustache akiml[...]
entertain.

NOT HAVE HEARD ABOUT

...ruce Forsyth in
...ment at Broad-
...all, the Winter
...obs of musical
... true clowning
...

...n as Berle was;
...ble jazz piano,
...ost of the time
... Victor Borge,
...s. When occa-
... for a bit of
...sive. He sings
...d; he dances
...s jokes range
...osely terrible.
...ousiance of the
...l entertainers
...showmanship.
...siderable style,

...he conferencier
...ium, dozens of
...in West End
...Simon's 'Little
...derably better
...Sid Caesar.
...d time to grow
... trust he can

...orld's funniest

THE HOLLYWOOD REPORTER,
Huntington Hartford, Dec 1
Frank Barron

Bruce Forsyth is a one-man show—an entertainer. He does patter and chatter, British humor, dances, sings and plays piano. His two nights here were far too short. Once he is known here, he will be playing longer engagements.

With a marvelous, captivating charm and personality, he endears himself to the audience immediately, and then captures them completely.

He is not a one-line comic, but does situations, anecdotes, and scintillating impersonations—particularly one of Sammy Davis. He is a light-footed soft shoe and tap dancer, had a warm, infectious manner in his singing, and then turns in a few numbers on the piano—even to the extent of clowning at the keyboards.

Forsyth, a big favorite in England for years, would make a wonderful host-M.C. of American TV specials, or even in pictures. It is a personality that can be captured easily on tape or film.

As a vocal impressionist, he neatly disposes of Tom Jones without even singing; he just thrusts his hips back and forth. He's passable as a sloshed Dean Martin, but misfires with his Frank Sinatra.

It sounds more like Sammy Davis Jr., whom he later brilliantly mimics with an out-thrust lower jaw, quick, nervous moves and superb tap-dancing and scat-singing in the familiar Davis manner.

He's a dandy singer in his own voice, too. He's got solid baritone pipes, good phrasing, can swing up-tempo wares with the best of them and is equally effective on ballads.

He comes here recommended by such Yanks as Neil Simon, Alan King and Davis the last was to introduce him to Tuesday's premiere-night crowd and is a trouper in the best, old-fashioned sense.

He's always working, always tries to give you your money's worth.

Forsyth has the talent, lots of it. But you occasionally feel he's holding back, still testing the American reaction. If he ever cuts loose, I suspect he'll have a great show, not just a good one.

Los Angeles Times
Lawrence Christon

Who knows how much Bruce Forsyth really knows about music or dancing, or joke telling or impressions? At the Huntington Hartford Friday and Saturday he gave us a bit of each, and it didn't take more than a minute or two for him to have charmed everyone. Forsyth has, up until now, been Bruce Who in Los Angeles (he's never worked here before). He is, and has been for some time, one of England's leading popular entertainers, a variety arts front-liner in a form that went out with vaudeville and has a certain residual life in Las Vegas.

But Forsyth is not catarrhal Archie Rice bludgeoning an audience into submission with tired jokes about knickers. He knows more than an elegant sufficiency about music (he plays "Clair de Lune," "Misty," with Errol Garner grunts, and-would you believe?—"Nola," with a light, sure touch); an adequate amount about tap dancing; and the salient characteristics of the objects of his impressions (Coward, Sinatra, and Sammy Davis Jr., among them).

Forsyth is a trim, dapper man with a bright, utterly persuasive smile. He's quick on his feet and possessed of the rare gift of turning an audience into eager children. You could call him slick except that he doesn't have the overweening narcissism of performers who want to remind us in rhinestone jackets or brassy arrangements that they're big stars. His relationship is with an audience, in which he is quick to spot the amusing oddities (who could have predicted a woman who said she came from Dublin, Scotland, for instance).

Forsyth's skills as singer, dancer and comic are all bound up in a formidable entertainment personality. His ability to brighten a room is as much a prodigy gift as, say, that of the adolescent physicist; that is, an endowment of nature. He has a 23-piece orchestra, under the occasionally wry Don Hunt, working behind him, but the audience is his metier. Los Angeles may not have known Bruce Forsyth, but he knew Los Angeles well enough to ask for, and receive, a standing ovation. Forsyth is in the best theater tradition of energized life, whether popular or serious, and since we've gotten plenty of the British dramatic heavies, we could use him, too.

...e, sharp wit,
...es and hoary
...syth, a star in
...has arrived on

...d by a 28-piece
...t the Winter
...Saturday, but
...in 36 years of

...revues, game
...variety series,
...n Palladium,"
... the departing
...ell?''

...give a qualified
...tall, energetic
...hite teeth and
...his tail off to

IN THE SWING

Time for a part of my life, which, when it's going well, I love to love, but when things go awry, like finding the bunker, I love to hate!

YES, GOLF.

I first learned to play way back when I was touring with Les Roy on the variety circuit. We were in Dundee, staying in some comfortable digs run by an elderly landlord, who did not approve of Les and me wasting our lives lying in bed half the day. What we needed, he repeatedly told us, was to play golf. Golf! I thought. That's an old man's game. He kept on and on at us, though, until eventually, just to shut him up, we agreed to have a game with him. He lent us some clubs and on a frosty Scottish morning, playing with red balls so we could see them on the white fairways, we played a round with our much older companion, and didn't win a single hole.

It didn't matter. Both Les and I had been well and truly bitten by the bug. We agreed later that just gripping a club had created a real sense in us of what golf was all about. We wanted more of that feeling. It surprised us, but we both knew we wanted to play. I've been trying to learn how ever since.

Now, I have so many golfing tales, all golfers do, that I couldn't possibly fit them all in here. For now, here are just a few highlights.

ONE OF MY FAVOURITE playing partners was Eric Sykes. Whether Eric would say the same about me is open to question. Eric was a delightful, gentle man, genuinely funny. It was a pleasure to spend three or four hours with him on a golf course. As you can see in the following photograph of Eric, myself and Jimmy Tarbuck from 1969, Eric has a cigar in his mouth.

He always played with a cigar.

He used to lay it down carefully on the grass before teeing off. If I was next up, I'd walk on to the tee and nine times out of ten I'd forget entirely about Eric's cigar. I cannot tell you how many I ruined by piercing them with my spikes. This went on for years until eventually Eric had had enough. 'From now on, Bruce, you are going to *hold* my cigar while I tee off. Have you any idea how much these cost?'

Many of my pals in the business played golf – Eric and Jimmy, of course, Kenny Lynch, Stanley Baker, Ronnie Carroll, Glen Mason and numerous others – but it was only when the BBC launched its *Pro-Celebrity Golf* series that I had the opportunity to partner some of the best players in the world.

THE SHOW WAS PRESENTED by Peter Alliss, who is a dear friend. We have spent many hours together in the nineteenth hole putting the world to rights and swapping stories.

Many people think of Peter purely in terms of commentating, but in fact he had a distinguished playing career, winning twenty-one professional tournaments and representing Britain in eight Ryder Cups. Long before we got to know each other, I used to travel to Wentworth or Sunningdale for big tournaments to watch him play. He was one of my favourite players, along with Dave Thomas, Neil Coles and Max Faulkner. Whenever I arrived at one of those tournaments I would

check to see which one of those four players was the nearest on the course and rush off to watch them play.

Peter presented 140 *Pro-Celebrity Golf* programmes for the BBC during the seventies and eighties, pairing up the world's best professionals with gifted amateurs (not necessarily gifted in golfing terms, you understand!). I took part in every series, over something like seventeen years. Two of the many great players I had the privilege of playing with were Lee Trevino and Seve Ballesteros.

IT GOES WITHOUT SAYING they were both brilliant golfers who wanted to win, but they also had a real sense of what the show was about – some mischief and a lot of fun. They would joke their way around the course, in Spanish naturally, but always explained what they were laughing about. They never excluded anyone and were a joy to be with.

It was not only the golfers who were at the top of their game in the *Pro-Celebrity* series. The 'amateurs' were all big names in their respective fields as well, with the likes of Christopher Lee, Terry Wogan, Ronnie Corbett, Henry Cooper, Kevin Keegan, Ian Botham, Bobby Charlton . . . The list could go on and on.

SEAN CONNERY WAS A regular on the show. Sean is a very keen golfer and a good one, thanks to Peter Alliss, so Peter likes to tell me. 'Oh, yes, I gave young Sean a few tips on the set of *Goldfinger*. He hasn't looked back since!'

Sean and I have known each other for many years. We have spent Christmas together and an *awful* lot of time on golf courses, particularly

during the sixties and seventies. I see less of him, these days, as he doesn't travel back to the UK as often. He's always a fun guy to be around but is also a very tough competitor.

A number of years ago I was playing in a group with Sean on the East Course at Wentworth and on each of the first seven greens he left his putt short.

'If I do that one more time . . .' he muttered, as he stomped off to the eighth tee in quite a temper. The rest of us couldn't wait to get to the next green to see what would happen. We were not disappointed.

Sure enough, Sean's putt settled about three feet shy of the hole. I won't repeat his next words, but after a number of expletives he took his putter and tried to break it across his thigh. Now, that is almost impossible, even for James Bond. All he achieved was a nasty welt on his leg. Undeterred he tried again, slowly bending the offending club until it eventually snapped. One half was then hurled into the rough to the right of the green, the other into the rough on the left. I don't think the sounds of stifled laughter from his playing partners helped his mood as he was forced to putt with his two-iron for the remaining holes.

We had arranged to play again the following day, and as I was driving past the putting green just before our tee-time I saw Sean on the practice green, with seven different putters. I wound down my window. 'Seven putters? Are we only playing seven holes today?'

I was glad I was in the car and able to make a swift getaway after that!

THIS PHOTO OF FORMULA One World Champion James Hunt on the opposite page reminds me of a great little story involving Peter Cook.

One year on the show James took his Alsatian dog along with him during his morning nine-hole match. In the afternoon Peter Cook was playing and when he walked on to the first tee he was carrying a goldfish in a bowl. Peter Alliss was naturally curious and asked what was going on.

'Well, James Hunt had his dog Oscar with him this morning, so I'm bringing my pet goldfish Ginsberg with me this afternoon. He loves the panoramic views.'

Peter carried the goldfish bowl for the entire round, chatting away to Ginsberg as he walked the fairways and gently placing him on the grass before hitting his shots. It was a wonderful comedy routine that only Peter Cook could possibly have thought of.

Still on the subject of 'swinging with the stars', Bing Crosby was another avid golfer with whom I had the pleasure of playing on a couple of occasions.

This is from September 1972, at the Southport & Ainsdale Golf Club in Lancashire, where Bing and I teamed up with Gary Player in front of a crowd of *six thousand*, for a pro-am charity match in aid of Cancer Relief.

I loved Bing Crosby as a singer and an actor, and I was thrilled to discover that day that he was also a very amiable man, with a delightful manner. He certainly did not play the 'superstar' in the least. Gary Player was much the same, a fantastic golfer and someone I admired greatly, but also very down-to-earth.

The three of us had such a laugh. On the first tee a group of fans were gathered around Bing, hoping for his autograph. 'Just remember,' I informed them, 'you can trade two of his signatures for one of Frank Sinatra's!' Fortunately Bing found that very funny. We were the last group, and just before we teed off I turned to the huge crowd around us and said, 'I don't know who else is playing but I bet we're the most famous!' That got a huge roar.

Playing with Bing was like being present at a masterclass in how to entertain crowds. He was such a natural, full of unprompted stories about Bob Hope and funny quips. I remember sinking a long putt for a birdie at which point Bing took off his trademark hat and gave me an exaggerated low bow. That received a bigger cheer than my hole-winning stroke!

On another green we couldn't decide who was furthest from the hole so we putted simultaneously. The gallery loved it. It was like that all the way around, Bing and I bouncing jokes off each other and enjoying ourselves thoroughly.

TAKE A LOOK AT this photograph. Yes, that really is *the* Burt Lancaster, with Cliff Michelmore on his right. Now, I wonder if you recognize the other guy (no, not me!). I suspect you won't, but I guarantee you'll have heard his name. I'll come back to that in a moment.

It was taken in August 1976 at the King's Course, Gleneagles, at a truly astonishing charity event organized by the Saints and Sinners Club of Scotland, in which a team of US celebrities took on a team of British stars. If I thought the turnout at Southport had been impressive, this was in a different league. I remember standing on the first tee and looking down the course. All I could see right up to the green were thousands of people lining both sides of the fairway. It was astonishing. *Sunday Night at the*

London Palladium and *Royal Variety Performance*s had nothing on this. All the players were nervous driving off that day.

It's no surprise that so many people turned out for the event. Here's just a taster of the line-ups: in the British corner we had the likes of Sean Connery, Jackie Stewart, Val Doonican, Henry Cooper, Max Bygraves and Jimmy Tarbuck, while the Americans featured Bing, Burt (I was now on first-name terms!), George C. Scott, Phil Harris, Robert Stack, Dick Martin and Jack Lemmon. I would definitely have travelled to see that match if I hadn't been playing.

Back to the photograph. You can see I have a slightly bemused look on my face. The reason for that, I think, is because of the conversation I have just had with the chap on my right. It went something like this.

'So let me get this straight. You are telling me that you hold the world record for the longest golf shot in history? Is that correct?'

'Yes, Bruce. I've already told you.'

'But I still don't get it.'

'Okay, I'll go through it one more time. It is 1971, zero gravity, and I hit a golf ball off the surface of the moon with a six-iron. It's probably still travelling today.'

'Yes, I've got all *that*, Alan. What I don't understand is why you didn't use a driver!'

Yes, it was the astronaut Alan Shepard, the fifth man on the moon. What an honour to meet him.

The Saints and Sinners event took place on a Sunday, and was followed by a big reception and dinner in the evening. Very early the following morning one of the hotel porters stumbled across George C. Scott fast asleep in the hospitality room, still in his dinner suit. Tentatively the porter shook the Hollywood star awake.

'Mr Scott. Mr Scott. Can I get you anything?'

'Get me a cab,' growled the star of *Patton*. 'I'm going home.'

'What about your clubs, Mr Scott?'

'Burn 'em.'

THAT GEORGE C. SCOTT story reminds me of my dear friend Howard Keel.

Howard and I became friends during his many cabaret and concert performances in London during the seventies, and we remained close until his death a decade or so ago. He was a marvellous man.

Remember my year away from the UK, in 1979? Well, I spent part of that time in Los Angeles and before I arrived I called Howard to tell him I was coming. He was thrilled to hear from me but unfortunately he wasn't going to be at home. He had committed himself to a summer show in the Hamptons.

'Listen, Bruce, if you want to play golf while you're here I can arrange a temporary membership at the Bel Air Club. I'm so sorry not to be joining you, but you can play there as often as you like. They'll give you a bill every week and as long as you pay up on time you'll have full access.'

It was so decent of Howard to sort that out for me. The Bel Air Country Club is one of the most exclusive in the world and I took full advantage, playing regularly with Sean Connery and the late Christopher Lee.

After the first nine holes at Bel Air you have to go to the clubhouse to reach the tenth tee. Now, the clubhouse is at the top of a cliff, and there's an elevator to take you up there. To reach the elevator you have to pass through a tunnel that has been dug out of the cliff-face, and is lined with sharp, jagged, protruding rocks.

Howard had one last thing to say to me: 'A word of warning, Bruce. I know you know George, and if you end up playing together, for God's sake don't get in a buggy with him. He drives through that tunnel like General Patton!'

WE ARE NOW INTO the twenty-first century and the All*Star Cup at Celtic Manor, Wales, in August 2006. This was a big televised event, featuring Europe versus the USA in a Ryder Cup format.

Just in case you can't quite make out everyone, this is the line-up of the US team: Meat Loaf, Patrick Duffy, Todd Hamilton (captain), William Baldwin, Chazz Palminteri, Aidan Quinn, Michael Brandon, Richard Burgi, Jane Seymour, Michael Johnson, Richard Schiff.

And here's Europe: Ruud Gullit, Jodie Kidd, Colin Montgomerie (captain), Damian Lewis, me, Chris Evans, Bradley Walsh, Ronan Keating, Ian Wright, James Nesbitt, Ross Kemp, Phil Tufnell.

I remember being asked on television whether I'd ever met Meat Loaf before. 'Oh, yes,' I replied. 'I met him years ago. In fact, I knew Meat Loaf when he was just a sausage roll!'

That helped set the tone for an enjoyable match, but it was also very competitive. There were lots of nerves out there. I certainly wasn't immune, but in that respect we comedians are lucky. If we mess up on a golf course we can often turn it into a joke. It's much harder for a straight actor or non-comedic person to do that. They tend to bottle things up, which just adds to their nervousness.

See if you can guess who won.

By the way, I sank the winning putt! *And* won Shot of the Match, a five-wood from a bunker on to the green (I knew you'd want to know). Perhaps I was inspired to stamp my authority on the match by the sign one of my teammates attached to my buggy: 'The Golf-father'!

As I draw this chapter to a close, for once in my life I'm going to give someone else the final say. Well, not some*one* exactly, but some*thing*. Why? Because I think it speaks for itself.

Who am I kidding? I always want the final say. Just so you don't think this was a fluke, I thought I should explain that, even though I only have certified proof for *this* ace, in fact I've had *four* in my golfing career!

Now that's the final word.

Chapter Thirteen

LADY IN RED

From the game I love, to the love of my life.

In November 1980 I received a telephone call that changed my life for ever. It came from the organizers of that year's Miss World competition, to be staged at the Royal Albert Hall on Thursday, 13 November. Would I be interested in being a member of the judging panel? *Would I?*

The only problem was, this was a very busy time for me professionally. I was in the middle of recording a series for ITV and on 17 November was due to appear in the *Royal Variety Performance*.

'Yes, I certainly am interested,' I told them, 'but it depends on how much of my time you require.'

They needed me for the semi-finals on Wednesday and the main pageant on Thursday.

'What a shame, but it's impossible,' I reluctantly explained. 'I could do the Thursday, but not Wednesday. Thanks for asking me. Maybe next time.'

I thought that would be it, but the following day they called back. 'We would very much like you to be involved, Mr Forsyth. If it was just the Thursday, from two in the afternoon, would that work?'

'That's perfect. I'll be there.'

I arrived at the Albert Hall as arranged and met my fellow judges in one of the reception rooms, prior to conducting interviews with the contestants. Well, I met *most* of my fellow judges. One had still to appear. We were just preparing to head off when *she* arrived. I saw her out of the corner of my eye, walking through the door, but then lost sight of her as she crouched down to search for something in her bag. When she stood up, there she was, a stunning vision in a red dress. My jaw dropped, and it's a big jaw to drop!

The interviews were being held in a large room under the stage.

> MY JAW DROPPED, AND IT'S A BIG JAW TO DROP!

There were ten judges in all, lined up in seats to ask the girls questions and have a bit of a chat. The stunning lady in red was sitting maybe three or four places to my right. I still had no idea of her name.

After a few interviews Miss Turkey came on, and when it was my turn to ask a question I decided to have some fun. I looked her straight in the eye and said, 'What *do* you eat for Christmas dinner?'

This got a big laugh from the judges and Miss Turkey. Most importantly, I looked along the line and caught *her* laughing. Oh, I thought, she's got the same sense of humour as me. I knew I'd made a small impression on her there.

We then went up to the main stage for the show itself. The judges were sitting in a row, with the founder of Miss World, Eric Morley, sitting between me and whoever she was. I would have loved to be next to her, but at least I could make some eye contact, and whenever Eric left his seat to make sure everything was running smoothly I managed a little chat.

The show began and the first order of business was introducing the

judges. When they came to me the announcer said, 'Now we have the famous television star who needs little introduction, Mr Bruce Forsyth.' I stood up and gave a short bow. Then came Eric Morley, and after him, the mystery woman.

Phew, I thought. Now at last I can find out her name.

'And from Puerto Rico, we are so thrilled she's here, former Miss World, Wilneliamerced.'

What? He spoke so quickly I was none the wiser.

I did, however, catch 'former Miss World'. Of course! Now I recognized her. I had actually watched on television the closing stages of the competition the year she won. I remember her standing onstage with her crown and thinking she was particularly beautiful. And now here she was. But what was her name?

WHEN THE PAGEANT WAS over we all attended the Miss World Ball, held on the top floor of the Hilton Hotel. I was on my own and among the first to arrive. After a spot of investigation I discovered there were two tables of ten allocated for the judges and their guests.

I hovered close by as the tables began to fill. Where would Whatshername sit? I continued to hover, politely declining invitations to take a seat. Something inside was telling me this could be a big moment in my life. Still there was no sign of her. I went downstairs to check. Nothing. Back up to the ballroom. No lady in red. The tables were now almost full but I continued to hang back.

Eventually she appeared . . . with a date! A good-looking Asian man, and they were clearly very close. They laughed and smiled naturally, at ease together. Well, that's that, I thought.

I sat across from her, in eye line. We had the meal, exchanged a few smiles, but not much else. Then the music started. I was signing a few autographs when I noticed her date had disappeared. She was sitting on her own. This is it, I thought. I walked around to her and said, 'Would your boyfriend mind if I asked you for a dance?'

'Oh, he's not my boyfriend. He's gone off to find Miss Hong Kong.'

'Well, I hope he takes a slow boat to China!'

It was the best ad-lib I could think of. Thank goodness she found it funny.

We danced and it was perfect. We fitted together. When I held her in my arms I felt as though I was in a dream, floating across the dance-floor. We danced for two hours. Even when the music stopped we didn't return to our table, choosing instead just to stand and talk. I discovered that not only was she totally gorgeous, she was very intelligent, well read, well travelled, and funny. We could have been twins! I'm just glad we weren't identical.

WE DANCED AND IT WAS PERFECT.

I asked her name. 'Please say it slowly,' I added. She told me, Wilnelia Merced, and that she lived in New York where she worked as a fashion model for Dior and other top labels. 'Everyone there calls me "Winnie". Please do the same.'

It was a magical evening, but one that had to come to an end. Her escort, Jonathan, finally reappeared and I walked them both down to the hotel lobby, then helped Winnie into a cab. As I did so, I held her hand.

'Thank you for one of the most wonderful, enjoyable evenings of my life.' I kissed her hand, then put it back in the cab with the rest of her. I said goodnight to Jonathan and off they went.

While dancing, Wilnelia had told me she was staying at the Tower Hotel, and would be there for a few more days before returning to New York. She also gave me the telephone number of one of her dearest friends, Teresa. Wilnelia explained that Teresa had been her chaperone in London when she won Miss World in 1975. 'We have been friends ever since. She is like a sister to me. If you want to speak to me, Teresa will know where I am.'

I did want to speak to her, and in between rehearsals for the *Royal Variety* I tried two or three times the following day, with no luck. She was a hard woman to get hold of . . . once she was off the dance-floor.

SHE WAS A HARD WOMAN TO GET HOLD OF

We eventually spoke on the Saturday and I invited her to dinner that evening. She had plans, of course she did. She was spending the weekend in London. Did I really think she would be free on Saturday night?

At around 9 p.m. I was lying on my bed at the Royal Garden Hotel, in my bathrobe watching *The Big Match* on television, when the phone rang. It was Winnie. 'Hello, Bruce. I am here with Jonathan and Teresa and we would love to go to Stringfellows, but we're not sure if we can get in. Do you think you could help?'

That was *the* big nightclub at the time, the place to go; you couldn't just walk in unless you knew people. 'Yes, absolutely. I can get you in. No problem.'

I jumped off the bed, pulled on some clothes in thirty seconds and off I went to pick them up. We had a great time at Stringfellows, talking, dancing, eating, sipping champagne, and at the end of the evening, when I dropped her back at the hotel, I again invited her to dinner. And again she was busy: she had plans to meet up with a group of Puerto Rican friends.

'Why don't you all come over to the Royal Garden?' I suggested. 'We can have drinks in the bar and a meal locally. There are some good restaurants in the neighbourhood.'

It was all arranged, but, over the course of Sunday, Winnie's friends began to drop out for a variety of reasons. 'Why don't we make it just the two of us?' I suggested hopefully. She agreed.

That evening over dinner we swapped life stories. Remember, she really had no idea who the devil I was. I told her about my career, and my marriages. As for her, I learned that she had been born and brought up in a city called Caguas, near the Puerto Rican capital, San Juan. Her parents were divorced and she had a brother called Kiko. Her mother, Delia, had encouraged Wilnelia to apply to modelling school, and from there she had found work in New York.

When she was chosen to represent her country in the 1975 Miss World, Winnie described it as a dream come true. Actually winning the competition was more than she ever imagined, but she had embraced the opportunities the title gave her with everything she had.

HAND IN HAND, WE WANDERED THE STREETS, LOST IN OUR OWN LITTLE WORLD.

At the end of the meal we decided to go for a walk. Hand in hand, we wandered the streets, lost in our own little world. Everything felt so incredibly right. I can't explain it better than that.

At the door of her hotel, at around three in the morning, I kissed her on both cheeks. 'On Tuesday morning, after the show tomorrow night,' I explained, 'I have to fly direct to Florida, for a job in Key Biscayne. I know you'll be back in New York by then. Can I come and see you there? Just to have a meal and to talk. Nothing else. I would love to spend more time with you.' She gave me the telephone number of her apartment and we said goodbye.

The following weekend I flew from Miami to New York. Everything blossomed from there.

The next two years were a mixture of telephone calls, letters and dozens of flights to meet up wherever and whenever our busy schedules allowed. It was exhausting, yes, the travel and different time zones, but much more than that it was exhilarating. I knew very early on that I must do everything possible not to let this amazing lady slip through my fingers. I am not exaggerating how I felt when I say that I knew my future happiness depended on her.

In time I visited Puerto Rico to meet her family – her mother, brother and her father Enrique, plus many, many cousins, aunts and uncles. Her escort on the day Wilnelia and I met, Jonathan Luk, was also over visiting

and we stayed in the same apartment block, which gave me the opportunity to get to know him. Jonathan remains very much part of our lives and our family. We see a lot of him, as this recent photo shows. He is a delightful man and a great friend to both of us.

IN THE SUMMER OF 1982 Winnie and I were in Turnberry, where I was filming *Pro-Celebrity Golf.* One evening, on the balcony of our hotel room, with a beautiful moon lighting the scene, I dropped to one knee and asked her to marry me. 'I know it's a huge decision, the most important of your life, and I'm not expecting you to answer straight away. Just, please, give it some thought. I love you, I want to make you happy and I want to be your husband for the rest of my life.'

Winnie looked at me, and smiled. I stood and she put her arms around me. 'I have thought about it, Bruce. I don't need to think any longer. I know the answer. I have never been in love before, but I am now. With you. My answer is *yes*.'

On 15 January 1983, at the Helmsley Palace Hotel in a snow-covered Manhattan, Wilnelia Merced and I were married. I was the happiest man alive.

IN THE LEAD-UP TO that incredible day one big question had been worrying me. Where do you take a girl from the Caribbean on honeymoon?

Winnie and I discussed this at length. We both wanted somewhere neither of us had been before, and it had to be somewhere we'd be anonymous, just a happy couple starting their lives together. We settled on Hawaii. We couldn't have made a better choice.

AFTER HAWAII, WE FLEW to New Zealand. I filmed a commercial there, but unfortunately the weather was so awful we saw very little of the country. From New Zealand the plan had been to travel to Australia where I was due to host a series of *Play Your Cards Right*, but at the last moment it was cancelled. Some crazy problem with obtaining my work permit was to blame.

With so much unexpected free time on our hands, we decided to take in Hong Kong, Italy and Spain before flying home. We ended up with an eight-week honeymoon. I wasn't complaining.

NICE TO SEE HIM!

In November 1986 Winnie gave birth to our son. Yes, our *son*! As the father of five beautiful daughters I would have been delighted, overjoyed, had I been blessed with a sixth. Winnie, I now know, was secretly hoping for a boy, for me more than anything, but, honestly, I didn't care which sex our child was going to be. I was just so thrilled that we were going to be parents. And then this wonderful little bundle of a boy arrived. I was thrilled and delighted.

We decided to call him Jonathan Joseph Enrique. All the firstborn males in my family have been either John or Jonathan, Joseph is my middle name and Enrique is after Winnie's father. We were rather pleased with ourselves, thinking this was a strong but relatively unusual name. Then we took him to Puerto Rico.

Our son must have been about six weeks old when he first visited the island. As his numerous aunts and uncles were admiring him in his cot, one of the uncles asked what his full name was.

'Jonathan Joseph.'

'Ah! Juan José!' Everyone started laughing and repeating his name. 'Juan José! Juan José!'

At that moment I realized it was one of the commonest Spanish names there is! Ever since he has been known as 'JJ'.

Who does he take after? I'll let you decide.

DANCING IS ONE OF the things that brought Wilnelia and me together, in that ballroom at the Hilton. She is a natural, and I believe she could have been a professional. She has the talent, no question. Whether she could have coped with all the rehearsals, that's a different matter.

During the nineties' revival of *The Generation Game*, Winnie agreed to appear with Rosemarie Ford in a dance routine I had written, a merengue, that was to feature as one of the games.

AT THE REHEARSAL ON Monday all went well. Winnie was pleased with how she had done. Then Jeff Thacker, the choreographer, said, 'And we rehearse again on Wednesday, here, and Thursday in the studio.'

'Oh,' replied Winnie. 'I have to do it again? I thought that was it until the show.'

'No, no,' said Jeff. 'I know you've picked up the routine very well but we still have to rehearse on Wednesday, then again two or three times on Thursday, before we record.'

Winnie couldn't believe it. She felt confident she had the number down perfectly. I had to reassure her that this was absolutely normal.

'It's what I do all the time, darling.'

I don't think she was entirely convinced, but she did agree to a number of additional appearances over the course of the next couple of series, so she must have enjoyed herself. Or perhaps the chance to work with me was an offer she couldn't refuse!

PEOPLE OFTEN ASK ME about our age gap. I always give the same reply: 'Oh, she keeps up with me very well.'

The truth, of course, is that it's Winnie who keeps me feeling and acting young. She is so full of energy and life that it's contagious. At this point I must confess that Winnie is not the sole reason I remain so active at my age. I have another secret. Wilnelia's mother!

Now, I KNOW THAT sounds a little odd, so let me explain.

Delia is a dream of a mother-in-law, so much so that I swear even Les Dawson couldn't have found a joke to make about her. That's saying something. Anyway, Delia has never once mentioned the age difference between her daughter and me. She has always been incredibly supportive of us as a couple and I'm very grateful to her for that. One day, however, back in the mid-nineties, she did give an indication that she was aware of my age.

She handed me a book by Peter Kelder entitled *The Ancient Secret of the Fountain of Youth*! 'Be sure to read this, Bruce,' she said. I'm so pleased I did as I was told. It was one of the best gifts I've ever received.

The book is based on secrets the author gleaned from Tibetan monks on how to remain young – both physically and mentally. I have followed the advice in that practical book since the day I read it.

I honestly believe the exercises it describes (plus a good diet, enough sleep and little alcohol) have helped me enormously. I don't think I would still be performing, and enjoying performing, if I hadn't made them part of my life.

I know, I know, that book has a lot to answer for!

IN 2007 WINNIE AND I visited Las Vegas, where I was making a programme for the BBC about the exceptional entertainers who have performed in that city. One of the segments involved a visit to an Elvis wedding chapel and my producer suggested that we find a couple who were actually getting married and ask if they would agree to be filmed.

I had a better idea. 'What about Winnie and me renewing our vows? We've often spoken about it. And as we're in Vegas, with a chapel, and an Elvis . . . But I do need to ask her first.' I did so.

'That would be lovely, darling, but I don't have a dress!' Panic!

To be fair, there were not a lot of options in Vegas, not in her style, but she really didn't need to worry. She found a simple dress in a hotel boutique, and she looked incredible.

I KNOW IT MIGHT sound terribly corny, renewing your vows, but I would recommend it to anyone. Winnie and I were full of emotion; it brought back such happy memories. In some ways I would even suggest it was a more meaningful ceremony than the original! What I mean is that this time we were able to listen properly to the words we said to each other. They had even more resonance because we knew we had already faced up to some of the challenges life inevitably throws at you. In New York in 1983 we had promised each other we would be strong and tackle everything together, and here we were in Vegas twenty-four years later, still together, still strong. We had kept our promises and we were proud to be reaffirming them.

ALMOST THIRTY-FIVE YEARS AGO I stepped on a dance-floor and fell in love with a beautiful lady in a red dress.

Well, that lady in red is still dancing with me, only now she is even more beautiful and I am even more in love with her.

Chapter Fourteen

GOOD DEALS

Picking up the story of my career again requires slipping back in time for a moment, to the year before I met Winnie.

It's December 1979 and, having enjoyed my two nights performing at Huntingdon Hartford, I decide to remain in Los Angeles for a week or so to unwind and think about my next move. In January I'm booked for one-man shows in Slough and Croydon, both good venues, and there is a *Big Night* special scheduled for April; other than that, my diary is relatively clear.

Relaxing in my hotel room one morning, I switch on the television and flick through the channels. Unlike at home, at this time of the day much of the schedule is given over to gameshows. I stop at one called *Card Sharks* on the ABC network. It's good . . . In fact, it's *very* good. Yes, this could work for a British audience.

Once *Card Sharks* ends, I return to channel-hopping, finally settling on another gameshow, this time on NBC. I smile when I recognize the host, British actor Dickie Dawson, Diana Dors's ex-husband. Now the host of *Family Feud*, he evidently likes to be called Richard Dawson. This is also a very good show.

Research reveals that the rights to both programmes are owned by a company called Goodson & Todman, and quite by chance, a day or so later at breakfast in my hotel, L'Ermitage, Beverly Hills, I bump into Paul Talbot, who is responsible for Goodson & Todman's overseas sales. Knowing the Americans love a breakfast meeting, I introduce myself and we sit down for a chat.

'Paul, I've been watching a lot of shows while I've been here and I'm very impressed with *Family Feud* in particular. I'd be interested in doing that back home.'

Paul gives me a wry smile. 'You might not believe this, but I've just done a deal on that. Only a few days ago. It's gone to Bob Monkhouse. Sorry, Bruce.'

'Oh, what a shame. That's the one I really fancied. There is another one I enjoyed, though, *Card Sharks*. What's the situation there?'

'Yes, that's still available.'

'Excellent. Paul, I wonder whether Bob might think about doing a swap? It's worth asking. If not, then I think *Card Sharks* will be equally good for me.'

'I'll make a call, Bruce. But don't pin your hopes on it. He seemed very keen.'

Paul was right: Bob didn't want to swap, which was fair enough. London Weekend Television did the deal (pun absolutely intended!) on *Card Sharks*, and we decided to retitle it for the home market as *Play Your Cards Right*.

The moment we began recording I knew I had ended up with the right show, and was genuinely pleased I hadn't managed to prise *Family Feud* away from Bob. (Which, of course, he made a great success of as *Family Fortunes*.) I would never have had such freedom and fun on that show as I had with *Play Your Cards Right*.

The first broadcast went out on 1 February 1980 and it proved to be quite a challenge for me. Here are some shots from that first series. Take a close look.

YES, THAT IS A bandage on my wrist. Here's what happened.

I mentioned having a couple of one-man shows booked for my return to the UK. Well, in Slough just as I was walking offstage I took a tumble. I'd noticed early at rehearsals the stage was slippery and asked for it to be scrubbed. They had obviously missed a bit. I landed hard on my wrist and, of course, the audience thought this was part of the act. I tried to explain what had actually happened but I don't think anyone believed me. Audiences rarely do when things go wrong. Somehow I struggled through my final song – on the piano, it hurt like hell – then took myself off to A & E where it was confirmed I had a fracture.

Now, IF YOU DON'T remember *Play Your Cards Right*, it featured oversized playing cards, as you can see below. When I chatted with the audience before the show began, someone would inevitably shout out, 'How do you shuffle those cards?' and I would always reply, 'We've got a ten-foot gorilla backstage!' Now, while that was obviously a joke (he was only about eight foot tall), it does reinforce the point that the cards really were quite large and difficult to handle. Especially with a broken wrist.

Like all the best gameshows, the format was fast-paced and simple. The contestants won by moving along the row, guessing whether the next card would be higher or lower, which I would then turn over. With my right-hand only good for holding my microphone, all the turning in the first few shows was done with my 'wrong' left hand. It wasn't easy, especially if the cards fell kindly and I had to move on to the next one very quickly, but I got through it.

The format also offered me the opportunity to launch a new range of catchphrases. As with *The Generation Game*, they were important in bringing both the audience and the viewers into what was going on. By calling out the responses, either in the studio or from their sofas, people felt they were investing something of themselves in the show.

For instance, when a pair was revealed as the contestants tried to move along their row of cards it brought the round to a halt. When that happened, I would turn to the audience and say: 'You don't get anything for a pair . . .'

And the audience would respond: 'Not in this game!'

Another audience-participation catchphrase featured in the second half of the show, when the winning couple played for prizes, and cash in later series. The idea in this final game was again to guess correctly whether the next card along would be higher or lower. This time, however, the contestants wagered points on the turn of each card, with the aim of accumulating four thousand points, which allowed them to go for the star prize, the car, because (here it comes) . . .

'What do points make?'

'Prizes!'

I was involved in three separate runs of *Play Your Cards Right*, all of which I'm delighted to say were extremely successful and ratings winners. The first nine series ran between 1980 and 1987, with the show then revived for a further six series between 1994 and 1999 and finally again for a last series in 2002–3.

Inevitably, the show evolved over this period, with each of the three runs reflecting the attitudes and sensibilities of their respective eras. For instance, from the nineties series onwards, as the rules restricting what gameshows could offer were relaxed, contestants were now playing for bigger prizes and large cash sums. This led to the introduction of the 'Brucie Bonus', originally referring to a prize, and later money, which was given to a couple when they won one of the first rounds.

But as one catchphrase arrived, another disappeared. Contestants in the final game were no longer playing with points, but instead were wagering cash. So, 'What do pounds make?'

'WHAT DO POINTS MAKE?'

'Rich people!'

It never took off.

ANOTHER EXAMPLE OF THE way *Play Your Cards Right* changed over the years is the way I referred to my fabulous assistants. In the photograph opposite, from 1980, I'm with Jan Michelle, Denny Kemp, Zena Clifton and Natalie Shaw, the 'Dolly Dealers', as I called them for a bit of fun. This expression, however, was deemed to be politically incorrect in the nineties – so I replaced 'dollies' with 'darling' – but then perfectly okay again in the noughties. Sometimes it's hard to keep up!

The most important element of *Play Your Cards Right*, and I think this applies to all successful gameshows, is that we had fun with the contestants. That's what I enjoy doing the most and it's why I loved *Play Your Cards Right*. As with *The Generation Game*, I didn't meet them until just before the show when I would briefly say hello. I didn't want to know too much about them. It's the spontaneity factor again. I wanted to be as surprised as the audience and viewers by the answers the contestants gave.

We would always have a much longer chat after the show. Over a drink in the Green Room there would be photos with friends and families and I would sign autographs. I always found this enjoyable, but I also

thought it was important. The contestants had given so much of their time to us that the least I could do was thank them personally.

THE INTERVIEWS I CONDUCTED at the start of the show were similar to those before Beat the Clock at the Palladium in as much as they were a buffer. The completely random nature of *Play Your Cards Right* meant that it was impossible to know how long each game would last. In no time the game could be over, or it could drag on, especially if we went to a tie-breaker. It all rested on the turn of a card, and as everything viewers saw on screen was absolutely genuine, we never knew what that next card would be.

As a consequence of this I could take my time over those chats, generating laughs and a lot of fun, knowing that if we had to, we could edit them down to fit the required length of the show. Usually we were able to keep in a lot of the banter, which meant that when the game actually began, the viewers and audience felt they knew something about the people they

were watching. They could empathize with them immediately, just as I did. I was as excited or disappointed as anyone on the turn of each card.

In the final round, when I explained the rules and reached the bit where I said that if they had accumulated four thousand points they had a chance to go for the car, I would turn to the audience expectantly and they would shout back, 'Wow-eee!' This helped to build an exciting atmosphere and again kept the audience involved in the game.

If the couple experienced an unlucky run, I was upset for them, but if they won, well, the look on their faces – that was priceless. I would take them over to their new car and open the door for them as the credits rolled. It didn't always go according to plan, mind you. In one of the early shows I brought the excited winners to their prize and went to open the driver's door . . . and it was locked. Someone backstage had walked off with the keys. People love these moments when things go wrong, and so do I. It gives me the chance to fake anger and outrage, much to the audience's delight.

Winning the car meant an awful lot to the successful couples, and it meant an awful lot to me as well. I wanted the contestants to be as happy playing the game as I was hosting it. And that was very happy indeed.

WHEN THE FIRST RUN *of Play Your Cards Right* came to an end in 1987, I already had a replacement show lined up.

You Bet! involved a panel of three celebrities introducing members of the public, who claimed to be able to complete unusual challenges in a set amount of time – pitching a scout tent in three and a half minutes while blindfolded, or a gymnastics team performing one hundred and fifty somersaults over a pommel horse in ninety seconds. The other celebrities would then bet on whether or not the challengers would be successful in order to win money for their favourite charities.

Many of the challenges took place in the studio and could involve a lot of people. As a result *You Bet!* was produced on a big scale – at Shepperton Studios, no less. It was broadcast at prime time on Saturday night, a slot I hadn't occupied since *Big Night* in 1978, and it was a hit. Yet . . .

I never felt I could make anything out of the show. I recognized that it was well thought-out and executed. It's just that it wasn't really for me; it didn't play to my strengths. I decided to leave after three series, to be replaced by Matthew Kelly, who did a fine job.

Despite what I've just said, I did enjoy myself during my time on the show. Some of the challenges were astonishing to witness and we had a host of excellent guests. One of my favourites appeared in the second series; I was a big fan.

Let me explain. Don't groan, but this goes all the way back to my school days.

You see, growing up, I loved playing football. My nickname at school was 'Spider Johnson' because I was all arms and legs and I moved quickly. At Brettenham Road Elementary School I was still a little tall for my age so I played centre half, and when I transferred to secondary school, aged eleven, I played on the right wing. I was fast on my feet and modelled myself on the great Stanley Matthews.

MY NICKNAME AT SCHOOL WAS 'SPIDER JOHNSON'

I carried on playing football right through my days in the RAF and beyond, although as my show-business career took off in the sixties my appearances on the pitch diminished in number. Diminished, but did not totally come to an end.

In the summer of 1967 I was appearing in a Blackpool show with Millicent Martin when Jimmy Tarbuck contacted me about a charity football match he was involved in to raise funds for the Cystic Fibrosis Research Foundation Trust. The game was to take place the following day, 19 July, with Jimmy captain of the celebrity team.

'You don't play, do you, Bruce?' Jimmy asked.

'As a matter of fact, I do.'

'Really? What position?'

'Right wing.'

'All right, then,' Jimmy said, then added, with perfect Tarbuck timing, 'That's probably the best place for you. Out of the way.'

EARLY ON IN THE match, I had the ball at my feet and flew down the wing, beating a couple of defenders before sending over an inch-perfect cross that led to our first goal. Walking back up the pitch, I noticed Jimmy standing stock still in the centre circle, with an amazed look on his face. 'Bruce, you really can play,' he said, as I passed him. I just smiled and took up my position. For once I didn't need a funny line.

The match was being played at the home of a local rugby-league team, and after it had finished one of the guys there offered to massage my legs. 'Oh, yes, please, that would be great.' I was delighted. I hadn't played football in a long time and knew I'd be suffering. Now, this guy was huge, a professional masseur, and when he put the oil on my legs and started to rub it felt beautiful. Just what I needed.

Back in my hotel room I decided to have a tiny rest before getting ready for the show that evening . . . and when I woke up my thigh muscles were red raw and on fire. I couldn't believe it. I phoned the secretary of the rugby club to find out what on earth his masseur had used.

'Oh,' he said, 'he always uses horse oil.'

'Horse oil! I know I've got a long face, but blimey!'

My opening number with Millicent Martin that evening was called 'Who?' This is a great song, with a lot of stops in it, during which, yes, you've guessed it, we had to slap out a rhythm on our thighs. The pain was excruciating. The things I do for show-business!

'Nice story, Bruce,' I hear you say, 'but what has it got to do with *You Bet!*?'

Well, the connection is my love of football. Joining Claire Rayner and Melvyn Hayes on the seventh show of that second series was the rising star of English football, Paul Gascoigne, who the previous year had signed with Spurs, a team I follow. As a fan, I had seen him play a number of times and admired him greatly. It was a genuine thrill for me to have Gazza on the show.

And, as you can see, I took the opportunity to offer him a few tips from the 'Spider Johnson' coaching manual. Given how well he played in the World Cup the following year in Italy, I think we can safely assume he took on board everything I taught him that day!

Following my three series of *You Bet!*, I returned to the BBC, first with the revival of *The Generation Game* and then, in 1992, with my own chat show. This was something I had been interested in doing for many years – I first talked about it back in 1971 with Bill Cotton, if you remember – and I wanted it to be a talk show with a difference.

For *Bruce's Guest Night*, the idea was that instead of the stars sitting passively on a sofa answering questions, they would be far more animated, giving performances and interacting with the audience.

The first series ran for six hour-long episodes on Friday nights, starting in April, and featured many marvellous guests, including Pat Cash, Leslie Grantham, Ronnie Corbett, Neil Sedaka, Bea Arthur, Jose Carreras and Dionne Warwick.

I was very happy with how it had gone: it sparkled with energy and fun and the sixty minutes allowed plenty of time for meaningful conversations with the guests. The public clearly thought so as well, as the ratings were good.

For some reason, though, the BBC were unconvinced and I honestly do not know why. They were unsure about commissioning another series, and when they eventually gave it the green light they played around with the schedule and format. We were now a thirty-minute Monday-night show. Unsurprisingly, such a display of confidence condemned that second series as the final one.

It was such a shame because the show was popular, and even with its reduced standing in the schedule it still attracted top-flight guests, such as Jackie Mason, Tony Bennett, Natalie Cole and Jack Jones.

One guest in particular comes to mind when I think of that second series, because his appearance sums up for me everything that was good about the show.

In April 1993 Howard Keel completed his farewell tour of the UK and agreed to come on to discuss his career. As always, he was a wonderful guest and the audience loved him. After discussing with Howard his various musical triumphs and his plans to open a theatre, I asked if anyone in the audience had a question.

A woman raised her hand. 'I'd like to wish you the best of luck with your new venture, Howard, and to ask if you've got a new leading lady yet. If not, can I audition?' I asked her what she would like to sing and she suggested 'Make Believe' from *Showboat*, a song Howard knew well from his starring role in the 1951 movie.

She then started to sing, with a gorgeous voice I must say, and, unprompted, Howard joined in. It was a delightful moment and must have made the woman's year. Imagine having the chance to sing with Howard Keel . . . and talk to me!

Howard and I then discussed doing a song together and he suggested 'Ol' Man River', with Howard singing the low notes and me the higher ones because, as I said, my voice hadn't yet broken.

We had put this number together in the BBC rehearsal rooms in Acton, which you can see here, where we fooled around with ideas until we had a very good comedy routine worked out. We had great fun that day. It was always a delight working with Howard. He had such a delightful sense of humour.

HAVE A THINK ABOUT 'Ol' Man River'. How many high notes can you remember? None. That was the point. Howard sang the song beautifully, on his own, while I tried desperately to join in. Finally, I resort to getting down on my hands and knees in a futile bid to be heard. Howard just sits on me and continues with his big finish. The routine was completely different from what anyone would have expected, and the audience loved it.

Guest Night was all about creating an atmosphere in which moments such as these could develop – I wish we'd been given the opportunity to create more of them.

Bruce's Price Is Right came about in a similar way to *Play Your Cards Right*, in that I was flicking through the TV channels, this time in Puerto Rico in 1995, thinking about what might work as a new show for me, when I came upon the US version. I knew Leslie Crowther had hosted it in the UK back in the eighties, highly successfully, but it had been off air for a number of years. Both the US and Leslie's version ran for sixty minutes, which I knew would be a problem. ITV in the nineties were looking for half-hour gameshows. But as I watched the programme that day it dawned on me that the two halves of the show were identical. Just cut it in half, I thought, and it will be perfect.

In September of that year the first *Bruce's Price Is Right* was broadcast. Just as we had on *Play Your Cards Right*, we taped two shows a day, with the same audience, which meant I could have a bit of fun. At the start of each second recording, I would mention how much better this audience was compared with the ghastly one from the previous week. Everyone loved being in on the joke and they always gave the line a big laugh, but I doubt we were kidding anyone at home.

'WE CAN'T HAVE YOU WITH FOUR FEMALE ASSISTANTS. IT JUST WON'T WORK NOWADAYS.'

As I have already mentioned, in the nineties political correctness was high on every broadcaster's agenda. When Ian Wilson and I first pitched the idea to Marcus Plantin, controller of ITV, I had anticipated what their major concern would be. I had a response prepared.

'We love the idea, Bruce,' they told me, 'but we can't have you with four female assistants. It just won't work nowadays.'

'I've already thought about that and I have a plan. Why don't we have three gorgeous girls and one handsome young man to display the prizes? That will stop any possible complaints, won't it?'

They agreed, as you can see here, with Emma Noble, Emma Steadman and Kimberley Cowell joined by Brian Tattersall.

THE FORMAT OF *Bruce's Price Is Right* consisted of contestants chosen at random from the studio audience; their task was to try to guess the price of various prizes through a series of different games. It was very popular and ran for six series between 1995 and 2001. It was an excellent show but,

as with *You Bet!*, it was never quite the same for me as *Play Your Cards Right*. Once again, I didn't have the opportunity for the same laughs with the contestants.

In truth, the most fun I had on the show was during the warm-up when I chatted to the audience, explained how the show worked and what people should do if selected to take part.

'If your name is chosen, come down and take your place. Please don't feel nervous or intimidated. Try to enjoy yourself. And when I talk to you, just forget you're talking to a superstar!' This always received a big laugh!

HONOURED

On 22 February 2015 the Dolby Theatre in Hollywood hosted the eighty-seventh Oscar ceremony . . . which happened to be exactly the same day as my eighty-seventh birthday!

Why do I mention this, other than the extraordinary coincidence? Well, as I sat at home in Puerto Rico watching it on television I was struck by a thought. Although over the course of those eighty-seven years the Academy had consistently overlooked my contribution to the world of cinema (although surely I had come close with *Heironymus Merkin*!), I realized I could still hold my head high should I ever find myself in the company of double Oscar-winners such as Maggie Smith, Tom Hanks and Dustin Hoffman.

You see, I am also the recipient of two Oscars – two *Bucket & Spade Oscars*!

These were presented by the famous comic actor Leslie Henson, who in the forties and fifties toured the English coastal resorts to review the Summer Season shows, in order to choose the best performer each year. I was the delighted winner in 1955 and 1956 when appearing at Babbacombe.

The top photograph here is Leslie presenting me with one of my awards, alongside the wonderful Hedley Claxton, in the white tie, who is receiving his own Oscar as producer.

The second shot gives you a closer look at the award itself, which is really a rather clever design I think – a starfish playing a spade like a guitar, posed on top of an orange . . . yes, the famous English seaside orange! (Well, the awards were sponsored by Outspan.)

I remember when I won I thought I had *really* made it. This was the gateway to stardom, as far as I was concerned. I wasn't entirely wrong, although it did take a few years before that gateway was fully opened.

I have been privileged to receive a number of awards and honours over the years and I cherish each one. It is a marvellous feeling to be recognized for the work you have done. I can't possibly list them all here, or properly thank everyone who voted for me, nominated me or considered me, or pay adequate tribute to all the people behind the scenes who made the awards possible – now I do sound as though I've won an Academy Oscar! So I'd like now to take this opportunity to say a heartfelt thank-you to everyone involved. I've been extraordinarily lucky and I am very grateful.

Which ones to mention here? Well, two industry awards come to mind in particular.

THE FIRST IS THIS silver heart Variety Club Award presented to me in March 1960. There are two reasons I have included this. The first is that I received the award for 'Independent Television Personality of the Year for 1959' in recognition of my work on *Sunday Night at the London Palladium*. I hardly need to say again how much I owe to that one show.

I also love the photograph. It reminds me of those heady early days when my career was taking off and I was starting to mix with entertainers

and personalities of this calibre. It was beyond my wildest dreams, it really was. We all look so young that I suspect you may not be able to identify everyone. Here's the line-up.

Richard Dimbleby, Richard Todd, me, Peter O'Toole, Bernard Miles, Anthony Newley, Elizabeth Seal, Harry Secombe and Peter Finch. Quite a gathering. I also find it very sweet that I have my hand on Harry Secombe's shoulder. We were such good friends, and I was thrilled for him that day as he had quite rightly won the big award: Show Business Personality of the Year.

THE SECOND INDUSTRY AWARD I would like to mention is the BAFTA Fellowship I received in 2008. This is the highest accolade in British show-business, and to be recognized in this way by my peers truly was an honour, made even more special by the fact that the ceremony took place at the Palladium. So much that is good in my professional life happened on that stage and to be able to add this to my memories, well, I couldn't have been happier.

In fact, this was my second BAFTA: I'd received a Special Award four years earlier. They now sit very proudly at either end of my piano at home. Just goes to show I don't get everything right – there *is* something in this game for a pair!

Now, while I am on the subject of the Palladium once again, if you're ever there to see a show, please do come and say hello. I'll be in the Cinderella Bar. I'm a permanent fixture there, you see.

THIS LOVELY BUST, UNVEILED in May 2005, was sculpted by my Julie's husband, Dominic Grant. Julie and Dominic were both in the hugely successful pop group Guys 'n' Dolls, who in 1975 had a smash hit with 'There's A Whole Lot of Loving'. They still perform as Grant & Forsyth, and in addition Dominic has carved out a second career as a highly regarded sculptor. He has a huge amount of talent, as this bust clearly demonstrates, and I'm thrilled at his success.

The official ceremony was conducted by Michael Grade, who was a perfect choice. Michael has been involved with my career for many years, probably more than he would like to remember. In 1966 he took over from his father, Leslie, at the Delfont Agency, sitting in the office next door to Billy Marsh. It was Billy who more or less showed Michael the ropes in the agency business and we subsequently worked a lot together, both through the agency and later when Michael joined LWT. I knew

Michael long before then, however. As a schoolboy he was a regular visitor to *Sunday Night at the London Palladium*. Whenever one of the big pop bands of the day was on the bill, young Michael could be found sitting in the stalls, loving watching his idols perform.

IN 1998 I WAS surprised and delighted to receive notification that I had been awarded an OBE in the Queen's Birthday Honours. The surprise was twofold. First, you never expect anything like that to happen to you, and second, surely I'd irreparably blotted my copybook many years previously.

It was a 1977 show in aid of the Prince's Trust, at the Theatre Royal, Windsor. I was top of the bill, and during my performance I had been having great fun teasing a young engaged couple. At the end of the evening, when the then single Prince Charles came onstage to thank me and everyone else who had been involved, he referred back to my earlier banter in his show-stealing opening line: 'Well, I must say, I am glad I'm not engaged! Although, according to some of the things I read – I am! To a different person each week!'

Prince Charles was a natural. He had a whole routine worked out, which was hilarious. He must have been onstage for ten minutes, very dignified, very professional and very funny indeed.

THIS CONTACT SHEET GIVES some idea of just how entertaining he was. But look closely at the start of the sequence. See the larger print in case you can't quite make it out.

YES, I'M AFRAID I was so carried away I put my arm around the heir to the throne. Now that is something you are meant never to do.

I am glad to say that Prince Charles and his family seem to have forgiven me, but even so, I feel I really should take this opportunity to apologize formally for my breach of protocol. I am sorry, Your Royal Highness. And thank you for not sending me to the Tower!

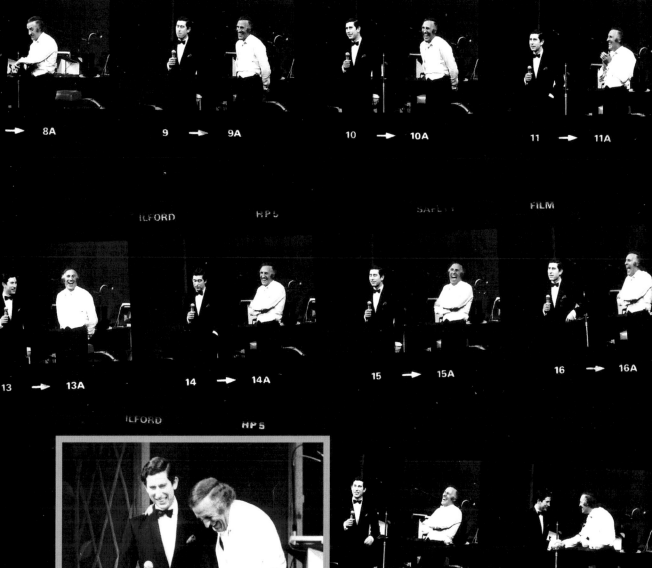

8A →   9 → 9A   10 → 10A   11 → 11A

ILFORD   HP5   SAFETY   FILM

13 → 13A   14 → 14A   15 → 15A   16 → 16A

ILFORD   HP5

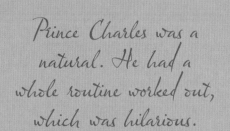

Prince Charles was a natural. He had a whole routine worked out, which was hilarious.

ON THE DAY OF the investiture, Winnie, pictured here with JJ and Debbie in the quadrangle at Buckingham Palace, was in some distress. Weeks before she had slipped, falling heavily, and was still suffering considerable back pain.

I was greatly honoured to receive my OBE, but after a family lunch at the Dorchester to celebrate, I was more than happy to take Winnie home. By then she was in agony, so much so that we arranged for her to be admitted immediately to hospital where it was confirmed she required an operation. Poor Winnie was house-bound for eight weeks afterwards but has since made a full recovery, to my great relief.

As for me, well, you can see I had no trouble with my back that day.

IN MAY 2006 I was again honoured by Her Majesty, with a CBE. Just before the official announcement of my award, a rather strange thing happened. News 'leaked' in the press that I was to be awarded a knighthood. This resulted in various people calling up to congratulate me and I had to tell them that the rumours were untrue. This proved very awkward for them, as you can imagine. As for me, I was thrilled with my CBE.

Fortunately this time Winnie, pictured with my daughters Julie and Louisa, was fighting fit and able to enjoy the occasion. I, on the other hand, was very nervous. Even with years of theatrical experience, an event such as this has a profound effect on you. I realized how privileged I was to be there, and that was a feeling I couldn't and didn't want to shake off. It was too big a moment in my life.

IN THE YEARS FOLLOWING my CBE a momentum built up, generated by both the public and the press, that I should receive a knighthood. I was extremely touched by this 'campaign', but I can honestly say that I was not in the least worried about whether I would become a 'Sir' or not. I was honoured to be mentioned in such a context, of course I was, but as I said, whenever I was asked about it, 'I'm in good company. If you think about it, Morecambe and Wise were never knighted, same for the Two Ronnies, Tommy Cooper, Les Dawson, Eric Sykes, Frankie Howerd,

Roy Castle . . . The list could go on and on. All marvellous entertainers and tireless supporters of charities, who were not recognized in their time with a knighthood.'

I have often wondered why that is. I think perhaps it's because entertainers and comedians are not regarded as having a proper job, so why would they deserve such an honour? Some people seem to think it's easy getting laughs. How little they know. The reality, especially for true comedians, is that it is one of the hardest jobs in the business.

First of all, there is a huge amount of work involved in preparing material you hope is funny. Then, if it doesn't go well for whatever reason, a performer whose sole professional existence relies on them getting laughs can go through hell. I am not affected in quite the same way as I can always go into a song and dance or impersonation or playing the piano. For comedians, though, they have to show such resilience and mental strength, to continue when things are tough and then pick themselves up and step back onstage for their next show. I have enormous admiration for those performers. So, as far as I was concerned, to remain part of a group that included, together with many others, the comedians and entertainers I mentioned above, was absolutely fine by me.

So when the letter actually arrived in 2011, I honestly thought it was a hoax. I assumed someone was playing a joke, and when I spoke to Ian Wilson about it, he thought the same. He even called up the Cabinet Office to confirm whether it was genuine or not.

A little later, I also had to put in a call to the Cabinet Office, after they sent me a form enquiring whether I wanted any publicity. I spoke to a very nice woman there.

'I really don't think I need any publicity,' I explained to her. 'There's been enough said already.'

'Hasn't there just . . . ' she replied.

There had been such extensive coverage in the press about my possible knighthood, with the Cabinet Office no doubt receiving a huge amount of mail on the subject, that I suspect they were delighted to see the back of me!

STANDING IN BUCKINGHAM PALACE as Sir Bruce Forsyth, with my wife of twenty-eight years next to me, Lady Forsyth, I was as pleased for her as I was myself. I could scarcely believe it had actually happened. I couldn't help thinking back on my life and career and all those people who meant so much to me and were no longer around. I saw my knighthood as honouring their lives, my parents, my brother and my sister, and also all the deserving performers who had not received the same recognition in their lifetimes. I like to think that those friends, with whom I had shared so much over the years, were looking down on me that day, as I stood proudly on their behalf, and smiling.

TO CELEBRATE, WE HELD a big reception with friends and family at the Westbury Hotel in Mayfair. It was a perfect afternoon, and very moving. As I made my entrance down the stairs, I looked out on a sea of faces that meant the world to me. In my speech I made sure to go round everyone, table to table, to say why each person was there and why they were important. I wanted all of them to know how special they were in my life.

Chapter Sixteen

STRICTLY

have now reached the point when the story of my career comes almost full circle.

As a boy I loved to dance and I dreamed of making people happy by doing just that. It wasn't such a fanciful thought. Back then, if you had enough talent and a lot of luck, you could hope to make a career through dance. With the variety circuit, the Summer Seasons, cabaret, West End and provincial shows flourishing, there were many opportunities for dancers. The main reason for that, of course, was that dancing was a very popular pastime with the public. They loved to participate and to watch. Ballrooms and dance halls up and down the country were full of couples enjoying themselves to the sound of big bands and even bigger orchestras.

And then, slowly, dancing – ballroom dancing – fell out of fashion. It's hard to pinpoint exactly when this change in fortunes began, perhaps in the mid-sixties, but certainly by the seventies the public seemed to have moved on from the quickstep, foxtrot and jive. It was sad to see. Dance was my passion, the backbone of my career, and although I and many others worked hard to keep it alive as a form of entertainment and a social activity, it seemed that it was in terminal decline in Britain.

Then, in 2004, along came a television show that would give a seventy-six-year-old man, who still adored to dance, the opportunity to be part of something that would resuscitate his great love, and place it firmly back in the public spotlight. What a wonderful thing to happen. When I first heard about the show, however, I would never have predicted that it would become such a phenomenon.

It came completely out of thin air. In 2003 I was filming an advert for the Sky+ Box with Kelly Brook at the Black Island Studios just off the North Circular Road in London. During my lunch break, Ian Wilson and I had been invited to meet with two senior executives from the BBC, Jane Lush, head of Entertainment, and the late Richard Hopkins, head of Entertainment Formats. We had no idea what was on the agenda as we crammed into a cubicle in a tiny Italian restaurant near Hanger Lane.

After some small-talk and a discussion about another show I was set to do for the BBC, Jane and Richard came to the main purpose of the meeting. They were developing a new format – for prime-time Saturday-night television – centred on ballroom dancing and wondered what I made of it. Well, if I'm honest, my first thought was this must be some kind of wind-up; it was such an unexpected idea. That might sound odd now, given the success of *Strictly Come Dancing* and the many other dance shows that followed in its wake, but you have to remember this was back in 2003.

Reality TV was king, although much of it was rather cruel for my taste. *Big Brother*, *Fame Academy* and other similar shows 'starring' members of the public were the big ratings winners. Entertainment shows – or, at least, what I thought of as entertainment shows – had practically ceased to exist. Yet here we were, talking about the possibility of a series with the working title *Pro Celebrity Come Dancing* in which well-known contestants would learn to ballroom dance (it could not have been less fashionable at the time) and compete against each other.

THEY WERE DEVELOPING A NEW FORMAT – FOR PRIME-TIME SATURDAY-NIGHT TELEVISION – CENTRED ON BALLROOM DANCING

As I realized Jane and Richard were serious, my thoughts were immediately drawn to *The Generation Game*, and the various dance-oriented games we had played. I began to imagine contestants tripping over each other, the chaos and laughs that would bring. I soon learned, however, that the BBC envisaged something that was far more of a genuine competition. In the end, *Strictly* brought together the best of both worlds – the fierce competitiveness of professional dancers, which I had overlooked when the concept was first discussed, combined with the more laid-back attitude of many of the contestants, people such as David Dickinson and Russell Grant, who were only participating to have a bit of fun. Indeed, I think it was this unique combination that made the show such a success. While viewers cared how well people danced, they also enjoyed supporting the celebrities who were just there to have a go.

From the start, *Strictly* was a very warm show and it has maintained that positive feel-good factor throughout, while still managing to create a strong competitive edge as each series progresses towards its climax. From early on this meant the contestants were reaching standards of dance that I would never have thought possible. Add to that some much-needed Saturday-night glamour, four larger-than-life judges and the best band on television, and this unlikely idea worked. Indeed, the bravery and vision of those responsible for *Strictly* still amazes me: Jane, Richard, Fenia Vardanis, who championed the format, and Lorraine Heggessey, controller of BBC 1 at the time, who commissioned it . . . as a LIVE show.

The BBC soon sensed they were on to a winner, so much so that we were starting to make our second series almost within days of completing the first. At seventy-six years old I was suddenly presenting one of the biggest shows on television. The echoes I could hear from *Sunday Night at the London Palladium* were not lost on me.

THE BBC SOON SENSED THEY WERE ON TO A WINNER

What no one could have guessed, however, was just how big a winner *Strictly* was to become. It has subsequently evolved into a monster hit, not only in the UK but worldwide. I believe it is now the BBC's biggest ever export as a format.

At this point, there is something important I would like to make clear. Much has been written over recent months about how I supposedly did not enjoy my time on *Strictly*. That is absolutely incorrect.

The point I was trying to make was that when I first started on *Strictly* it was difficult for me because I had to learn a new craft. I was being asked to do something I had never done before in my career – to be just a presenter.

What I mean is that in the *Strictly* format I did not really have very much interaction with the public, contestants or professional dancers. Instead, I was repeatedly on and off camera, introducing the show, linking a very rigidly timed series of set-pieces, then saying goodbye. There was little chance to slip in any fun 'business' and very few opportunities for me to ad-lib because *Strictly* was so well produced. It is a totally live show, often running at more than two hours, incredibly complicated to stage, yet there were and are hardly any mistakes.

VIRTUALLY THE ONLY TIME anything went wrong in my presenting eleven series of the show was during series four when former cricketer, and firm favourite with our female viewers, Mark Ramprakash was performing a salsa with his partner Karen Hardy and Mark's microphone came loose. They had to stop the dance and Mark and Karen were worried that they might not be given a second chance. I walked over to check what was happening and to reassure them that everything would be fine. Just then one of our floor producers appeared to see if she could help.

'Who's this? Who are you?' I said, and started to dance with her, announcing to the studio audience, 'I love this! This is what it's all about! Live television!' I meant it. That was the interaction I thrive on, but such opportunities were scarce because my role on *Strictly* was more removed than I was used to.

For a start, the audience sat miles away from where I stood so I couldn't interact with them. Even the judges were really only in my peripheral vision and my time with them was limited. I could comment only briefly on what they had said, and even then we had to tread a fine

line. If we had too much fun it was seen as being disrespectful to the dancers and the dances. The serious dancing public took issue with that. And if we were too serious, where was the entertainment? As for talking to the contestants, I only ever spoke to them when they had just finished dancing and were exhausted.

All this was initially alien to every bone in my entertainer's body. I'm a performer, but I found in *Strictly* it was the camera that was my audience. It was a different way of working that, yes, I did find hard, but even so I still regarded it as a privilege to have been given the opportunity to learn this new craft.

I like to think I made it work. Taking on new challenges is something I have never shied away from; in fact I relish it, and that applies as equally in my seventies and eighties as it did when I first stepped on to the Palladium stage, presented *The Generation Game* or put together my one-man shows. In truth, it is being able to take on these new challenges, and to enjoy doing so, that is one of the biggest reasons I have remained young at heart for so long.

I ALSO FOUND THE role of presenter to be quite a lonely one. I didn't even see much of my co-host Tess Daly – we would have our opening joke, say good night, and that was it.

Right from the start Tess was a joy to work with and, over the years, we shared many, many laughs. Even in the very early days, before the show had properly found its feet, when we were still putting it together and things could be hard going, Tess and I would laugh at what was happening over coffee and a sandwich. She has a wonderful sense of humour and was always great fun at the script read-throughs, constantly coming up with suggestions and adding funny bits and pieces. She has a very active mind and I couldn't have wished for anyone better to present with, I really couldn't. Thank you, Tess.

Now, OVER THE YEARS, I was asked many times who my favourite contestants were, but I never said. As host, it would have been both unprofessional to do so, and disrespectful to the integrity of the show.

Incidentally, how long do you think that catchphrase 'You're my favourites' has been around? Since the early days of the show, when I would say it to *all* the semi-finalists and finalists? (By the way, when I first used the expression on *Strictly* it gave everyone sitting in the production gallery kittens. They were worried that I was trying to influence votes. Perhaps because I looked so fresh-faced they thought it was my first time on television!)

If you are thinking that the phrase originated around then, you would be wrong. Instead, you have to go back a long, long way, to 1961, in fact, and Nat King Cole's appearance on *The Royal Variety Performance*. After he had finished his numbers, I spoke to him onstage.

'Well, Nat, thank you so much for being with us this evening and for your wonderful performance. It has been lovely having you here. I hope you have enjoyed working for ATV.'

'Oh, yes,' he said, 'they're my favourites.'

I used it on a couple of occasions after that at the Palladium and it received a nice response, but it wasn't until I brought it out again for *Strictly* that it caught on. That must be the longest ever gestation period for a catchphrase!

Anyway, now that I've left the show, I think I can break my rule and actually talk about some of my favourite dancers and moments. As so often in this book, I can't mention all the great stars and dancers who appeared: there just isn't space. I hope those I've been forced to miss out will forgive me. I used to say at the beginning of each programme, 'It's time to meet the *stars* of our show.' I meant it then and I mean it now. Each one of them – not only those mentioned here, but all the contestants and professional dancers – were stars. They put so many hours and dedication into their performances. Without them there would have been no show.

IN THE FIRST SERIES, because *Strictly* was an unknown quantity, a lot of celebrities who were asked to take part were unsure about coming on board. The BBC needed some high-profile popular names and that's why I *think* a little pressure was put on Natasha Kaplinsky to agree to appear. What I know for *sure* is that initially she was sorry she had done so.

Natasha and I were standing at the top of the stairs, the ones I walked down to make my entrance. We knew each other a little from working together on *Have I Got News For You*, and she said to me, 'Bruce, you have got to get me out of this show.'

'What do you mean, Natasha?'

'I want to be voted off. Can you do something?'

'What can I do? I'm not a judge. I'm only the presenter.'

'Surely you can do something to get me out of this.'

'I'm so sorry, but I can't. I can see you feel strongly about it but there is nothing I can do.'

I think the enormity of what Natasha was undertaking had just sunk in and she was feeling overwhelmed. It is a big commitment. Thank goodness she overcame her concerns and chose to stay, because she ended up loving the show and, of course, went on to win. I remember her saying to me towards the end of the series that she was now really enjoying ballroom dancing. She was a great champion and I was so pleased when I heard that.

IN THE SAME SERIES, the very popular *EastEnders* star Christopher Parker proved we could have comedy on the show, even when we weren't expecting it. Christopher was great for *Strictly*, but his paso doble, bless his heart, was one of the worst dances ever. It was dreadful. I hope he doesn't mind me saying so, but it's true.

The great thing about Christopher was that he gave his all, and the public loved him for that. When Arlene Phillips criticized him, he would say. 'But, Arlene, I am trying, I really am.' And he was! It was just that the more he tried, the worse he became! That was why people adored him so. He always gave his best, but he just couldn't do it. The judges produced terrible scores but the public kept voting him back because he was so lovable. He had a touch of pathos about him. 'I'm trying, I really am trying.' It was very endearing.

In that first series, the final was down to a viewer vote and Christopher came second to Natasha. I always wonder what would have happened if he had actually won. Would we have had a totally different TV programme on our hands afterwards? I think it's possible because future contestants wouldn't have taken the show seriously.

Voting for the underdog is part of the fun of *Strictly* and I hope it remains so, even as the standard of dancing improves year on year and the format is tweaked to give the judges more of a say. It is a great aspect of the programme, but sometimes it has created situations in which we've had to say goodbye to some very good dancers much earlier than they deserved.

In series five, for instance, the judges were forced to cut either Gabby Logan or Penny Lancaster in week four, and they were two of the best dancers we've had. Then in series seven tennis champion Martina Hingis was first out, even though she was terrific. I guess you can't have everything.

IT WAS ANOTHER *EastEnders* star, Jill Halfpenny, who started us thinking that *Strictly* could be a serious dance competition. She was a very worthy winner, and the first contestant to score four tens, with her jive. That really was something. I don't think anyone has kicked or flicked more than she did. Because of Jill, in what was only the second series, it became clear that someone who is a good dancer could be properly recognized. That was a very important step in the evolution of the show.

CRICKETER DARREN GOUGH WAS probably the biggest surprise we had in the early series. He made me realize for the first time the extent to which the contestants' training could improve their performance. I remember asking Darren, off camera, 'Do you go out dancing a lot?'

'Oh, yeah,' he replied. 'I go to discos. But just to have a drink with the lads. I never get on my feet!'

Watching Darren in the first couple of weeks, I knew he was telling the truth. There was nothing there. Then gradually he began to find his feet and the improvement kept on and kept on until he ended up a fine dancer and the series winner, no less.

Perhaps I shouldn't have been as surprised as I was. After all, it has been proved time and again that sports stars have a natural gift for *Strictly* – they have control of their limbs, they know what to do with their arms and legs, and they have timing. Most important of all, however, is that they are all incredibly competitive; every sports person wants to win.

Darren's partner Lilia Kopylova was perfect with him. It is very important that the contestants have the right partner. You need a strong chemistry between celebrity and professional dancer. If you're someone like Darren and do well in the show, the relationship is going to last a full three to four months. That's a long time to be in someone's company, especially in such a physical environment.

The producers spend a lot of time deliberating on the pairings. They take it very seriously because they understand how critical the matches are, not only for the contestants but for the show itself. They do an excellent job.

MODEL AND ACTRESS KELLY Brook is our most unfortunate contestant. Kelly is an extremely good dancer, very elegant, and would have given the eventual winner of series five, Alesha Dixon, a run for her money, I have no doubt. Kelly was that good. Unfortunately, however, poor Kelly had to retire when her father died. It was an awful time for her. Everyone on the show was so sorry for Kelly.

ALESHA THOUGH WAS A great champion. I was delighted for her. I think she had reached a bit a crossroads in her pop career and her win on *Strictly* helped her to focus on what she wanted for herself. I am very fond of

Alesha and was delighted when, after she won, we performed a number together . . . although quite where the idea for us to dance to Sinatra's 'Something's Gotta Give' came from I do not know. There is a line in the song that mentions an irresistible force meeting an old immovable object . . . I can't see how that had *any* relevance to Alesha and myself!

Normally, at the end of such dances, it is the female who kicks up her leg, but for a bit of fun we reversed the traditional roles, with me kicking up mine. I can tell you, at my age that's harder than it looks!

In 2009 Alesha became a *Strictly* judge but was very unlucky with the timing. A decision had been taken to refresh the judging panel, and when it was announced that Arlene Phillips was being replaced by Alesha,

some people took that to mean that Alesha was responsible for Arlene's departure. That simply wasn't true. At the time I said that if change was required, we should do it by having five judges instead of four, with Arlene still on board. It wouldn't have been unprecedented to do so. In some of the South American versions of *Strictly* they have as many as ten judges. They all score each dance but they don't all speak every time. It's a different way to do it and it works. However, the decision was taken not to go down that route.

It was a difficult situation for Alesha but she coped beautifully, winning over the public by being a very competent and interesting judge. She brought a new dimension to the panel, seeing things from the perspective of the contestants and, indeed, a champion who knew what it took to make it through an entire series.

As for Arlene, well, I was very sorry to see her leave. She was an excellent judge with a wicked twinkle in her eye when she commented on the effect some of the male dancers were having on her while they performed particularly sensuous or passionate routines. Arlene was always very entertaining, enjoying playing up having crushes on some of the boys – but only those who were attractive and good!

FORMER BBC POLITICAL CORRESPONDENT John Sergeant danced a number of entertaining comedy routines with Kristina Rihanoff, providing some extremely funny moments. These proved popular with the public, who continued to vote him back even though he couldn't dance. At all. As I have said, that is part of the fun. However, John saw things differently and chose to withdraw after the ninth programme, claiming the 'joke had gone too far' and that he might end up winning. That disappointed me because it messed up subsequent rounds, including how the semi-final would be determined. I didn't think it was fair. So when I look back on it, it's not really a favourite moment after all, but it was definitely a significant one.

SERIES EIGHT SAW THE arrival of politician Ann Widdecombe and boy did she, and all of us, have fun while she remained on the show. There were many delightful comedy moments, but I will never forget when she flew in on a harness! No one who witnessed it ever could. It was priceless.

I particularly liked Ann's attitude. She took everything in the right spirit. The judges' comments could be shockingly scathing but it was water off a duck's back to Ann. Typical politician. She would just look them in the eye and say, 'Well, I'm having a lot of fun, and I'm enjoying myself.'

I WAS ALSO VERY pleased that Ann had been paired with Anton du Beke. I knew they would be great together and so it proved. I always loved it when Anton was matched with a funny lady, because something special was bound to happen. Anton brings his own brand of mischievous comedy to the dance-floor.

Of all the professionals, he's the one I know best. We often have a game of golf together. As I've mentioned, I didn't spend much time with the dancers or the celebrities, but in an early series I performed a routine with Anton and his professional dance partner Erin Boag. It was a fun number, a combination of dancing and singing, which went down very well with the audience. In fact it was so popular that a few series later I enjoyed one of my *Strictly* highlights when Anton and I duetted on 'Me and My Shadow'. Guess who was the shadow? We had to rehearse both numbers, of course, which was how I got to know Anton. I wasn't in the least surprised that we clicked.

As we were preparing for the first series, looking through photographs of the professional dancers who would be featuring, the moment I saw Anton I knew I would have fun with him. It was like looking in a mirror! In fact, there is such a likeness between us that we have developed quite a running gag about whether we could be related. 'How's your mother?' I liked to ask him, as if she and I once had a thing going . . .

IN THE OPENING SHOW of series nine, when the contestants were introduced to their partners for the first time, and Lulu was paired with Brendan Cole, I could see instantly she wanted anyone but him! He had a bit of a reputation then. He could be a little mouthy with the judges, stroppy in rehearsals and a hard taskmaster. I think Lulu was genuinely concerned that he would be fire to her water.

Poor Lulu didn't stand a chance. The moment the announcement was made, Brendan rushed over to her, threw her over his shoulder in a fireman's lift and whisked her off up the stairs, with Lulu shouting, 'Let me down! Let me down!'

A terrific start to the series. Thank you, Brendan.

BEFORE THE BEGINNING OF series nine I had doubts as to how TV astrologer Russell Grant would take to the show. Then he walked out for his first dance and I knew in that instant he was going to be one of our stars, not in a dancing sense, but in terms of pure entertainment. Just as performers have command of the stage, Russell has command of the dance-floor. He stepped out with one purpose, to perform, regardless of how he was dressed or what he was about to do.

Somehow, Russell managed to create this wonderful façade of being a better dancer than he was, and the public quite rightly loved him for it. He broke down the barrier between artist and audience; he made a connection. The public then accepted him for who he was on the dance-floor – someone who was trying to reach beyond the limits of his talent and was willing to give anything a go that might help achieve his goal.

Being fired out of a cannon at Wembley certainly counts as 'giving anything a go'! It could have been the end of his show. It could have been the end of everyone's show.

He was a delight as a contestant and gave me many laughs on and off camera. A lovely man.

Olympic gymnast Louis Smith provided us with a different type of champion in series ten because of his wonderful athleticism and gymnastic ability. When he did that lovely Patrick Swayze lift from the film *Dirty Dancing* it was one of the big moments in the series.

I remember thinking when he came back to appear in one of our specials that he had changed since he first appeared on the show. There was a different, positive aura about him. I thought it was great. He was very focused on what he wanted to do, very professional, but still great fun. That's what *Strictly* can do for some people. It can help them develop their own personalities week on week as they grow in confidence with their dancing. Even if they don't win, as Louis did, I am sure the show does a lot of contestants a lot of good.

Finally, what of our judges? Well, I certainly don't have a favourite among them – they are all wonderful!

It is the mix of personalities and styles that makes the judges so endlessly entertaining. They all clearly have a genuine passion for dance and want the most talented contestants to proceed through each round, but at the same time they understand the crucial element of family entertainment, which makes *Strictly* what it is. It was a great pleasure to work with them and I'm thrilled that the show has given them all a chance to shine and embark on new careers that a dozen years ago would not have been possible. Good luck to them all.

I have already discussed Arlene and Alesha, so taking the current judges in the order in which they sit, first we have Craig Revel Horwood. Now, what can I say about Craig? Well, Craig is Craig. Although his marks, let alone remarks, can seem cuttingly low at times, I believe that, of all the judges, when Craig moves into the middle range of scores, his marks are the fairest of all. He's very discerning. And if a contestant receives a ten from Craig, he or she will most certainly have deserved it.

I also love the way Craig talks, especially how he calls everyone 'darling'. I never normally like a fella saying that to me, but I'll always be happy to hear it from Craig!

When Darcey Bussell replaced Alesha in 2012, she brought a new and exciting element to the panel's range of experience – a worldwide reputation as a sublime ballet dancer. Darcey has true legitimacy in the

world of dance, although I don't know if she knew a lot about ballroom dancing when she first arrived. That didn't matter, though. Over her career Darcey has been so thorough in her approach to dance that she recognized all the moves the contestants were attempting; and she certainly now knows what a 'fleckerl' step is in a Viennese Waltz, and all the kicks and flicks in the jive. I think it's fabulous when, during her critiques of the routines, Darcey uses her arms and hands to illustrate exactly what she is talking about. To me that shows she really cares, and wants to help.

THEY ARE ALL
WONDERFUL!

Next to Darcey sits Len Goodman. Len is probably the judge I spent most time with on *Strictly*. He would often pop into my dressing room for a chat, which I always appreciated. As a judge, I see Len as having a dual personality. On the one hand he can be like the wicked uncle in a pantomime, quite stroppy and prone to coming out with remarks now and again that can be shocking. On the other hand, he also takes on the persona of a kindly father figure who is very supportive, especially if he knows a contestant is really trying. Those two sides to Len make him a key personality on the show; you can never predict quite what he is going to say next.

Finally there is Bruno Tonioli. To say Bruno is flamboyant is the biggest understatement of all time. Enthusiasm and energy burst out of him, which is another huge addition to the panel's make-up. I love the way he can't stop himself leaping up to demonstrate how the contestants *should* have been moving. He is always very funny but also constructive.

I actually spoke to Bruno more than anyone else during the shows because of where he sits. After each piece to camera, I would have to move quickly to my off-stage position (actually hiding behind a pillar up the stairs!) so that I couldn't be seen while the contestants were dancing. To get there I would have to pass Bruno and we always exchanged a few comments and laughs about what was going on in the show or about what one of the other judges might just have said. I loved those moments with Bruno. It was great banter.

I should also mention that Bruno and Len are the two hardest working of the judges, as they both appear on the US version, *Dancing with the Stars*. I bet back in 2004 neither of them could have even dreamed of becoming such big names on the other side of the Atlantic or getting so many airmiles. During the autumn the two shows run pretty much simultaneously, which means Bruno and Len have to fly off to the States directly after finishing on *Strictly*, be on camera for the Monday and Tuesday in *Dancing with the Stars*, then back to the UK for the weekend. I wonder if that schedule pickles Len's walnuts . . .

ALL THROUGH MY ELEVENTH series of *Strictly* I had been thinking about the possibility of it being my last. The adrenalin drain you suffer after being on your feet for two hours plus, live in front of ten million people, is physically exhausting. The BBC had been really understanding of this pressure for some time, and had gone out of their way to help. They gave me more time off and in 2010 handed over the Sunday results show to Tess and Claudia Winkleman. I appreciated that very much and it certainly allowed me to remain on the show for longer than I ever thought I would.

I HAD BEEN DOING *STRICTLY* FOR TEN YEARS

However, by the time we put out the final show of series eleven, on 21 December 2013, I was seriously considering the possibility that the time had come for me to stop. I decided to think it over carefully while Winnie and I took our three-month break in Puerto Rico at the start of 2014, and the more I thought about it, the more the correct decision became clear. I had been doing *Strictly* for ten years and I didn't want to start feeling stale. And I didn't want the show to stop being fun.

I ALSO KNEW THAT if I did step aside I would be leaving *Strictly* in very good hands. I saw a seamless transition from me and Tess to Tess and Claudia. I had complete confidence in Claudia even though we have never actually worked together, which is a pity as we always have a laugh when we do meet up. As I mentioned, she and Tess started to co-host the results show, and prior to that Claudia hosted *It Takes Two*, a companion programme to *Strictly* in which she had done very well indeed. I had also seen her on the main show on a few occasions, when I'd had time off, and I always enjoyed how quick she was. Yes, I had no doubt that *Strictly* would continue to prosper with Tess taking on my responsibilities, and Claudia stepping into Tess's job, chatting with the contestants upstairs in what I called 'Tess's Penthouse'.

With all this going through my mind, when the time came to make my final decision, it really wasn't hard. It was the right thing to do, the right time to go.

Strictly has been a wonderful show *for* me, and it has been wonderful *to* me. I am proud to have been a part of it and thrilled that I could contribute in some way to bringing dancing back to the British public. There is a large increase in attendance at adult dance classes and I'm told that dance as entertainment is now the fastest growing art form in the country. *Strictly* has played its part and that means an enormous amount to me.

I am not gone from *Strictly* for ever, though. Not a bit of it. It is part of me now and I will be back. I look forward to seeing you all when I do. In the meantime, Keeeeep Dancing!

My paternal great-grandfather,
Joseph Forsyth-Johnson.

Chapter Seventeen

AFTER ALL THESE YEARS

A nd so to the final chapter . . . of this book, not my career! There's still plenty of that to be enjoyed in the years ahead. Now into my eighth decade as a performer I am as active as I wish to be – which is a truly marvellous thing to be able to say.

Strictly played a major role in my professional life between 2004 and 2013 but, in addition to that fantastic show, in what is now the second decade of the twenty-first century, I continue to take on fresh challenges. I couldn't wish for more.

Here, then, is a snapshot of what I've been up to in recent years.

FIRST IS A VOYAGE of discovery. In 2010 I took part in the BBC show *Who Do You Think You Are?* in which well-known personalities are assisted in tracing their family history. The show focused on my paternal great-grandfather, Joseph Forsyth-Johnson, pictured here, whom my father rarely mentioned. I knew he had been a gardener, but that was about it . . . until my interest was ignited by an astonishing letter I received from a lady in America. In the note, she suggested that not only might we be related through Joseph Forsyth-Johnson but that he had died at sea and was possibly a bigamist! Needless to say, I was fascinated to learn more.

My cousin Alan Johnson – our family historian – set me on the trail with some information he had found out about our great-grandfather, and from there I was in the hands of the producer and director. I had no idea where they, or the story, would lead me.

Now, there is a huge amount of work that goes on behind the scenes, but that was all kept entirely from me. As one surprise and shock followed another, I was continually astonished at what I discovered. I knew nothing about what had been uncovered until I was told on camera. That's one of the reasons enjoyed the show so much. Everything that the viewers saw was totally genuine.

'Today, Bruce, you're going to meet Katherine Hughes, a social historian at the Arts Club in Mayfair.' Oh, lovely!

And then, further into filming, I would be introduced to 'Ken Cobb, senior archivist at the New York Municipal Archive' or 'Paul Crater, senior librarian at the Atlanta History Center' – just a couple of the many experts who played their part. In meeting these various people, all on film, I had to have an instant reaction, to ad-lib if you like.

As you can imagine, I loved every moment of it.

Now, I'm not going to go into all the twists and turns of Joseph's story here. I don't want to ruin the show for you, should you have a chance to see it. I assure you it's worth it. I don't say that because I'm involved, not at all. It's the life Joseph led that makes the programme so fascinating, and the hard work put in by the *Who Do You Think You Are?* team, as well as all those amazing archivists and experts who contributed. They are the stars of the show.

As a taster, however, I will say that the original letter I received was partly correct. I *did* meet a whole new side of my family, which was incredibly moving, but Joseph was not *legally* a bigamist, and he did *not* die at sea. For a time he became quite a famous figure in the US, and then his life took a very different turn. That's all I'm saying.

NOW I KNOW WHERE THAT LOVE CAME FROM.

One last thought on this. Way back at the beginning of this book I mentioned my love of the flowers growing in my mother's garden. Well, now I know where that love came from. Great-grandfather Joseph turned out to be quite a landscape gardener. That's something I can thank him for.

IN 2011 I RECORDED an album called *These Are My Favourites* to celebrate my forthcoming seventieth anniversary in show-business. I had a brilliant team of producers and arrangers behind me, and a superb group of musicians to accompany me. It was fabulous to be back in a studio, at the piano, singing some of the greatest songs ever written.

There are two duets on the album, both remarkable to me in different ways. On the very appropriately titled 'Smile', it was an absolute joy to sing with my granddaughter Sophie Purdie, Julie and Dominic's daughter. Here we are rehearsing. My expression says it all.

AS FOR THE SECOND duet, I still shake my head in amazement when I think about it. I can't quite believe it's true. Yet it is. The song is 'Paper Moon' and I'm singing with Nat King Cole. Yes, Nat King Cole. And this is not a case of two tracks being spliced together. *I am actually singing with Nat King Cole.*

How is that possible? I only ever met him on those two days in May 1960, at *Sunday Night at the London Palladium* and *The Royal Variety Performance*. Let me explain.

A neighbour of mine, Margaret, received a parcel containing a CD. The parcel was sent by someone Margaret knew, who was aware that she and I were friends. This person thought I might be interested in what the CD contained.

Might be!

It astonished me.

At this point in my story the facts become a little hazy, but somehow, on the night of 15 May 1960, when Nat and I sang together on the stage of the Palladium, someone recorded us. That person must have been in the broadcast truck. The sound quality is too good to have been taped off the television. Whoever did it, I have no idea. Why they did it, I have no idea. And where the recording has been all these years, I have no idea. But thank you, whoever you are.

We recorded new music for the album version, but the voices you hear are Nat's and mine, singing on that night. You can even make out Nat laughing at one point when I do a slight impersonation of him singing. More than fifty years on from the only time I sang live with one of my all-time heroes, we are once again duetting. A moment in time I thought lost for ever is now part of the present. As I said, it's hard to believe.

Over the course of this book I have discussed some of the playbills that have represented milestones in my career. Well, here is a final one for you, which I think goes to show that if you remain in show-business long enough you never know what might happen – you see, the times they're always a-changin'!

What a day it was at the Hop Farm. Another new challenge to relish: my first festival, performing outdoors, in the afternoon, on a big open stage in front of a huge audience. I do hope they stuck around for Bob.

I really did not know if this was going to be a success. Was it a venue too far for me? It turns out it wasn't. The reception I was given was extraordinary. Yet another thing I found hard to believe.

A year later I was back on the festival trail, this time at the biggest one of all – Glastonbury. When my appearance was announced, the reaction was generally one of astonishment.

So many people contacted me and said, 'What are you going to do at Glastonbury? What are you going to do?'

'I'm going to do what I always do,' I replied. 'I'm going to sing, dance, play piano, do some impersonations, have fun with people from the audience.'

I may have sounded confident, but just before I walked out on to the Avalon stage on the afternoon of 30 June 2013, I was very nervous. My audience consisted of twenty-, thirty- and forty-year-olds. Virtually no one older. I knew how my show went down with my regular audience, but this crowd? They were so young, to me at least. How would they react? Would they give me a chance? And could I transform such a different venue for me into a variety theatre?

I could. The Glastonbury crowd proved to be a well-versed variety audience and a marvellous one at that. Honestly, I have never been so well received. Going right back through the ages, as far as I can remember, they were the best I have experienced. I was absolutely stunned.

Listening to BBC radio on my way home, I heard that the organizers had been forced to close the gates at the Avalon stage during my performance because so many people wanted to get in. What a thing to happen.

THE MOMENT I EMERGED onstage the reaction was staggering. Suddenly, I felt at home. It could have been a small Summer Season theatre that I knew well, or a huge venue like the Palladium, it didn't matter. I had a sense that I belonged out there. That in itself astonished me.

Now, AS YOU KNOW, I love audience participation. I especially enjoy persuading people to come up on to the stage to dance and have some laughs. However, I wasn't sure it would work at Glastonbury, given that most people were wearing wellingtons or heavy boots. But as I have said, I was determined to do what I always do.

'Now it's time for the big Hollywood musical number,' I announced. 'I'm dying to do it, but I haven't got any backing.'

Then, at random, I picked four guys from the audience and asked them to help me.

'I've always thought you can tell if someone is a good dancer by the way they walk,' I explained, as the guys lined up on the stage. 'Will you please walk over to the side there, where you'll be given a hat? I'm going to study you . . . to see if you can be a dancer. Now, who do you want to be? Fred Astaire or Mick Jagger?' The guys would then make up their mind and individually walk across the stage imitating whoever they had chosen. I, of course, had a bit of fun with each of them in turn.

WHEN THEY REAPPEARED, WE did the Fred Astaire number 'Top Hat' together, with the guys copying my moves. There is definitely a touch of *The Generation Game* in this, and audiences always respond very well to that. It was no different at Glastonbury. The crowd loved my new backing dancers and they loved the show. And I loved the Glastonbury crowd.

When I came off a journalist tried to interview me. I could barely speak to him. 'Bruce,' he said, 'this has really affected you, hasn't it?'

It had. I was completely blown away. All these young people had come to see my performance and given me such an overwhelming and positive response. They made me feel ten feet tall.

I'm approaching the end of the book now, but before I go I briefly want to mention one of the best things I've been involved with in the past few years – the television show I did in September 2013, *When Miranda Met Bruce*.

Miranda Hart was terrific to work with. She's a delightful person and a fabulous entertainer. She's game to give anything a go, and she does it all with infectious enthusiasm.

The show was a lovely idea, looking back on my career and reliving some of the funniest moments, such as Daphne Cox from *The Generation Game*. We even recreated one of the games from *SNAP*, with Miranda trying to throw a shuttlecock into a cup I was holding.

In particular, I enjoyed the piano routine we worked out, which we are rehearsing here.

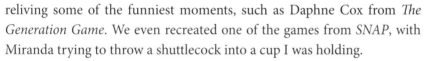

When we both messed up our duet, I turned to the studio audience and said, 'I used to think Les Dawson was bad!' They loved that. It was the kind of show, pure Saturday-night family entertainment, that still works and is still funny. Being capable of achieving that is one of Miranda's many talents.

As she herself would say, it was 'such fun'.

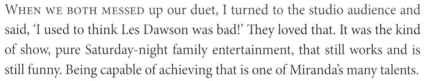

Finally, as a song-and-dance man at heart, I'm going to round off this look back on my career to date with some recent memories of my one-man show. That seems fitting, given it is the accumulation of so many of the elements that have made up my professional life.

In May 2012 I returned to the Royal Albert Hall where I first appeared in 1964, when I presented a show called *The Baird Festival of Television*. I had been back many times since, but never as a solo performer.

YOU CAN SEE ME here, on one of the grandest stages of all, seventy years after 'Boy Bruce, the Might Atom' arrived at the Theatre Royal, Bilston, to perform in a page-boy uniform. Remarkable. This time I didn't have my ukulele with me. Lucky audience.

DURING THE EVENING I was joined by a member of my 'family'. When I was halfway through singing 'Young And Foolish' my 'love child', Anton du Beke, appeared with his partner Erin Boag. They danced beautifully as

I continued with the song. I then stepped in to dance with Erin, with Anton looking on, no doubt hoping to learn some new steps. But when Anton made a move to sing, I wasn't having any of it. I grabbed the microphone back from him. After all, I'm in charge.

It was a lovely little comedy routine and I was so pleased they had agreed to do it with me.

LATER IN THE SHOW, to add to an evening already so full of wonder, a very, very special guest accompanied me onstage, this time a real member of the family – my granddaughter Sophie. We sang 'Smile' together. It was an unbelievable experience for this grandfather. I couldn't have been more proud of her.

Then in June this year, at the age of eighty-seven, I returned with my one-man show to the London Palladium. As I stepped out on to that famous stage once again . . . *SNAP!* The years melted away.

The magic of the Palladium will always be a part of me.

HOW TO END?

Well, as you know, I usually like to have the last word. This time, however, I am going to take my bow first and leave my family onstage. No, really, I am.

Left to right, here they are: Charlie and George; Tommy and Poppy; Jeremy; Josie (my first granddaughter to tell me I was going to be a greatgrandfather!) and Noah; Julie; Charlotte and Harry; Jamie; Louisa; Winnie and me; JJ; Debbie; Richard; Laura holding hands with Libby; Dominic; Sophie and Luke. Since this photo was taken, our family has increased even further. Tommy and Josie have a third child, Joel; Jamie and Louisa now have two little girls, Emma and Vivien; Jeremy, my grandson, now has a little boy called Carrick, plus two stepdaughters with his new wife, Kate.

Thank you to all of you who have supported me all these years, and thank you to my family for being, well, for being everything I could ever have wished for.

Picture Acknowledgements

Every effort has been made to trace copyright holders, but any who have been overlooked are invited to get in touch with the publishers.

BF = author's collection

BF: 8, 10, 11 both, 12, 13 , 14, 16 both, 17, 18 both, 19, 21, 23, 24 all, 25, 28, 30 both, 31, 36, 41 both, 43, 44, 46, 47 both, 49 both, 51 all, 53 all, 55, 56, 57 both, 58, 59 both, 60, 62 both, 64 both, 66, 67, 70, 71, 73, 75, 74 bottom right, 86, 90, 91 top right, 92, 93, 96, 99 all, 100, 101, 104, 105, 106, 110, 115, 121 bottom, 122 both, 128, 129, 130, 132 both, 134, 139 bottom, 141, 142, 151, 152 top, 160, 167 both, 171, 173, 174–75, 176 both, 178–9 all, 180, 181 top, 184, 185, 186 both, 192–6 all, 204, 207 all, 210 both, 215 both, 225, 248.

Alamy: 34–5 (© Douglas Carr), 152 bottom (© Trinity Mirror/Mirrorpix), 169 (© Trinity Mirror/Mirrorpix).

David Wilson: 36 inset.

ArenaPAL: 50 (courtesy of the Windmill Theatre Collection), 154 top (Ronald Grant Archive).

Rex: 65 (ITV/Shutterstock), 68 (ITV/Shutterstock), 69 (ITV/Shutterstock), 72 (ITV), 75 top (ITV/Shutterstock), 78 (ITV/Shutterstock), 80 (ITV/Shutterstock), 83 (ITV/Shutterstock), 85 (ANL/Shutterstock), 89 top (Shutterstock), 94 (*Daily Mail*/Shutterstock), 95 (ITV/Shutterstock), 111 top (ITV), 112 bottom (ITV/Shutterstock), 111 (*Daily Mail*/Shutterstock), 112 (ITV/Shutterstock), 113 (ITV/Shutterstock), 118 (ITV), 119 (ITV/Shutterstock), 121 top (ITV), 124 (ITV/Shutterstock), 125 both (ITV/Shutterstock), 127 (Dezo Hoffmann/ITV/Shutterstock), 131 (ITV/Shutterstock), 136 (Everett Collection), 150 (ITV/

Shutterstock), 162 top (*Daily Mail*/Shutterstock), 188 (ANL/Shutterstock), 198 (ITV/Shutterstock), 199 (ITV), 201 (ITV/Shutterstock), 202 (Ltd /Shutterstock), 205 (ITV/Shutterstock), 209 (ITV/Shutterstock), 213 top (David Fisher/ Shutterstock), 213 bottom (Andy Paradise/Shutterstock), 217 top (*Daily Mail*/ Shutterstock), 217 bottom (Paul Gover/Shutterstock), 219 top (*Standard*/ Shutterstock), 244 bottom (Bruce Adams/ANL/Shutterstock), 246 (Shutterstock), 247 (Shutterstock).

Topfoto/UPP: 75.

Getty Images: 79 (Popperfoto), 114 top (William Lovelace/Express), 114 bottom (Popperfoto), 117 both (Popperfoto), 170 (Ron Galella/WireImage), 181 bottom, 246 (Christie Goodwin/Redferns).

PA Archive/Press Association: 88, 91 (top left), 126, 139 top, 212 S&G Barratts/ EMPICS Archive, 216 PA Archive/Press Association Images.

Mirrorpix: 89 bottom, 91 bottom, 102.

© BBC: 140, 154, 156, 161, 220, 224, 227–34 all, 237.

Courtesy Poseidon films: 146 both.

The Scotsman Publ. Ltd: 182.

Mike Prior: 219 bottom.

Kindly supplied by Wall to Wall: 238.

Ian Wilson: 241, 242 both, 243, 244 top, 245.

Christie Goodwin: 247 top and middle.

Acknowledgements

This book relies on photographs, and therefore would not have been possible without the photographers to capture these moments. Thank you all. Much of my research has involved looking through boxes and boxes of photos that have been sent to me over the years, or searching online for the perfect shot to illustrate a story. This unearthed many photos I had either forgotten about or never seen before. It was a joy to do and brought back countless happy memories.

In deciding what stories to tell, I adopted a basic rule: if I couldn't find a relevant photo, the tale would not be included. This has meant, inevitably, many people who otherwise would have appeared in these pages have unfortunately been left out. To all of you, I apologize.

Thank you to David Wilson, whose help in putting this book together has been invaluable. We began the process in February, while I was in Puerto Rico and David in London. Over the course of a month we spoke for over twenty hours on Viber, before my return to the UK. It was a strange sensation, therefore, when we did finally meet – like seeing an old friend whom I had never met before.

Thanks also to my manager Ian Wilson, who has been enormously helpful in reading the text and either confirming (or denying!) the accuracy of the stories since he and I first began working together in the 1970s.

Another invaluable collaborator is Cora (my housekeeper). Without the lovely lunches, coffees and teas she supplied, the writing and editing would have been a far less enjoyable experience.

I'd also like to thank my golfing pals at Wentworth for providing some much-needed breaks from working on the book. I enjoyed our rounds together, regardless of whether the golf itself was good, bad or indifferent. Thank you Russ (Abbot), Keith, Conner, Kenny and Karim, who is still my bodyguard. Don't go looking for any photos of yourselves, though. I see enough of you as it is!

My publishers, Transworld, have been extremely supportive. Thank you to the whole team there, and in particular Andrea Henry, Sheila Lee and Helena Gonda for all your help.

A huge thanks to everyone who has supported my career over the years. An entertainer is nothing without an audience. Thank you for being there.

Finally, my biggest thanks go to my family, for putting up with my endless questions on people, places and dates as I worked on the text. And, of course, for so much more.

Index